Center for Basque Studies
Basque Politics Series, No. 9

The Basque Experience

Constructing
Sustainable Human Development

By Juan Jose Ibarretxe

Translated by
David Griffiths

Basque Politics Series, No. 9

Center for Basque Studies
University of Nevada, Reno
Reno, Nevada

Library of Congress Cataloging in Publication Data pending

Center for Basque Studies
Basque Politics Series, No. 9
Series Editor: Xabier Irujo

Center for Basque Studies
University of Nevada, Reno
Reno, Nevada 89557
E-mail: basque@unr.edu
Web: http://basque.unr.edu

First edition printed in the United States.

First Edition ISBN: 978-1-935709-63-3

Contents

Introduction

First of all I have to say this work has been carried out with the intention of settling a moral debt with the Basque People, from whom I have received so much affection and recognition over the last few years. My gratitude to Basque society is infinite. They know many things were done well and some things were done not so well, however, they were always done with awareness of our identity and with the intention of solving problems and making progress. This is how Basque Society has always considered our work, wisely, intelligently, and with deliberation. It is to Basque society itself, before the University or myself, to whom I owe this contribution.

This work aims to provide a serious and serene analysis of the legal-political and socio-economic aspects, which, in the efforts to achieve sustainable human development, have been evident in Basque society from the recovery of self-government via the Statute of Gernika in the 1980's up to today. This work specifically focuses on the period between 1998 and 2008.

The timeliness of this work is clear at a time when we are experiencing an economic, social and institutional crisis on all levels. These crises require new political, economic and social proposals, which have at their center respect for individual and collective Human Rights and the cultural identity of peoples. Changing the emphasis from the economy to economic ethics, from growth to sustainable human development, committing to equality between men and women, and recovering the protagonism of individuals by returning to them the power to make decisions. Mr. Addarii states that the Basque Case document (we will use both "Basque Experience" or "Basque Case" as synonymous) is "clear proof that it is possible to have both growth and social equality in a challenging environment" and expresses a belief that "the Basque Case is not just important as evidence, but also as an inspiration in the search for alternative models of development"[1].

The dilemma is very clear, radical in fact: to continue constructing from a position of power, handing over more and more areas to the market, or to find a clear response in order to guarantee the rights of individuals and peoples.

We know that every work of research, and this is no exception, when answering a question generates another two questions, and in this way, we are able to advance. With all sincerity, I believe that it is our duty to reflect profoundly upon the theory behind the measures and initiatives taken over this period and to present them to the academic community and, of course, to Basque society. Given that they were conceived to solve the problems of society and individuals they may be an asset and a contribution to the construction of the future. Mr. Seaford exquisitely describes the Basque Case as "a moral story about a moral country".[2]

I would like to end this introduction by expressing my gratitude to various parties. Thank you, first of all, to Columbia University and George Mason University as well as the Euclid Network of London, without whom none of this would have been possible. I will always be grateful for the opportunity they have afforded me to direct this research program.

Thanks in particular to Andrea Bartoli from George Mason University, to Peter Coleman from Columbia University, to Filippo Addari from the Euclid Network, whose committed support for my research visits to Washington, New York and London was essential. And special thanks to Tom Richardson the brilliant and diligent coordinator of this research program during my stays in

---

[1] ADDARII, F., Executive Director, Euclid Network, London. A contribution made in relation to "The Basque Case: A comprehensive model for Sustainable Human Development" research program at the bilateral meeting held in London, 31 March 2011.

[2] SEAFORD, C., Head of the Centre for Well-Being, New Economics Foundation, London. A contribution made in relation to "The Basque Case: A comprehensive model for Sustainable Human Development" research program at the bilateral meeting held in London, 30 March 2011.

Washington, London, and New York and who has become a great friend of mine and of the Basque Country.

Thanks must also go to the many academics and third sector leaders who have lent their valuable time to studying and contributing to this project: Noel Johnson, George Mason University (WDC); Tyler Cowen, George Mason University; Robert Rogowsky, George Mason University; Chris Mitchell, George Mason University; Robert Clark, George Mason University; Josep Colomer, Georgetown University (WDC); Charles Betsy, Howard University (WDC); John Gray, Howard University; Paul Aligica, George Mason University; Andrew Hughes-Hallet, George Mason University; Alex Tabarrok, George Mason University; Karol Boudreaux, George Mason University; Diogo Vasconcelos, Director Cisco Systems Ltd. (London); Mark Napier, Managing Director, Center for Public Innovation (London); Baroness Noala O'Loan, Member of the House of Lords (UK); Nicola Cobbold, Managing Director, Portland Trust (London); Mathew Pike, Chair, Substance (London); Mathew Taylor, Chief Executive, Royal Society for the Arts (London); Indypaul Johar, Owner, Project 00 (London); Charles Seaford, Head of the Center for Well-being, New Economics Foundation (London); Dr. Alasdair McDonnell, Member of Parliament (UK); Alex Murdock, London South Bank University; Filippo Addarii, Executive Director, Euclid Network (London); Colin Campbell, Founder & Executive Director, Assist Social Capital (UK); Joanna Weschler, Deputy Director & Director of Research, Security Council Report (NY); Jacqueline Klopp, Columbia University (NY); Mark Stover, Columbia University; Lucy Goodhart, Columbia University; Brendan O'Flaherty, Columbia University; Macartan Humphreys, Columbia University; Shanker Satayanath, New York University; Oeindrila Dube, New York University; Teresa Whitfield, New York University; and Kenneth Melchin, Director of the Lonergan Center, Saint Paul University (Ottawa-Canada).

All of you, whether your research program reflects your opinions or otherwise, have helped to enrich this work through your contributions and, above all, your criticisms, many of which have been incorporated in the final document.

And finally, many thanks to all the people everywhere who are struggling to change an unjust world, the only cause worth living for.

1
Progress with "Roots", "Eyes" and "Faces"

Our world is complex, with complex problems, complex solutions, profound changes, and massive transformations. As Edgar Morin says that from now on it is necessary to "gérer la complexité"[3] and as if this were not enough, we are experiencing a profound global crisis with different characteristics than all other crises we have experienced to date. Because, from the outside, this crisis appears to have a polyhedral shape. It is a crisis of the legal, political, economic, sociological, environmental, and cultural systems. It is a crisis that is, above all, axiological.

Over the last three decades of the 20th Century, in Western Society, the neoliberal conception based on the postulates of the School of Chicago became the political order of the day. Now, neoliberalism is on a full planetary offensive. The market rules the roost, and ultimately this means that, with the individual displaced, any moral justification proceeds from a moral of means, having a utilitarian foundation identified as the market system[4]. Faced

---

[3] MORIN, E., *The method: The nature of nature*. Madrid, ed. Cátedra, 1981, p. 436, says: "From here on I am convinced that all simplifying and, therefore, mutilated knowledge, is mutilating and can be translated as a manipulation, repression, devastation of that which is real, from the moment it is transformed into action and particularly into political action. Simplified thought has come to mean the barbarism of science. It is barbarism specific to our civilization. It is the barbarism which today is allied to all historic and mythological forms of barbarism." A particular example on which "gérer la complexité" consists in relation to Law can be seen in: ARNAUD, A. J., *Pour une pensée juridique européenne*, Paris, ed. PUF, 1991, ps. 241 and following.

[4] HAYEK, F. A., *Law, legislation and liberty*, v. II, Madrid, Unión ed., 1988, p. 201, states: "The suggestion that (...) social links corresponding to the Great Society are 'merely economic' (or more specifically, 'catallactic') and produce a vigorous emotional rejection. And yet, it is something that is difficult to deny, as one also cannot fail to conclude that, for a society with the dimensions

with this reality, denouncing the "homo aeconomicus" it is necessary today to restore the kind of ethics for which the subject is an end in itself.[5] We must return from the totalizing market to economic practices with ethical foundations, knowing, as we do today, that there is no economic project without a life project that takes into account the human aspect in its widest sense.

The motto of this 'ideological globalization' seems to be: everything for individuals and peoples, but without their participation and ownership. The data shows this in an increasingly harsh manner. Reports and declarations by United Nations experts to the effect that "every five seconds a child dies in the world due to avoidable causes"[6] should make us all feel ashamed. At the same time, studies such as those by the renowned North American linguist Merritt Ruhlen[7] warn that of the 5,000 languages currently spoken in the world, only around 500 will still exist by the end of this century. He adds that one of these will be the Basque language, and clearly explains the strategy of destruction of cultures and peoples on which 'this globalization' is based.

---

and complexity of a modern society, there is no alternative social solution. It is repugnant to most of our kind to accept that the 'pecuniary' link is the element capable of drawing together the members of the Great Society; that, ultimately, the grandiose ideal of the convergence of all human beings must be based on established relationships between persons motivated by the desire to reach a more fulfilled satisfaction of their material needs."

[5] This concern is clearly reflected in DUFOUR, D. R., "In times of total capitalism: The new servitude of the liberated man." Le Monde Diplomatique, Spanish edition, Madrid, October 2003, p. 4, when he states: "We are experiencing a capital change as, if the shape of the subject is affected, it will not only be the institutions that we share that will be endangered, this will also affect, above all, 'what we are.' Then, nothing can stop total capitalism, in which everything, without exception, forms part of the commercial universe: nature, the living and imaginary world."

[6] CARDONA, J., United Nations expert, Panama City, October 2014.

[7] RUHLEN, M., Department of Anthropological Sciences, *The Origin of Languages; An Interview with Merritt Ruhlen,* Stanford University, May 2009.

We can begin to see that the idea of the 'global village' is not such a pretty idea after all; it is 'ugly' because it abandons its children to their fate. It is increasingly unequal and leaves the most vulnerable people unprotected in an inhuman way. Recently (2014), the NGO Oxfam Intermón stated, "economic inequalities are growing fast in most countries. The world's wealth is divided in two: one half is in the hands of the richest 1% of the population and the other half is shared among the remaining 99%", adding, "governments overwhelmingly serve the economic elites to the detriment of ordinary people."[8] The International Labor Organization (ILO) recently published a report stating, "73% of the world's population does not have social protection."[9] It is not surprising that discontent and 'indignant' social movements are gaining ground and are out on the streets on the five continents. The fight against inequality that works to favor everyday people is the revolution of the 21st century. It is a revolution for 'human dignity.' It is not a crisis but the "I don't love you anymore" sentiment that appeared on a recent protester's poster. Indeed, institutions such as the World Economic Forum recognize that "inequality is affecting social stability within countries and represents a threat for security on a world scale."[10] Even today, the International Monetary Fund (IMF) — whose economic plans seem to say, "So what if people are not doing well if the economy is going well?' — recognizes that "reducing inequality helps to achieve faster and more sustainable growth."[11] Personally, I agree with the Spanish poet Luis Garcia Montero when he recently said: "I don't believe in a theoretical project that is not based on a sentimental commitment to the happiness of others."[12]

---

[8] OXFAM INTERMÓN, *Gobernar para las élites: Secuestro democrático y desigualdad económica*, Barcelona, 2014.

[9] ILO, *World Report on Social Protection 2014-2015*. Geneva, June 2014.

[10] WORLD ECONOMIC FORUM, *Perspectivas de la Agenda Mundial 2014*. Geneva, November 2013.

[11] INTERNATIONAL MONETARY FUND, *Redistribution, Inequality, and Growth* (Jonathan D. Ostry, Andrew Berg, Charalambos G. Tsangarides), Washington DF, February 4, 2014.

[12] GARCIA MONTERO, L., Agencia EFE, Madrid, 14.02.2015.

The "Basque Case" humbly demonstrates that another kind of world is possible. In this sense, Diogo Vasconcelos describes it as "A very timely piece of research, we are asking how we can create new social and economic governance models that will pave the way to a new golden era. Normally when looking for alternatives we end up in the Nordic countries when we seek examples, Swedish model of adaptation, Finnish model of restructuring. Now we have the Basque model of innovation, cooperation and competition." Vasconcelos adds that the Basque Case "offers a model for 21st Century development, a merger of Keynesian and Schumpeterian approaches; social change enhanced and entrepreneurship."[13] This is also supported by Prof Betsy's comments on the existence of alternatives to the neo-liberal model: "Academic questioning of the neo-liberal model is a pressing necessity and there is a need for examples such as the Basque Case to highlight the existence of alternatives for holistic, social and economic progress."[14] Moreover, Mark Napier states, "looking across the model, it seems very timely. We have invested very heavily in the neoliberal model, it is a busted flush, it does not work. Which begs the question, what is the next economic paradigm? Behind the scenes over the past 30 years the Basque People have been working away, there is something already tried and tested."[15] Professor Melchin affirms, "there has been a wide division in the field of economics between those who see the financial markets as part of the productive elements of an economy and those who see this as a serious flaw that has been

---

13 VASCONCELOS, D., Cisco, London. A contribution made in relation to the Basque Case. A Comprehensive model for Sustainable Human Development research program at the bilateral meeting held at Euclid, London, 28 March 2011.

14 BETSY, C., contribution made in relation to the "Basque Case: A Comprehensive model for Sustainable Human Development" research program at the bilateral meeting held at Howard University, Washington, 25 January 2011.

15 NAPIER, M., Managing Director at the Center for Public Innovation, London. A contribution made in relation to "The Basque Case: A Comprehensive model for Sustainable Human Development" research program at the bilateral meeting held in London, 28 March 2011.

demonstrated by the current crisis," arguing that "Dr. Ibarretxe's report comes at a critical moment, offering an alternative model based on a record of success when other experiments have not been as successful."[16] Finally, Mathew Taylor recognizes "the importance of the human model of decision-making used by the Basque Country, in contrast with the market model prescribed by neo-liberalism. The Basque Case offers a valuable contribution to the need for authentic public conversation as to what policy will mean for government, the public and private sector of a society."[17]

Today, as Eduardo Galeano says, "development is a journey with more castaways than sailors."[18] It is the first lesson of this 'new era': "a market without values is a flea market" or, in the recent words of Pope Francis: "... this economy kills."[19] F. Hayek's concept of 'self-regulation'[20] has

---

[16] MELCHIN, K., Director of the Lonergan Center, Saint Paul University, Toronto. Contribution made in relation to "The Basque Case: A Comprehensive model for Sustainable Human Development" research program at the bilateral meeting held in New York, 13th May 2011.

[17] TAYLOR, M., Chief Executive, Royal Society for the Arts, London, a contribution made in relation to "the Basque Case. A Comprehensive model for Sustainable Human Development" research program at the bilateral meeting held in London on 29 March 2011.

[18] GALEANO, E., *Las venas abiertas de América Latina.* Madrid, ed. Siglo XXI, 2005, pp. 224 and successive pages. On p. 363, he writes: "Underdevelopment is a not a phase of development. It is its consequence"; on p. 323, "In each country the international system of dominance country is repeated"; on p. 234, "The entry of Latin America in the British orbit, which it only left to join the North American orbit, took place within this general framework, and in it the dependence of the new independent countries was consolidated". In no. 23 he quotes MARX, K, *Discourse on the new change, in the Poverty of Philosophy,* Moscow, undated, "It is not at all strange that the free-marketers are incapable of understanding of how a country can get rich at the expense of another, because nor do those same people want to understand how one class can get rich at the expense of another within a country."

[19] HOLY FATHER FRANCIS, *Evangelii Ggaudium*, *Exhortación Apostólica,* Point 53, Vatican City, Nov 2013: "As the commandment 'thou shalt not kill' imposes a clear limit in order to

therefore been debunked. This is the first evidence, but is not the only one.

Almost everything is shrouded in uncertainty. We do not have a clear diagnosis, we do not know what is happening to us… and it is precisely this uncertainty that is happening to us, as Ortega y Gasset would say. In these circumstances, nothing would be more negative than returning to the "situation prior to the crisis," a view that has too many advocates in the Western world, which often impatiently yearns for "the old good days." Whatever has to happen will happen, but it will be new and different, not inspired by nostalgia but intellectual tension and multidisciplinary reflection — nothing can escape from rational challenge — and the search for new pathways and spaces for encounter. This process will allow the dissemination of knowledge and thought, helping us to see the light in the distance as the exit from the tunnel and not as a train rushing towards us, as the genial and universal Basque sculptor Jorge Oteiza once said.

Today we know that Culture, understood as the mass of shared understanding and an ongoing learning process, forms "silver bridges" between politics, the economy, and life. At the end of the nineties, Baudrillard stated, "the universal has had its historic opportunity. However, confronted today with a world order without an alternative to indisputable globalization on the one hand and, on the other, the loss of direction or the tenacious insurrection of singularities, the concepts freedom, democracy and human rights have an extreme paleness which corresponds to their condition as ghosts from a disappeared universe. And it is difficult to imagine that they can be reborn from their ashes through a simple political game, as this has also become a victim of the same deregulation and has no other foundation than moral or intellectual power." Following this statement, a door is opened to hope, with the declaration that "however, the die

---

guarantee the value of human life, we now have to say 'no' to an economy of exclusion and inequality… that economy kills."

[20] On this question, see HAYEK, F. A., *Derecho, legislación y libertad*, v. II, Madrid, Unión ed., pp. 75-108.

is not yet cast, although nothing now works for universal values. Achievements have been strengthened and globalization has not won in advance. Faced with its solvent and homogenizing power we see heterogeneous powers arise everywhere, not only different, but conflicting and uncompromising."[21] Lately we have become witnesses and protagonists of a paradigm change in the globalized world that, again, in the interest of universalization has tried to achieve standardization.[22]

Pope Francis recently said, "[...] globalization that enriches is like a polyhedron. Every side is connected but each one conserves its particularity, its richness, its identity," and he added that "Globalization understood wrongly — the present one — is like a sphere: all its points are equal, all equidistant from the center."[23] I agree. This is the real dilemma of our time: to be a sphere or a polyhedron. I have no doubts about my choice: a polyhedron.

Today, in the "global society" it is "the local" that embodies real hope that another world is possible. We have passed from the "old" paradigm of "global cancels local," to the "current" paradigm: "local moves the world." For some time people have started to reject the process of transformation and change, and to passively intervene.[24] It is

---

[21] BAUDRILLARD, J., *Total screen*, Barcelona, ed. Anagrama, 2000, p. 183.

[22] BAUDRILLARD, J., "From anti-terrorism to war: The violence of globalization." Le Monde Diplomatique, Spanish edition, Madrid, November 2002, p. 17, states "the mission of the West (or the ex West, as for many years it has not had its own values) is to submit, by all means, multiple cultures to the ferocious law of equivalence. (...). The creation of a world system is the result of immense jealousy: that felt by an indifferent and low definition culture in relation to highly defined cultures — that felt by disenchanted cultures, lacking the intensity of high intensity cultures."

[23] HOLY FATHER FRANCIS, *La Vanguardia Internacional*, Interview with the journalist Henrique Cymerman, Vatican City, 13 June 2014.

[24] OSBORNE, D. and GAEBLER, T., *The reinvention of government: The influence of the business spirit in the public sector.* Barcelona, ed. Paidós, 1995, p. 62 to 66, reflect on the question "smaller, but stronger," highlighting: "communities enjoy good health when their

not passively accepted, rightly, that "modernity carries the mark of another."[25] Faced with the catastrophic vision of Immanuel Wallerstein on the individual in search of identity, "identity encrusted in an evasive concept called 'culture' or, to be more exact 'cultures,"[26] today we are experiencing, as stated by F. J. Caballero Harriet, the "return of cultures,"[27]

---

families, neighborhoods, schools, volunteer organizations and enterprises enjoy good health, and also know that, in order to achieve this, the essential function of the government consists of taking the helm in these institutions (…) becoming the catalyst that helps communities to strengthen their civil infrastructure. (…). Governments that focus on taking the helm shape their communities, States and nations. They take *more* political decisions. They set in motion *more* social and economic institutions. Some even carry out *more* regulation. (…) there is a greater demand for *government management*, i.e. to `drive' society, to convince the different interest groups to embrace common goals and strategies".

[25] MAALOUF, A., *Killer identities*. Madrid, ed. Alianza, 1999, ps. 88 to 91, reflects that anywhere in the world modernization means westernization and states: "This reality is not lived in the same way by those born in the heart of the dominant civilization and those who were born outside it. The former can be transformed, advance in life, adapt, without losing their identity (…). For everyone else (…) modernization has always meant abandoning part of their identity. Even when on occasions enthusiasm arises, the process is never developed without certain bitterness, without a feeling of humiliation and denial. Without a painful question mark over the risks of the assimilation. Without a deep identity crisis. (…). Yes, at each step they take in life they hit upon deception, disappointment, humiliation. How will they not have a bruised personality? How could they not feel that their identity is being bruised?"

[26] WALLERSTEIN, I., *The future of capitalist civilization*. Barcelona, ed. Icaria, 1997, ps. 91 and 92, adds: "The new geo-cultural theme has already been proclaimed: it is the subject of identity. (…) we can expect explosions in all directions."

[27] CABALLERO HARRIET, F. J., *Some keys for Globalization: Global, Democracy and Development Foundation*. (FUNGLODE), 2009, ps. 196 and 197, says, "It is necessary to accept that the return to `cultures' does not mean a conflict of civilizations (…), the return to "cultures" cannot be understood as something tragic and regressive in the process of maturing and liberating the individual throughout history, but as the return to the axiological deposit in which the lost

not only from a social and political point of view, but also from an economic point of view. That is to say, "to do what you know how to do", indeed, incorporating new knowledge, new technologies... starting each day by "innovating with values," "innovating with roots." This means opposing with noble resistance the capitalist economic order, Max Weber's[28] "capitalist cosmos." the new way of understanding progress.[29]

We also know, now better than ever, in the area of the multinational business networks, the strategic value that industry, "with its feet firmly on the ground," and the native productive economy have for a country and for the future welfare of its people. Today we speak of "looking at the real economy" as the best recipe to escape the crisis and face the future, when it is clear that countries with an "income" culture, not a productive culture, on which the speculative economy was built, cannot change their economic structure from one day to the next. There is an economic culture, just as there is a legal culture, the result of shared understandings about the economic or legal question in the more general framework of the culture of a people. Individuals, companies, and countries are all the product of the "accumulation" of training, decisions, and adaptations carried out in a constantly changing cultural reality. What we will be tomorrow will be directly related to the decisions, correct or incorrect, which we take today.

In the case of the Basque Country, the recovery of self-government with the approval by referendum of the Statute of Autonomy of Gernika was what enabled the first

---

identity can be found again following the frustrated hope from not achieving absolute individual liberty in a world in which universal values, ultimately, turned out to be market chains."

28 WEBER, M., *Protestant ethics and the spirit of capitalism.* Barcelona, ed. Peninsula, 1989, p. 49, states: "an extraordinary cosmos in which the individual is born and in which, at least with regard to the individual, he is given a practically un-reformable building, in which he must live, and in which the norms of economic behavior are imposed, as soon as he is involved in the fabric of the economy."

29 On the idea of progress it is interesting to consult NISBET, R., *History of the Idea of Progress.* London, ed. Einemann, 1980.

Basque Government in the 80s, presided over by President Garaikoetxea, to make the strategic decision to commit the country not to a speculative economy but to a productive one. This decision was taken by the democratic Basque institutions, not without difficulties, and inspired by the productive tradition of the Basque people. We must not forget that it was the determination and tenacity of our society (cultural element) and our leaders (political resolution in tune with the former) which made it possible, then, to commit to our own industrial framework, to the "real economy," the success of which we can see today. A commitment to the real economy which, it should be highlighted in the interests of memory, was severely criticized by social, political and media agents, fascinated at the time by those neoliberal theories which, following the oil crisis of the seventies, were in vogue in every Western society. In Spain and in Europe neoconservatives were delighted, finally, to see the disappearance of the "dangerous" storm clouds provoked by the philosophy of Keynes[30] which had laid down a velvet carpet for the "social State." Now, they saw their great opportunity. Without doubt, the spirit of this neoconservative opportunity could be synthesized in the words of the Spanish Minister of Industry of the time: "the best industrial policy is to not have one."[31] Fortunately, the Basque People did not do the same.

Building peace, advancing self-government, personality as a People, and furthering the achievement of sustainable human development have been the objectives of society and the Basque democratic institutions at this turn of

---

[30] See KEYNES, J.M., *General Theory of Employment Interest and Money*, 1936 (in English); FIORITO, A. AND MURGA, G., *Keynes and his interpretations II,* Madrid, Ediciones cooperativas, 2006 (in Spanish), where we find the fundamental thesis of John Maynard Keynes which is, in short, the fact that governments cannot trust everything to market forces.

[31] SOLCHAGA, C., Minister of Industry of the First government of Felipe Gónzalez (December 1982- July 1985) Premonitory phase ahead, by several years, of what we could understand as the "formal" formulation of the neoliberal dogma made by John Williamson in 1990 and which is commonly known as the Washington Consensus.

the century. These efforts, along with the achievements obtained, have not gone unnoticed, not only by other countries governments and different prestigious institutions that see in the "Basque Case" a reference model,[32] but also by Universities in different parts of the world.

It is with the creation of its own new models — different and original in political, legal, social and economic areas — that a country longing for peace attempts to make its right to freely decide its own future and bring to fruition the policy of sustainable human development for the benefit of the men and women of its country a reality.

"Grand Passion at the Service of a Great Idea"

We present the analysis of the Basque experience within the thematic framework of multi-national societies, of the 21st Century.[33] Euskadi is an example of sustainable human development that is open to the world. It is a modern country that has not forgotten its roots. A People who, despite suffering the inhuman violence of ETA, occupy one of the leading positions in the world in the Human Development Index (HDI) carried out by the United Nations.[34] A Basque model which has demonstrated that Self-Government, that is the capacity of self political and social regulation, can be a synonym for welfare.

The Basque People — one of the most ancient peoples of Europe — has been able to stay on the cutting edge of progress in Europe. This progress is understood in a particular way as not only economic but also social progress.

---

32 - LOPEZ-RODRIGUEZ, J., FAIÑA, J.A., and MONTES SOLLA, P., "*Case Study Basque Country*" "*The Basque Country: Strategy for Economic Development.*" Published by Jean Monnet Group on Competition and Regional Development, Harvard, 2009.

33 RAMÓN Y CAJAL, S., Opening speech at the Royal Academy of Exact Physical and Natural Sciences. 1897, stated, "Every great work, both in arts and in science is the result of a grand passion at the service of a great idea."

34 UNITED NATIONS, "Human Development Index," Report 2007.

Progress at the service of the people, progress at the service of the community.[35]

The Basque People is a modern people who have historically defended their national identity before the Spanish state. Aside from this historic and democratic defence, the Franco dictatorship unfortunately provoked the rise of the terrorist movement ETA which, in accordance with our hopes and expectations, is today on the point of disappearing. The violence of ETA has caused pain and suffering for over 50 years and has brought about a unanimous cry for Peace in the Basque Country. Peace understood, not only in terms of the absence of violence, but Peace built on justice and liberty.[36] The future of the Basque People should be built upon the foundation of the Ethical Principle,[37] building Political Normalization[38] and so making

---

[35] This is the idea of AUZOLAN: to clarify this Basque term we can say that AUZO means neighborhood, physical and, above all, social and community unit. LAN is work. And AUZOLAN is common work, between everyone, for the good of the neighborhood and to benefit all the community. It is the basis for communal work in Basque farmhouses, villages, councils, towns and communities, and it has been considered the basis of this original way of understanding work that constitutes Basque cooperatives.

[36] Presentation TRUYOL and SERRA, A., in KANT, I., *On perpetual peace*. Madrid, ed, Tecnos, , 1998, ps. 15 and 16.

[37] KANT, I., *Groundwork of the metaphysics of morals*. Barcelona, ed. Ariel, 1999, p. 199 when he states, "in the kingdom of ends, everything has either a price or a dignity. Instead of having a Price something else, equivalent, may be placed; on the other hand, that which is above all price and consequently does not admit an equivalent, has a dignity." The concept dignity, therefore, is an absolute concept that makes up the Ethical Principle.

[38] This is implementing political autonomy as a consequence of the existence of an individual autonomy. In this sense, CASTORIADIS, C., "From autonomy in politics: The privatized individual." Le Monde Diplomatique, Spanish edition, February 1998, p. 27, states: "There is, then, a political autonomy; and this political autonomy means knowing that men create their own institutions. This requires the attempt to consider these institutions, with knowledge of cause, with clarity, following a collective

the true Democratic Principle the basis for democracy. As Nicola Cobbold says, "the challenge to sustainable development in conflict-affected societies is, as it is in the Basque case, to create a 'triple helix' structure of economic development, democratic political process, and the creation of security and the shift towards non-violent political engagement."[39]

The reason for the research on the Basque model does not lie in emotion or mere intuition but, ultimately, in the importance that responsible work and intellectual-scientific rigour have to find the solutions to the great problems we face in the 21st century. The problems of poverty, health, water, energy, climate change, intolerance, terrorism, fundamentalism, equality, and identity will have no solution with less science, but with more science and more education.[40]

Science today, leaving aside the risks involved through instrumentalization and manipulation,[41] is a human

---

deliberation. It is what I call collective autonomy, which has individual autonomy as an inalienable companion."

39 COBBOLD, N., Managing Director, Portland Trust, London. A contribution made in relation to "The Basque Case: A Comprehensive Model for Sustainable Human Development" research program at the bilateral meeting held in London 28 March 2011.

40 ETXENIKE, P.M., "Appearance in the Spanish Senate to carry out an assessment of the scientific policy of the State and the European Union." Record of Proceedings, 18 June 2007, states, "the wealth of nations will depend more and more on the wealth of notions."

41 In this respect, the words of HOBSBAWM, E. J., *Interview about the XXI century,* p. 170, are sufficiently illustrative when to the question: "Do you never fear the power of science? The possibility of cloning a person, or crossing animal and vegetable genes in a tomato; or the possibility of killing in a war waged on the computer screen?" He answered: "Of course I am horrified. Not only by the dimension of power it confers, but because the apprentices of the wizard often do not know how to use it. If a guarantee existed that the people who handle progress know what to do with it, how to use it for the benefit of others, or when never to use it, I would be less frightened, but such a guarantee does not exist. Immense natural forces are manipulated and are not always well known, and

adventure, an intellectual adventure, and an essential part of humanism and modern culture which in recent years has changed our perception of both work and ourselves. Modern science, beyond the excesses committed in its name — more eloquent perhaps is the statement of the scientist, Jacob Bronowski, for its depth of thought about what happened in Auschwitz[42] — is the most important collective cultural work of humanity. The importance of scientific, technical, and social research does not lie solely in the economic aspect but in its contribution to the training of individuals, to the generation of a climate of permanent searching, innovation, creativity and demands, rigour in the treatment of problems, which affects, as if by osmosis or by "the domino effect," the rest of the activities of a society.

Today there is a wide consensus, at least in public discourse, about the importance of science and technology, of social and technological innovation for our development. It is the advance caused by scientific and social knowledge that explains why we continue to exist as the human species and which guarantees our survival in the future.

The importance of the analysis of the Basque case lies in the awareness of the existence of a problem and tries to recover attitudes, habits, behavior, and values of science that are useful and, we believe, are necessary. Firstly, optimism, faith, and the conviction that problems have solutions. Secondly is the idea of long term thinking, believing that we are all links in a chain and, therefore, each

---

norms or institutions do not exist to tell us what we must or must not do. The only rule that exists in free market conditions, the maximization of economic growth and profit, is almost certain to produce negative effects."

[42] BRONOWSKI, J., *The Ascent of Man.* Boston, ed. Little, Brown and Co., 1973, p.374, states: "It is said that science will dehumanize people and turn them into numbers. That is false, tragically false. This is a concentration camp and crematorium in the style of Auschwitz. This is where people were turned into numbers. Into this pond were flushed the ashes of some four million people. And that was not done by gas. It was done by arrogance. It was done by dogma. It was done by ignorance. (...). We have to cure ourselves of the itch for absolute knowledge and power."

little contribution we make is important.[43] And thirdly, complexity and cooperation and the avoidance of the simplification of problems.[44] Today, more than ever, we need to confront the problems of the citizens of each and every community using new styles of governance. The Basque case teaches us that it is necessary to seek a solution for social, political and legal problems and even the problems of violence with legal-political initiatives and also that political leaders must pay attention to the facts and the complexity of reality and not be swayed by one-dimensional simplifications promoted by ideology or by particular interests.

Seen from this point of view this work becomes even more interesting as the last years of the 20th century and first years of the 21st century saw important changes in the Basque Country when constructing ethical, democratic and sustainable human development principles; i.e. paradigm changes.

Thus, 1998 was a key year to understand the construction process of the ethical principle for future years. The paradigm change occurred when all the political and social agents in the country, and also ETA, accepted in theory and in public pronouncements — unlike the negotiation processes of the Spanish Presidents Aznar and Rodríguez Zapatero held since then — that we should differentiate between peace and politics. That peace is peace and political agreements are political agreements. The latter corresponds only and exclusively to political parties. It was

---

[43] In this sense, with an aim to illustrate, it is useful to see what, MONDOLFO, R., *Problems and research methods in the History of Philosophy*, p. 71 says referring to the understanding and interpretation of philosophers in the History of Philosophy: "we must always bear in mind this double demand, to recognize a dependence on them, on the one hand, and an independence on the other. The dependence is represented by their relations with previous thought and Independence by their new thought which is insinuated in the very adhesion to the authority of a previous system."

[44] As MORIN, E., *Method: The nature of nature*, p. 434 says, "The first positive basis of the method is in the first universal statement of complexity. The problem is, from here on, to transform the discovery of the complexity into the complexity method."

also concluded that it was necessary to open a new stage in the relationship and approach to the victims of violence and terrorism. Support structrues were established, help and recognition from the Basque Government itself, and declaring all together solemnly — again in practice this was a different matter — the commitment to "remove" victim support policy from the political-electoral agenda.

It was also the turn of the century that saw a paradigm change in relation to the construction of the democratic principle. The "Ardanza Document" in 1998, and later the programs of the Basque Government arising from the elections in 1998 and 2001, clearly established the legitimate claim for the democratic principle — the right to decide — as the "keystone" for the social, political, and economic construction of the Basque People in the 21st century.

These years have also meant a paradigm change in relation to the construction of sustainable human development. From 2001 social, scientific, and technical innovation was clearly defined as the new lever for the socioeconomic transformation of our society. In the 80s, the lever for the transformation in our Country was "the spirit of survival," which helped us learn how to compete. Then in the 90s, it was the commitment to quality, to opening up, which enabled us to learn to compete and cooperate. Only because we learned to compete in the 80s and learned to compete and cooperate in the 90s, were we able to tackle the paradigm change of the 21st century: "to learn to innovate in cooperation."

This book aims to analyze the initiatives that, from the beginning of self-government in the eighties, and specifically from 1998 until 2008, were presented and defended in democratic forums and institutions. These initiatives worked to decipher the changes in political, social and economic focus that caused and suggested them, learning from the experience to offer future models to advance the ethical principle, democratic principle, and sustainable human development.

Like every work of research this one generates another two questions when answering one. It is in this way that we are able to advance. We will try to demonstrate with this analysis that the Ethical Principle[45] cannot be renounced by Basque society, that peace is possible for the Basque People, that we can tackle a "dialogued end to violence,"[46] that there is no road to peace because peace is the road,[47] that self-government is a synonym of welfare for this country, that building the Democratic Principle — the right to decide for oneself — to develop self-government fully, to advance in one's identity as a moral person[48] and as a people,

---

[45] Ethical principle founded on the principle of personality, which is well described by MONDOLFO, R., *Rousseau and the modern conscience*, p. 45 when he says: "Receiving (the principle of personality) from the intimacy of the conscience its content and value, raises the feeling of dignity of human nature and the harmony or identity between ends of the personality and the universal system: this "feeling" anticipates, thus, the Kantian "concept" of the human person as an "end in itself" and of universal harmony in "the kingdom of ends."

[46] AGREEMENT FOR THE NORMALIZATION AND PACIFICATION OF THE BASQUE COUNTRY, *Ajuria Enea Pact*, Vitoria-Gasteiz 12 January 1988, Point 10: "If suitable conditions arise for a dialogued end to violence, based on a clear will to put an end to violence and on unequivocal attitudes that can lead to this conviction, supported by dialogue processes between the competent powers of the State and those who decide to abandon violence, respecting at all times the un-renounceable democratic principle that political questions must be solved solely through the legitimate representatives of the popular will."

[47] With regard to peace, for example, ROUSSEAU, J.J., *Extrait du Projet de Paix Perpetuélle de Monsieur l'Abbé de Saint Pierre*, O.C., v. III, p.563, states that the most honourable question must be the object of occupation of a decent man.

[48] MARITAIN, J., *Man and the state.* Madrid, ed. Encuentro, 2002. The unquestionable existence as a People, as a political society or, perhaps, in the words of MARITAIN, as a "political body" is what confers the character of "moral person." And it is not a case of creation but of advancement. This has nothing to do with the conception of the atomized "political society" expressed by Locke (fundamental to the model of liberal State). LOCKE, J., *Second essay on civil government.* Madrid, ed. Aguilar, 1969, chap.VII, paragraph 99, says, "We have, then, what starts and constitutes any political society, it is none other than the consent of any number of free men capable of forming a majority to get together and integrate into a similar society. And this and only this is what could lead to a

not with backs turned nor in confrontation, but in coexistence with all other identities, is behind not only a legitimate political aspiration but at the base of the construction of Sustainable Human Development for Basque society. As Joanna Weschler states "the violent and political conflicts have been a factor in the Basque people becoming acutely aware of a need to maintain their identity. This has resulted in significant levels of solidarity and almost a spiritual belief in strengthening society at all levels."[49]

Looking Backwards to Understand, Looking Forwards to Live: 1998–2008

The end of the 90s and the start of the 21st century witnessed an era of special interest and political, economic, and social significance for the world. Perhaps we lack the historical perspective with which to assess the extent of these changes, but their effects are continually being demonstrated at an uncommon speed in the lives of people and of nations.

The acceleration of technological innovations in every area, not only in the business world but also in genetics, communication, energy, new materials, biotechnology, and countless others are shaping the future world that will scarcely resemble the one we lived in only 10 years ago. But, as well as technological innovation, other additional factors are causing acceleration in this process of change without precedent.

---

legitimate government." Really, this is nothing more than simple "individual self-determination" that, in the case of the Basque People, had already been carried out at a remote moment when they were constituted as a People, as a political body and, therefore, as a "moral person." From then on, "advancing in your identity as a moral person" requires, in Kant's words, the "united will of the people" i.e. "collective self-determination." Therefore, "individual self-determination" and "collective self-determination" result in a true democratic State.

[49] WESCHLER, J., Deputy Director & Director of Research, Security Council Report, New York. A contribution made in relation to "The Basque Case: A Comprehensive model for Sustainable Human Development" research program at the bilateral meeting held in New York, 9th May 2011.

There are emerging nations demanding a new strategic role in the world. Globalization and the lack of control of speculative capital flows can the whole world economy in jeopardy and bankrupt entire countries in under a week. The proliferation of security risks provoked by injustice and the lack of dialogue and the threat of terrorist actions in any country in any part of the globe. Poverty and social inequality are growing not only in the so-called third world but also in the developed countries.

All these factors are giving shape to a scenario of transition which in some cases may be seized as an opportunity, but for many people who are directly or indirectly threatened by these changes, it generates a situation of insecurity and threat, even misery.

Under this new scenario people are demanding from their governments a new style of leadership and a different way of doing politics. The relentless pursuit of growth and abandonment of a significant part of society by the wayside is no longer enough. It is no longer possible to turn a blind eye when the environmental balance of the planet is being put at risk.

The citizens of every nation and country are demanding a new model of development, one which incorporates social and environmental balance. Development, in short, based on investment in social capital and innovation which increases happiness and security. With regard to this Professor Melchin points out that "the philosophy of Lonergan economics is reflected throughout the themes of the Basque model. Lonergan economics emphasises the importance of investment in social capital and innovation which are central to the Basque model."[50]

The Basque Country demonstrates the possibility of successfully applying a new model of Sustainable Human Development under extreme and unfavourable circumstances. That is, having to overcome a process of

---

[50] MELCHIN, K., Director of the Lonergan Center, Saint Paul University, Toronto. A contribution made in relation to "The Basque Case: A Comprehensive model for Sustainable Human Development" research program at the bilateral meeting held in New York, 13th May 2011.

restructuring its traditional economy with the background of an ongoing political and violent conflict.

The Basque analysis of Sustainable Human Development and the keys to its success are of particular relevance as they can reveal a path to follow for other communities and nations searching for a new model of government with the objective of facing up to the challenges of economic growth, social balance, and respect for the environment. In this regard Baroness Noala O' Loan suggests, "the model could be useful in other places around the world, but being able to apply it will depend on whether or not they can adapt it to their own culture."[51] In short, the Basque case could be a point of reference for those countries or regions which, more so than economic growth, are seeking welfare and happiness for each and every one of their citizens.

Therefore, it is extraordinarily important from a social, political and economic viewpoint to understand the recent past of the Basque case and to support us in building its future.

The 80s were years of recovery for the Basque democratic Institutions and self-government, keys in the political, economic, and social development of the Basque Country over the following 25 years. This was also a period when it was necessary to undergo a period of restructuring of the economic and productive base of the Basque Country. It was an era full of hope, serious economic crisis, and political turbulence with incipient instruments of self-government. Nevertheless, it was also an era in which a strategic national decision was made by the recently re-established Basque Government. With a vision of governmental intervention to "control the worst excesses of the economic cycle" in the grateful words of Paul Samuelson to John Maynard Keynes,[52]

---

[51] BARONESS O'LOAN, N., Member of the House of Lords. A contribution made in relation to "The Basque Case: A comprehensive model for Sustainable Human Development" research program, at the bilateral meeting held at the House of Lords, Westminster, London, 28 March 2011.

[52] SAMUELSON, P. and NORDHAUS, W., *Economics,* (16th ed.). Madrid, ed. McGraw-Hill, 1999, p. 37, said: "Nowadays, thanks to the intellectual contribution of John Maynard Keynes and his

and on the basis of a strategic public-private alliance: "industry is the economic and social engine of our people, we must look after it."

Dynamic socio-industrial policies were set underway. In short, the first phase of the Sustainable Human Development model adopted by the Basque Country was "learning to compete." This was based upon our existing strengths, the industrial core of the country. The formula "zapatero a tus zapatos" literally *cobbler to your shoes* and meaning *stick to what you know best* became the foundation for economic development.

This all occurred at a key moment for the future of the country, as it coincided with structural changes in the lives of Basque people and companies. The most important change was joining the European Common Market along with the Spanish State on January 1, 1986. This date also coincided with the Single European Act and meant a stage of reorganization of the productive activities as a result of joining the European markets. From then on, at different speeds and with a delay with regard to the rest of the European countries, the integration of our markets and our lives with the European markets and lives began to take place.

Later, in the 90s, already integrated into what was to become the European Union, society started to "learn to compete and cooperate." New types of organization were adopted, markets were opened, and there was a dynamic expansion of our international presence. A commitment was made to quality[53] through Cooperation and through

---

followers, we know how to control the worst excesses of the economic cycle. Governments can influence the levels of production, employment and inflation by carefully using fiscal and monetary policy."

[53] In December 1992 EUSKALIT was set up (Basque Foundation to promote Quality) with 21 large public and private organizations. In 1993 the first activity was to design and start up an advanced course in Quality for technicians. In 1995 the first edition of the Training Program for Action for industrial companies was held. In 1996 the program was for educational centerscenters, non-profit making organizations, and Public Health Network Centres (Osakidetza). In 1995 work was started in the club of assessors

Clusterization. The concept of Cooperation is key to explain past success and to build the future: the commitment derived from the strategic public-private alliance is the cornerstone which, together with self-government and training, explains the level of development as a country over recent years.

Subsequently, the Basque Country tackled a third strategic phase over a period of approximately 10 years, between 1998 and 2008 when it "learned to innovate," which we will discuss in detail in this paper. Furthermore, studying this period will also enable us to analyze the immediate effects of the "fifth" — and most important to date[54] — extension of the European Union in 2004[55] on the Basque Country and the incorporation of ten countries from the east and the center of Europe (PECOs) to make up the EU-25 (later in 2007 two more inclusions would make up the current EU27).[56]

The new additions brought in countries with a lower per capita income than the EU-15, but with similar characteristics regarding human resources, cultural heritage, or geographical situation, being countries with interesting characteristics in various sectors. For these reasons the initial forecasts indicated likely negative consequences for the

---

according to the EFQM Excellence model. Currently the Basque Country has the greatest concentration of Excellence centers in Europe. According to data on the webpage, at present there are 131 diplomas of commitment to excellence, 154 silver Qs, and 37 gold Qs all awarded by Euskalit. There is 1 Award, 10 prizes, and 9 finalists for EQA excellence, following the EFQM model.

[54] The EEC (European Economic) of the Treaty of Rome 1957 comprising Belgium, Holland, Luxemburg, West Germany, France and peripheral, was later joined by the United Kingdom, Denmark and Ireland in 1973. Then Greece became a member in 1981. Greenland, which is part of Denmark, decided by referendum to abandon the EEC in 1985. In 1986 Portugal and Spain joined. In 1990, with the application of the Right of Self-Determination, the Reunification of Germany meant an automatic widening of EU borders with the integration of the provinces of the former GDR. In 1995 Austria, Finland, and Sweden all joined.

[55] Estonia, Latvia, Lithuania, Poland, the Czech Republic, Hungary, Slovakia, Slovenia, Malta, and Cyprus made up the famous "fifth" broadening of the EU in 2004.

[56] In 2007 Romania and Bulgaria entered the EU.

European "peripheral regions," such as the Basque Country. These forecasts were tempered by an economic boom — which in many cases has helped to hide competitive deficiencies which have augmented during the current crisis — as well as by a strong business and social response to the challenges arising from the new socio-economic situation caused by the processes of extension.

Two additional arguments give weight to the importance of the analysis of the Basque Case between 1998 and 2008. During this period there were the two most recent attempts to negotiate with ETA. Additionally, legal-political initiatives were presented and approved by absolute majority in Basque democratic institutions with the aim of separating peace and politics in order to channel the political conflict.

With regard to the first argument, it is necessary to underline that precisely during these years, following the breakdown of the Ajuria-Enea Pact in March 1998, the most intense attempts to negotiate with ETA were made: The agreement between the political parties and social agents of Lizarra-Garazi in September 1998, the negotiation by President Aznar in 1998–1999 who took advantage of the ceasefire declared by ETA in response to the Lizarra agreement, and the last by President Rodríguez Zapatero between 2004 and 2007. All of them have been honest attempts to seek peace, others, such as the State terrorism of GAL developed by the Socialist Party of the Spanish Government, were not so.[57] They failed, but the effort was worthwhile. It is necessary to underline, too, that it was in this period of time (1998–2008) when more progress was made in the development of the ethical principle, the approach to an ethical and moral recognition of the victims of violence and terrorism and the culture of peace (Victims Office, Agreements on Victims of the Basque Parliament, Peace Plan, Law on Victims, etc.).

With regard to the second argument, based on the questioning whether or not ETA exists, the Basque people need political agreements for coexistence. Whether political

---

[57] To quote an example of the literature on the subject, see MIRALLES, M. and ARQUÉS, R., *Amedo: The State against ETA*. Barcelona, Plaza y Janés, 1995.

agreements exist or not the violence of ETA must disappear immediately, and the fertility of the 1998–2008 period must be recognized in relation to the democratic approval by the Basque Parliament of legal political initiatives to tackle the solution to the so-called Basque political problem. Thus, separating the negotiation to achieve peace from political agreements for coexistence between the Basque Country and Spain — with regard to this question, Prof Aligica states that "the separation of political conflict and violence has been an important lesson learned from the Basque experience"[58] — initiatives were passed by absolute majority in the Basque Parliament.

These initiatives, which still have a long way to go in the future, represent a qualitative leap for Basque self-government regarding the right to decide and the depth of political power and competence that is required in order to achieve sustainable human development. These initiatives also represent for the Basque people, the Basque Country or Euskal Herria, our Basque culture and Basque language — Euskera —their rightful place in Europe and in the world. Moreover, Professor Satayanath suggests that the Basque case could offer applications for other identity disputes throughout the world "due to its social democratic liberal model focussed on the rights of the individual and the non-violent efforts to secure decentralization of political power from the national government."[59]

Looking to the future without forgetting our roots. Compete with roots. Innovate with roots. The last 30 years have shown us that self-government — "burujabetza" in Euskera — is equal to welfare. The Basque Model demonstrates that strengthening the identity of Peoples does not mean rejecting globalization or the modern world but in fact means the contrary: Innovation and Identity, self-

---

[58] ALIGICA, P. Contribution made in relation to "The Basque Case: A Comprehensive model for Sustainable Human Development" research program at the bilateral meeting held at George Mason University, Washington, 26 January 2011.

[59] SATAYANATH, S., New York University. Contribution made in relation to "The Basque Case: A Comprehensive model for Sustainable Human Development" research program at the bilateral meeting held in New York, 13th May 2011.

government and welfare are linked to the achievement of Sustainable Human Development today, they were so in the past, and they will be more so tomorrow. Teresa Whitfield agrees that "social cohesion in the Basque Country and unifying sense of identity has been critical to its success in terms of economic and social growth; this sense of identity has resorted in a nation-building project defined by sustainable human development which unites the populace."[60]

Sustainable Human Development: A Global Reflection from a "Human" and a "Local" Perspective.

It is necessary to point out that between the ethical principle, the democratic principle, and the principle of sustainable human development, there is a logical identification and an inherent fusion that gives sense and life to the model.

Thus, beyond rhetorical definitions of sustainable, lasting development emphasizes the responsibility of one generation to another, pointing out the objective of "satisfying the needs of the present generation without compromising the ability of future generations to meet their own needs." Our definition of sustainable human development stems from the fact that development cannot, in any way, be understood as merely a generic appeal to responsibility, not even in terms such as "a rationalization of needs satisfaction, economic growth." It is necessary to bear in mind realities such as the fact that "cultural diversity is as necessary for humankind as biological diversity is for living organisms." On this matter Jacqueline Klopp agrees stating, "the Basque Case demonstrated the success of a holistic approach through a deliberate attempt to integrate economic, social and environmental agendas, and then bring in, often excluded, cultural elements."[61]

---

[60] WHITFIELD, T., Centre on International Cooperation, New York University. Contribution made in relation to "The Basque Case: A Comprehensive model for Sustainable Human Development" research program at the bilateral meeting held in New York, 13th May 2011.

[61] KLOPP, J., Center for Sustainable Urban Development, Columbia University, New York Contribution made in relation to

This means, holding firmly to the belief that, if we so wish, a different kind of model is possible, if not "the principle of democracy itself would be under threat."[62] To restructure the State and the Government, to develop, in the words of Anthony Giddens, "a new social contract" that "reconnects the three spheres — State, market and civil order," as only a society that reaches a balance between these will be a "healthy society."[63] Not allowing, as stated by Jürgen Habermas, that "socially powerful corporations participate in the exercising of public power, without being subject to the usual responsibilities which are associated with

---

"The Basque Case. A Comprehensive model for Sustainable Human Development" research program at the bilateral meeting held in New York, 9th May 2011.

62 JULIEN, C., *Le suicide des democraties,* París, ed. Grasset, 1972. Reflects that the very principles of democracy are weakened when the great majority of the citizens are convinced that they cannot influence policies of the government; CHOMSKY, N., *El beneficio es lo que cuenta: Neoliberalismo y orden global,* Barcelona, ed. Crítica, 2000, p.145, writes: "democracy works whenever individuals participate in a significant way in public matters, at the same time as they concern themselves with their own affairs, both personal and collective, without illegitimate interference from the concentrations of power."

39 GIDDENS, A., *The third way and its critics,* Madrid, ed. Santillana, 2001, pages. 176 and 177, states: "The loss of power of the in the last two or three decades has not been caused only be globalization. It is also fruit of an endogenous crisis. The reconstruction of State and of Government may recover this power. It continues to play a fundamental role, both in the economic life and in other areas. It cannot replace the marketplace nor civil society, but it is necessary that it intervenes in both. (…). A healthy society is one in which there is a balance between the State and the market and civil order. (…). Without a stable civil society, with rules, standards of trust and social decency, it is not possible for either the markets to flourish or for democracy to be maintained."

organs of the state."[64] Democracy and the Social State according to Ignacio Sotelo "depend on each other."[65]

In this respect the comments of Mark Stover, Lucy Goodhart, and Oeindrila Dube on this research are worthy of mention. Mark Stover expresses a strong interest in the social resilience of the Basque Country suggesting,"it could make a valuable contribution to a study of dynamic systems," adding, "the document could form a vital contribution to the construction of a dynamic systems theory (DST) model of the Basque Country."[66] Lucy Goodhart says, "in the Basque Country the role of social and economic innovation in coordination with research and development is profound and could make a valuable contribution to the varieties of capitalism literature."[67] Professor Dube remarks, "in the Basque case it was a unique combination of research,

---

64 HABERMAS, J., *Between facts and norms Contributions to a discourse theory of law and democracy.* Madrid, ed. Trotta, 1998, p. 519, who also added: "social protagonists endowed with a paraconstitutional power shatter the framework of the Constitution."

65 SOTELO, I., *El Estado social: Antecedentes, origen, desarrollo y declive.* Madrid, ed. Trotta, 2010, pages. 391 and 392 point out: "Democracy and Social State depend upon each other. The weakening of the Social State renders democracy more fragile and the collapse of the Social State augers the end of democracy, at least to the extent in which we understand it in Europe. (...). The invention of a new kind of Social State is based on the same supposition that sustains democracy, to discover, that the citizens self-govern better than when ruled from above by the wishes of someone or some group of people."

66 STOVER, M., Advanced Consortium on Cooperation, Conflict and Complexity, Columbia University, New York. Contribution made in relation to "The Basque Case: A Comprehensive model for Sustainable Human Development" research program at the bilateral meeting held in New York, 12th May 2011.

67 GOODHART, L., Columbia University, New York. Contribution made in relation to "The Basque Case: A Comprehensive model for Sustainable Human Development" research program at the bilateral meeting held in New York, 12th May 2011.

development and innovation that boosted both economic and social growth."[68]

In short, sustainable human development does not lend itself to a closed definition but one that is open, resulting from the dialectic between dignity/equality, political autonomy/freedom, cultural identity/intercultural relations. That is, "progress with roots,"and "progress with a face and eyes."

We will see in the following section how, from a local level in a "small" country such as The Basque Country, a strategy for sustainable human development can be applied. Following the thinking of Anthony Giddens, "day to day decisions" and "global consequences" are increasingly interrelated,[69] contributing to the environmental equilibrium of the entire planet.

Lamentably, the reality we are faced with today is far from this equilibrium. Economic growth and technological advances have not managed to reduce our "ecological footprint." Neither have they made significant headway in the fight against climate change or even increased our "well-being" in parameters of increased social and personal happiness and satisfaction.

In the first decade of the 21st century we can see that world GDP and the per capita income of the developed countries are higher than ever before in the history of humanity. We now enjoy more material goods and a higher purchasing power than we ever have. Furthermore, more than 1,500 million people, that is an ever increasing percentage of the population of the new emerging countries,

---

68 DUBE, O., New York University. Contribution made in relation to "The Basque Case: A Comprehensive model for Sustainable Human Development" research program at the bilateral meeting held in New York, 13th May 2011.

69 BECK, U., GIDDENS, A. y LASH, S., *Reflexive Modernization: Politics, tradition and aesthetics in the modern social order.* Madrid, ed. Alianza, 1997, p. 77 states: "This extraordinary inter-connection (which is accelerating even more) between everyday decisions and daily consequences, together with the converse, the influence of global orders in individual live, constitute the key theme of the new agenda."

are rapidly becoming part of the so-called "consumer society."

The advances brought about through the development of science and technology in the last fifty years have probably been greater than those accumulated by humanity throughout all the rest of human history. Economic globalization, international commerce, and multi-national financial flows are now a reality.

It is true that since the end of 2007 — although it cannot be said that this has been a surprise for everyone[70] — we have been undergoing a profound crisis. The economic and financial authorities "reassure" us, claiming that sooner or later things will settle and we will once again enjoy significant growth rates thanks to technological innovation and to the thrust of the emerging nations. Enormous efforts are made to get the message across that "everything will be all right." We have to keep running to avoid being left behind. This is the prevailing social thinking and the economic philosophy in politics and in the media. This "singular" line of thought gained tremendous strength after the fall of the Berlin wall and the failure of socialism. We

---

[70] KRUGMAN, P., El gran engaño: Ineficacia y deshonestidad: Estados Unidos ante el siglo XXI. Barcelona, ed. Crítica, 2004, p. 103, his forecast anticipating events which we have experienced at the end this first decade in of the 21st century, he writes: "1st February 2002 (…) How many more cases like Enron are out there? Even now, the general opinion is that Enron was not a very clean company. Well, other companies have also adopted 'dynamic accounting', an art previously known as fraud. But what is the probability that other important companies turn out to be, behind their imposing facades, little more than pyramid selling scams? Ah, the probability is high. I cannot tell you which business icons will reveal themselves to be made of papier-mâché, but I would be very surprised if we don't end up having two, three or even several Enron cases in the future"; SOROS, G., The crisis of global capitalism. The open society in danger, Madrid, ed. Debate, 1999, p. 21, points out: "We see ourselves as having missed out (…) from counteracting the excesses of the financial markets. Without these controls, it is likely that the global economy will collapse."

have reached the "end of history," according to the spokesman for liberalism F. Fukuyama.[71]

We run and run but just like Alice in Lewis Carrol's[72] story we have the sensation of staying in the same place. The time has come to pause for a moment to reflect, to show some humility, to listen to the different voices from all over the world which are asking us for prudence.[73] These voices are proposing other ways[74], are suggesting the need to set

---

[71] FUKUYAMA, F., *The end of history and the last man.* Barcelona, ed. Planeta, 1992, based on an essay, which turned out to be very controversial, which was published in 1989, after the fall of the Berlin wall, in which he defends the idea that Human history as a struggle between ideologies has concluded, and a world has begun based on the neo-liberal policies and economics which have been imposed on the utopias. The ideologies are no longer necessary and have been substituted by the economy.

[72] CARROL, L., *Alice Through the Looking Glass.* Madrid, ed. Gaviota/Everest, 2010. In this book — the follow-up to Alice in Wonderland — Carroll puts forward a principle, voiced by the Queen of Hearts, who says to Alice: "To stay in the same place you need to run as fast as you can. And if you want to reach somewhere else, you have to run at least twice as fast." This can be read in chapter 2, which is entitled "The Garden of Live Flowers."

[73] SAMPER, E., *El salto global: Retos de América Latina ante la globalización.* Bogotá, ed. Taurus, 2004, p. 299, states: "At the beginning of the 21st Century the world was not going well for the majority of its inhabitants. The lives of many are controlled by just a few who take decisions about 85% of production, control 84% of trade and hold almost 90% of savings. As long as this situation remains the same, globalization will continue to be a game of winners and, a dangerous game in which everyone plays but only a few can win."

[74] RIFKIN, J., *The hydrogen economy: The creation of the worldwide energy web and the redistribution of power on earth.* Barcelona, ed. Paidós, 2002, p. 263: "Reglobalization from the bottom. Our future lies in hydrogen. But who will control this 'ever-lasting fuel'. By virtue of its very ubiquity, hydrogen opens the way to democratise energy and give access to power to all human beings on earth." And then goes on to warn: "But the fact is that this possibility does not guarantee that hydrogen will be distributed equally and with justice among every nation. It depends to a great extent on how we 'value' hydrogen. Will it be seen as a shared resource, just like sunshine or

limits on growth itself, to oppose this "self-inflicted fate," which, in the words of Jürgen Habermas, may even endanger finding a "new identity" for old Europe.[75] We have to ask ourselves simple questions, although they may be uncomfortable ones for the neo-liberals. We must ourselves questions about where we are, and above all, where we are going in this never-ending race. Where is "this vast procession" leading us, just as the eminent physicist Sir Alfred Ewing[76] asked in 1932. Juan José Sánchez Inarejos wondered, "What are the targets of our civilization, of our nations, of our lives?" and submitted with conviction that "the lack of the answers to this question is terrifying, because the fact is that the world today does not know where it wants to go."[77]

---

the air that we breathe? Like a good which is bought and sold in the market place? Or something in between?"

[75] HABERMAS, J., *The philosophical discourse of modernity.* Madrid, ed. Taurus, 1989, p. 432, writes: "Old Europe will only be able to find the way to a new identity when a short-circuit of economic growth, arms race and 'old values' offers it a vision of breakaway to its fate, which is in fact a self-inflicted fate."

[76] EWING, J.A., Presidential speech to the British Association Assembly, 1932. Printed in the *Daily Telegraph*, London, September 19, 1932. He said "We are aware that in the attitude of the thinking person in our times a change in spirit has taken place with regard to what is called mechanical progress. Admiration is tempered by criticism; complacency has given way to doubt; doubt has turned to alarm. There is a sense of confusion and frustration just as someone might have who has walked a long way only to discover that he has taken the wrong direction. Turning back is impossible. What way should he go? Where will this or that path lead? An old representative of applied mechanics may be forgiven if he expresses certain disappointment when, finding himself now left aside, he observes the dizzying march of discoveries and inventions that used to delight him so much. It is impossible not to ask: Where is this enormous procession heading? What, in the end, is its target? What way might it influence the future of the human race?"

[77] SÁNCHEZ INAREJOS, J. J., *La globalización al desnudo.* Madrid, ed. Chaos-Entropy, 2001, pages 205 and 206, further point out: "it is said that the immense majority of people want to be rich, that the desire to possess and to enjoy as many goods as possible, is the true objective which drives most of our contemporaries. But if it is true, that it is money that moves so many people, it is a false logic to

Simple questions that different people, academics, philosophers, economists, politicians and ecologists[78] are already asking to seek a more complete sense to our life, beyond the facet of "consumer-soldier" which uncontrolled and unregulated marketing and capitalism have insisted in turning us. What a wonderful reflection from José Saramago, quoted in his article "Centro" in *La Caverna*: "We would sell everything you needed if we didn't prefer you to need what we have to sell,"[79] which invites us to change life for a change of life.

In short we have to be able to ask ourselves questions as simple as these:

- Is continuous economic and population growth possible in a finite world?
- Have we crossed the boundaries of the capacity for regeneration of the planet?
- Do economic growth and compulsive consumerism make us happy?
- Why and how are we here?
- What road should we take to guarantee a better future for the whole of humankind?
- How can nations and local communities preserve the biological diversity of the planet?

Evidently, we do not aim to defend utopian or catastrophic ideas; it is simply a matter of putting forward urgent questions for their reflection, with the objective of

assume that those anxieties to store riches constitute an objective; in fact they are more a drive, a kind of animal appetite which takes hold of the simplest of souls."

78 See for example the references of Steve Dodds, David Myers, C. Hamilton, Carol Ryff, E.J. Mishan, Herman Daly, William Lawrence, André Gorz, Serge Latouche, Nicolas Georgescu-Roegen, Vincent Cheynet, Francois Schneider, Richard Meinberg, James Howard Kunstler, Carlos Taibo, Edward Goldsmith, Federico de María, and Giorgio Mosangini, among others.

79 SARAMAGO, J., *La caverna.* Madrid, ed. Santillana, Suma de letras, 2002, p. 353.

rescuing critical thought[80] and the freedom of the individual from the dream of consumerism and utilitarian materialism in which we are submerged.

It is not our intention to provide a complete answer to each and every one of these questions. Among other things it would be impossible, just as it was for Giovanni Arrighi when he asked in an excellent study if the history of capitalism might be at a point of decisive inflection.[81] Nevertheless, we will try to approach their underlying theme, because we are convinced that the economic, political, and social development of the 21st century will depend upon the individual and collective answers given to these and other similar questions regarding the future of humankind.

---

80 By way of example we consider it interesting to consult RAMONET, I., et al., *Critical Thinking vs. Unique Thinking*. Madrid, ed. Le Monde Diplomatique, 2001, in which there are also works of esteemed authors such as ARMAND MATTELART, J.M. NAREDO, SAMIR AMIN, JUAN GOYTISOLO, BERNARD CASSEN, NOAM CHOMSKY, K.S. KAROL and EDUARDO GALEANO among others.

81 ARRIGHI, G., *The long twentieth century: Money, power and the origins of our times*. Madrid, ed. Akal, 1999, pp. 13, 427, 428 and 429, in which he states: "the resources needed to construct the State and organize the war of the traditional centers of power of the western capitalist world have grown to such an extent that they can only increase through the formation of a truly global world empire. (…) this requires control over the most prolific sources of surplus world capital, which is currently located in Asia", and he goes on to ask: "Why not, in other words, allow East Asian capital to set the terms under which it would lend its help to the western world in order for it to conserve power? Is this not the kind of agreement which has been made historically by capitalism?" Then, paraphrasing Schumpeter, he adds: "before humanity drowns (or revels) in the dungeons (in paradise) of a post-capitalist world empire or a world post-capitalist market society, it may well burn in the horrors (or the glories) of the intensification of violence which has accompanied the liquidation of the world order of the Cold War. (…). It is impossible to say if this will mean the end of the world or the end of humanity."

Is Continuous Economic Growth Possible in a World with Limited Material Resources? Have We Overrun the Limits of the Earth's Capacity for Regeneration?

> "If the present growth trends in world population, industrialization, pollution, food production and the use of natural resources are not adjusted, the growth limits of the planet will be reached within the next one hundred years."

This is the conclusion to the report entitled "The Limits of Growth," presented more than 30 years ago in 1972 by the Rome Club.[82] The report was a huge blow to the environmental conscience of political, economic, and social leaders.

---

[82] MEADOWS, D., "The limits of growth." Report commissioned by the Rome Club to be drawn up by the MIT (Technological Institute of Massachusetts) in 1972. The principle thesis of the report is, "in a limited planet, the dynamics of exponential growth (for population and GDP) are not sustainable." The report by Donella Meadows, with the collaboration of Dennis Meadows and Jorge Randers, pointed out figures which were, even then, most concerning:
- The exponential growth of population. In the last two hundred years, the population of the planet has grown from 1 billion in the year 1800 to 6 billion in the year 2000 (at an estimate).
- The excessive consumption of mineral reserves and non-renewable energies "per capita," as well as the increase in dumped waste, result of the economic growth without limits, places at risk the capacity of the planet for generation. "The relationship between the limits of the Earth and human activities is changing." The exponential growth curves add millions of people and thousands of millions of tonnes of contaminated waste to the ecosystem each year. "Mankind's plundering is going beyond the limits of what the Earth is able to bear."
- The report added a global recommendation: "it is still possible to modify these growth tendencies and to establish conditions of ecological and economic stability, in such a way that growth is prolonged and sustainable in the future. For this to happen it is necessary to go through a great transition: the transition from growth to global equilibrium."

In 1992 the same team published a new report, "Beyond the Limits," and in 2004 it was updated,[83] confirming the process of deterioration of the planet and the failure to fulfil the recommendations made in 1972.

Is this merely ecologist propaganda? It would not be entirely wise to qualify it as such. The reports themselves and posterior empirical data duly corroborated by official research confirm that the evidence can be found all around us.

- Sea level has risen between 10 and 20 cm since 1900, and the area of the polar circles is progressively shrinking.
- In 2000 the FAO announced that 75% of fish stocks were beyond a level which could guarantee their conservation.
- According to a study by the World Resources Institute[84] the total amount of waste products and contaminated substances increased 28% between 1975 and 1996 despite greater efficiency in the use of materials.[85]

---

83 MEADOWS, D., MEADOWS, D.L., and RANDERS, J., "The limits of growth: 30 years later." Published June 1, 2004 by the Chelses Green Publishing Company. The report states, "there cannot be unlimited population, economic and industrial growth in a planet with limited resources."

84 THE WORLD RESOURCES INSTITUTE (WRI) is an independent center set up in 1982 with its headquarters in Washington, D.C. It is devoted to policy research and to technical assistance in environmental and development areas. WRI provides subjective information and formulates practical proposals aimed at promoting a change in the policies which lead to healthy and social equitable environmental development. WRI works with institutions in more than 50 countries to bring the discoveries of scientific research, economic analysis and practical experiences to leading organizations in the fields of policy, business, and global level non-governmental activity.

85 WORLD RESOURCES GUIDE 2000–2001: *People and Ecosystems: The fraying web of life.* The full report is a joint publication on behalf of the United Nations Development Program (UNDP), the United Nations Environment Program (UNEP), the World Bank and the World Resources Institute (WRI). In the report the statistics

- Human beings appropriate 40% of the net product of photosynthesis (the planet's vegetable growth) when just 70 years ago we only used 10%.[86]
- Different reports indicate that non-renewable resources are being over exploited, causing an increase in the price of raw materials, especially in the case of petrol and uranium.[87]
- Researchers have compared the annual demand for resources with the area of the earth necessary to generate them and to absorb the corresponding waste products.[88] According to calculations, human demand for resources in 1961 approached 70% of the regeneration capacity of the planet. By the end of 1990 it was 20% more than the capacity of the earth to sustain the demand. The biosphere needs, therefore, one year and three months, to replace

---

presented are overwhelming and the report warns that stopping the deterioration of the life support systems of the planet is probably the most difficult challenge which humankind has had to confront.

86 In the reports of the United Nations Fund for Population Activities statistics have been provided concerning these subjects. In the report corresponding to the 2001 "*State of World Population: Footprints and milestones; Population and environmental change*. See chapters 1 and 3. Similarly in the final report, corresponding to 2009: *Facing a changing world: Women, population and climate* we are alerted to the consequences for the planet of increasing population and consumption of natural resources.

87 See SEMPERE CARRERAS, J., and TELLO ARAGAY, E., *The end of the era of cheap petrol.* Barcelona, ed. Icaria, 2007; La OCDE and the OIEA publish the periodical report: "Uranium: Resources, production and demand," known as the "RED BOOK." Another report, published by the Administration for Energy of the US Government entitled "International Energy Outlook 2005" (IEO 2007*)*.

88 WACKERNAGEL, M., and REES, W., have designed a measurement of ecological impact known as the Ecological footprint. They warn that the ecological impact of humanity, at the start of the 21st Century, is 20% higher than the earth can support. This impact is far above the capacity of natural regeneration and will lead us in the short term to an ecological deficit.

what humanity consumes in just one year, according to studies from 2008.[89]

- Climate change is a reality. According to various reports from the Intergovernmental Panel on Climate Change (IPPC) of the UN[90] and the US National Academy of Science by the end of the century we will have witnessed an increase of six degrees centigrade in the temperature of the earth.

If this was not enough, the list of contradictions continues to a scandalous extent. Economic growth has failed to achieve social convergence throughout the planet, in fact the gap between the richest and the poorest is growing in the global economy as Robert Wade's[91] famous "glass of Champagne" graphically demonstrates. In 1998 more that 45% of the inhabitants of the earth had to live on an income of no more than $2 a day. Meanwhile, the wealthiest 20% of the world's population possessed 85% of the global GDP.[92] The gap between the rich and the poor continues to widen, despite globalization being advocated as an opportunity for poor countries. In practice — paraphrasing M. Castells, A. Hoogvelt, David Held, and Anthony McGrew — the world is no longer divided as it once was along geographical lines, that is to say, between north and south, but reveals a new social architecture. This architecture, which divides humanity into the elites, the bourgeoisie, the underprivileged and the impoverished, cuts across territorial and cultural frontiers and

---

[89] *LIVING PLANET.* Report, 2008 of the World Wide fund for Nature (WWF).

[90] *Climate Change 2007: Physical Science Basis* is the contribution of Working Group I to the fourth Assessment Report of the Intergovernmental Panel on Climate Change (IPCC). This report is the point of reference for all UN decisions, discussions, and studies. Climate experts at MIT have calculated recently that the temperature increase of the earth's surface by 5.2 degrees in 2010 was more than double the rise that had been predicted in 2003.

[91] HELD, D. and McGREW, A., *Globalization / Anti-globalization: On the reconstruction of the world order*, Barcelona, ed. Paidós, 2003, pages 97 and 98.

[92] United Nations Environment Program (UNEP) GEO process of World Environment Perspectives l. GEO Report- 3, 2002.

reorders the world into two categories: the winners and the losers of globalization.[93]

It is nothing more than scandalous that we consent to a daily expenditure of 3,000 million dollars on military arms when more than 60,000 people die from hunger each day.[94] In fact, we have recently witnessed the multi-million dollar rescue of financial institutions that only a few years ago led us to disaster, right when the objectives of the millennium were being fixed, the governments of all the world pleaded a lack of funds with which to fight against world poverty. "There is no money," they said. There was no money to resolve famine and, as if by magic, hundreds of thousands of millions of dollars appeared to "rescue" the banks which had caused the financial crisis which has brought unemployment and poverty to millions of people since 2008.

In short, numerous official indicators are signalling that the limits for growth are about to be reached, if they have not been reached already.

Evidently not everyone is of the same opinion. There are those who maintain that the constant process of technological innovation will provide a solution to the environmental problems, reducing the consumption of raw materials and waste per unit of product and, thereby, guaranteeing growth rates sufficient to keep increasing the welfare of citizens.

Even accepting this as a possible thesis, it is no less certain that, at least over the last fifty years, this assertion is not backed by empirical evidence. In fact, technological progress that has taken place over the last fifty years has been exceptional. At the same time, perhaps, as maintains Ernest Gellner, it is because to a large extent we have had to concentrate on mitigating the effects created by ourselves[95]

---

[93] HELD, D. and McGREW, A., *Globalization / Anti-globalization: On the reconstruction of the world order*. Barcelona, ed. Paidós, 2003, p. 97.

[94] MAYOR ZARAGOZA, F., "More of the same? NO." Article published on his blog January 8, 2010.

[95] GELLNER, E., *Culture, Identity and Policy: Nationalism and the new social changes*. Barcelona, ed. Gedisa, 1989, p. 133, on reflecting on the shared weakness of the great ideologies inherited from the 19th

as the use of material resources and the level of waste dumped on the planet have increased[96].

Nevertheless, and setting aside the discussion as to whether we have passed the limit for planetary regeneration or not, it would be no more than common sense, and even coherent with the laws of physics and entropy of any system,[97] to answer the first questions by declaring that continuous and indefinite economic growth is not possible in a finite and limited world. The "capacity" of the earth is reaching a limit, which will oblige us to come up with new visions for the future, or at least to bring them to the table. In this respect the suggestion of Demetrio Loperena to consider sustainable development as a global ideology appears particularly attractive.[98]

Does Economic Growth and Compulsive Consumerism Increase Personal Happiness?

The consumer society of today is sustained upon the following economic and social philosophy, one in line with the defenders of the neo-liberal market: An increase in the consumption of material goods means greater happiness because consumption enables us to satisfy our needs. More consumption means higher economic growth. Higher

century, and the power of modern technology and its side-effects: "man is no longer struggling against nature but is fighting against the side-effects of man's conquest of nature."

[96] BECK, U., GIDDENS, A. and LASH, S., *Reflexive modernization: Politics, tradition and aesthetics in the modern social order.* Madrid, ed. Alianza, 1997, p. 101, states: "Evidently natural disasters still happen, but the current socialization of nature means that a diversity of systems which were once natural are now products of human decisions. The concern for global warming arises from the fact that the earth no longer follows a naturally given order. If global warming does exist, it is the result of the excesses of 'greenhouse gases' which have been added to the atmosphere over a period of no more than two hundred years."

[97] See GEORGESCU-ROEGEN, N., *"The entropy law and the economic process."* Cambridge, Massachusetts: Harvard University Press, 1971.

[98] See LOPERENA, D., *Globalization and sustainable development.* Pamplona, ed. Aranzadi, 2003.

economic growth means greater individual wealth. More individual wealth means more consumption. More consumption means greater happiness. And so the circle is complete.

For this reason, beyond the social and environmental repercussions, the reflection with regard to growth and its relationship to happiness is a question which makes many economists uncomfortable. Yet, it is a question we must ask as more and more citizens in different parts of the world are becoming reluctant to accept that higher growth is necessarily, always and everywhere, a good thing. Many people are beginning to ask if the craving — permanently unsatisfied — for more material goods and greater wealth with which to satisfy this craving, is in fact synonymous with greater happiness.

It is an uncomfortable question because if the market is no longer the provider of happiness, the logic of consumerist capitalism is brought into question.[99] The debate concerning happiness and the economy[100] begins to unsettle the sole prevailing line of thought, as any kind of reflection on this matter implies questioning the contribution of consumption and the "supremacy" of the market as a source of personal satisfaction and happiness.[101] The phenomenon

---

99 SOTELO, I., *El Estado social: Antecedentes, origen, desarrollo y declive.* Madrid, ed. Trotta, 2010, p. 392, "the citizen, turned into consumer, limits more and more the scope of the consumption, expecting less of the State and other social authorities. With the intermediate networks (family, neighborhood, company) weakened, we will become used to struggling for survival, a situation which little by little we will become to accept as our inexorable fate."

100 See BRUNO, F., and STUTZER, A., *Happiness and economics.* Princeton: Princeton University Press, 2002.

101 JAUREGUI, G., *La democracia en el siglo XXI: Un nuevo mundo, unos nuevos valores.* Oñati, IVAP (Herri Arduralaritzaren Euskal Erakundea), 2004, p. 218 states: "Liberal philosophy conceives the political protagonists as rational individuals and, in the best of cases, under the restrictions imposed by morality. In brief, it reduces the scope of the political to what is useful: the economy and, in the best of cases, ethics. If only public liberties are true rights, the rest of our needs are satisfied in the marketplace."

of downshifting, which is spreading in the rich countries, is a demonstration of this questioning.[102]

In fact, above a certain level of income or growth, there is no research that supports the equation: more wealth = more happiness. If this equation were true the following three correlations would also be true:

- People in the richest countries would be happier than people in the less well-off countries.
- Within each country the richer would happier than the poor.
- People would be happier the richer they got.

Our own experience and popular wisdom accumulated over the years, tell us that "money does not buy happiness." It is true that when one is on the threshold of poverty, money certainly helps to achieve happiness, but above a certain level of wealth, the tautology that more wealth, more consumption, more growth, more happiness begins to break down.

Following Frey Bruno and Alois Stutzer, if we consider the 20 leading countries where income per capita is above 15,000 dollars, there is no direct relationship between the higher incomes and a greater evaluation of the level of life satisfaction.[103] In general, rather than economic growth, personal and social happiness are related to aspects such as: education, human rights, and tolerance. GDP is quite low on the list.[104]

Other studies reach the conclusion that in those societies which inequality indices are lower, levels of happiness are higher. The most egalitarian societies are

---

[102] See LATOUCHE, S., *Supporting de-growth: How to get out of the presiding imaginary?* Barcelona, ed. Icaria, 2008. The main ideas of this book were previously expressed by the same author in "The Absurdity of productivity and waste: For a society of de-growth." Le *Monde Diplomatique*, November, 2003.

[103] BRUNO, F. and STUTZER, A., *Happiness and Economics*, Figure 2.2.

[104] See WEARING, A. and HEADEY, B., "Who enjoys life and why?", in ECKERSLEY, R., (ed.) *Measuring Progress: is life getting better?*, Coollingwood, Victoria, CSIRO Publishing, 1998.

happiest because inequality is associated with poor health, even in rich countries.[105] Furthermore, in relation to inequality and trust, Richard Wilkinson and Kate Pickett, "Changes in inequality and trust go together over the years. With greater inequality, people are less caring of one another, there is less mutuality in relationships, people have to fend for themselves and get what they can — so, inevitably, there is less trust. Mistrust and inequality reinforce each other. As de Tocqueville pointed out, we are likely to empathize with those not seen as equals; material differences serve to divide us socially."[106]

As wealth rises, income and economic factors lose importance for well-being. This is the consequence of the "decreasing marginal importance of the economy," as defended by the British economist Sir Jon Hicks.[107]

From a more individual perspective, happiness is associated with aspects of the sense and the finality of life itself, acceptance of one's self, personal-achievement and, especially, with a certain degree of spirituality, understood as a transcendental search for the most relevant aspects of human potential.[108] In this sense, Richard Wilkinson and Kate Pickett state, "As we showed (...) further improvements in the quality of life no longer depend on

---

[105] See ARGYLE, M., *Satisfaction levels in the Good Life,* London, CHRISTIE, I. and NASH, L., ed., 1998.

[106] WILKINSON, R. and PICKETT, K., *The Spirit Level. Why Greater Equality Makes Societies Stronger,* New York, ed. Bloomsbury Press, 2010, p. 56.

[107] Quote attributed to HICKS, J.R., Nobel prize winner for Economics in 1973 and included in DODDS, S., "Economic growth and human well-being", Ecological Economics, v.23, November 1997, pages. 95-111, and also in DIESENDORF, M., and HAMILTON, C., *Human ecology, human economy*, Sydney, Allen and Unwin, 1997.

[108] See EMMONS, R., HORWITZ, J., and DIENER, E., "Happiness of the very wealthy", *Social indicators research.* vol. 16, 1985, pages. 263-274; MYERS, D., "Does economic growth improve human morale?" Centre for a New American Dream. www.newdream.org , 1997; RYFF, C., "Happiness is everything, or is it?", Journal of Personality and Social Psychology, v. 57, 1989, ps.1069-1081.

further economic growth: the issue is now community and how we relate to each other"[109]

Evidently these kinds of analyses and conclusions are perfectly understood by the creators of marketing[110] and are used as incentives to motivate the drive for consumption in modern society. Thus, this sense of importance and of searching for an identity is what lies behind the image of consumer products. The publicity is efficient because it is capable of responding to this search for an identity, to build the "me" of each person, not from what we are but from what we consume. Consumption, in this sense, no longer has the target of the satisfaction of human needs; its current target consists of manufacturing identities.

The system based on compulsive hyper-consumerism will continue to work while people still have unsatisfied needs. It is a permanent state of unhappiness or lack of satisfaction which is the engine of economic growth. Hope invested in material wealth to fill the existential vacuum was described by Goethe when he declared, "We lurch from desire to enjoyment, and in enjoyment we long again for desire."[111]

We are immersed in the society of marketing, a society of people who try to give sense to their lives filling them with goods and merchandise. We live, as stated by Kjell Nordström and Jonas Ridderstråle, in the "age of more," in the "world of excess."[112] Human beings have turned into

---

109 WILKINSON, R. and PICKETT, K., *The Spirit Level. Why Greater Equality Makes Societies Stronger,* New York, ed. Bloomsbury Press, 2010, p. 247.

110 On this question the following examples of studies have had a great impact: KLEIN, N., *No logo: taking aim at the brand bullies,* Barcelona, ed. Paidós, 2002; FOX, R.W. and LEARS, J., *The power of culture: critical essays in American History,* Chicago, University of Chicago Press, 1993.

111 GOETHE, J.W., *Fausto.* Madrid, ed. Cátedra, 2005. This seminal work of the German Enlightenment describes a legendary character, Doctor Faust, who sells his soul to the devil in exchange for the pleasures of life through the fulfilment all his earthly desires.

112 NORDSTRÖM, K. and RIDDERSTRÅLE, J., *Funky Business.* Madrid, ed. Prentice Hall, 2000, p. 84, "We are so small and there is

consumers looking for happiness in the modern temples that are the shopping malls, but we can see from our own experiences that people are not any happier for possessing more goods.[113]

All things considered, and to answer the question that initially provoked this reflection, *Is economic growth equivalent to greater welfare?* We can conclude that the inhabitants of the richest countries are not necessarily happier than those who have less (as long as the latter have overcome a minimum threshold of wealth) and that people do not achieve happiness through obtaining more material possessions. Evidently these conclusions have to be made while keeping in mind that growth and an increase in income are of fundamental importance, in terms of personal satisfaction, for the poor and for those deprived of basic needs in nourishment, housing, health and access to education.

How Did We Get Here?

The philosophy of growth at any cost makes it, as put by Paul Krugman, "the nucleus of economic promise."[114] The

---

so much of everything. Look at the stars and count them. Look at the earth from an airplane and gaze at the lights. We are insignificant; we are drowning in a sea of choice and in the seas of change. We have too much. And the problem is that we keep asking for more. This is the age of more. More to choose. More to buy. More enjoyment. More fear. More uncertainty. More responsibility. More opportunities. We have entered into the world of excess: in the age of abundance."

113 HAMILTON, C., *Growth Fetish*. Iruña, ed. Laetori, 2006, pages 43–76.

114 KRUGMAN, P., *Selling Prosperity*. Barcelona, ed. Ariel, 1994, p. 113, "The nucleus of the economic promise of the conservatives can be summed up in just one word: growth. The staunchest defenders of supply economics, such Jude Wanniski and Arthur Laffer, sustain that if taxes are lowered, growth would accelerate in such a way that everything — including fiscal revenues — would increase. The most moderate conservative economists, such as Murray Weidenbaum or Michael Boskin, did not go so far, but did maintain that the tax burden and legislation were one of the principal explications for the deceleration undergone by growth in

liberalization of the markets and the economic globalization, no longer a new concept,[115] imposed especially from the 1970s onwards at the hand of a particular branch of economic thinkers and followers of the neo-liberal or neo-classical school.

The neo-liberal school has been the undisputed leader of economic thought and policy-making since the fall of the Berlin Wall. According to this philosophy, anything that hinders the free working of the market — be it of goods, services, people or capital — is counter-productive to growth and therefore must be sacrificed. Thus, the objective of growth as a path towards greater welfare is a priority objective. As Jürgen Habermas states, "the apologists of the Social State are everywhere in retreat, while the neo-conservatives advance freely in their attempt to do away with the Social State."[116]

Neo-liberal economic thought, used amongst others by Milton Friedman, believes that "an ever-increasing interventionist public sector will destroy both the prosperity which we owe to the free market system and human liberty itself."[117] This belief has been responsible for a historic

---

the United States during the decade of the 1970s, thereby implying that the elimination of the State would bring about bountiful rewards. There were even many liberals who believed that liberalization and the introduction of some reforms to the tax system could increase growth rates in the United States".

115 WALLERSTEIN, I., *Utopistics: Or historical choices of the 21st Century*. México, ed. Siglo XXI, 1998, pages. 11 and 12, "the modern world system, which is a capitalist world-economy, has existed since the 16th Century. It was originally created only in one region of the globe, in almost all of Europe and in part of the western hemisphere. (…). The modern system was globalized from a geographical point of view just before the end of the 19th Century and only in the second half of the 20th Century have the furthest flung corners of the globe been integrated. The creation of the structure of the States was part of the creation a capitalist world and economy, and was a necessary element in its structuring."

116 HABERMAS, J., *The philosophical discourse of modernity*. Madrid, ed. Taurus, 1989, p. 421.

117 FRIEDMAN, M. and FRIEDMAN, R. D., *Libertad de elegir: Hacia un nuevo liberalismo económico*. Barcelona, ed. Grijalbo, 1980, p. 22.

transfer of the political power of the state to the free market. Thus the political projects, both from the right and the left, have undergone a process of convergence. However this, according to Norberto Bobbio, should not lead us to accept the simplification that the difference is obsolete[118] and that they have succumbed to the totalitarianism of the market. If this is so, the most significant feature of the current modern world is globalization which has facilitated almost unhindered mobility to goods and capital. Fruit of this process, which has transformed the economic policies of the nations, has been the extraordinary size and influence of the international capital markets. We can measure their strength by their capacity to change the stability of a national economy in a matter of days or hours, such as we have recently witnessed in the cases of Greece and Spain.

The current economic crisis, therefore, clearly shows us that a new focus is necessary to control the power of the finances, a power which is largely a consequence of this globalization. Robert Skidelsky wrote in a recent article — a biography of Keynes — that, "Keynes observed that 'the precariousness of the financial markets is, to a great extent, the cause of our contemporary problem to generate sufficient investment.' This is even truer now — 70 years later — than in his time. Instead of obtaining investments for the productive sectors of the economy, the financial industry has become expert in generating investments for itself," thereby requiring an active governmental policy. Skidelsky adds, "however, as Keynes would have pointed out, it is important that government participation is based on solid economic foundations and not on political ideology, be it social democratic or of any other kind."[119]

The processes of globalization are mechanisms by which a specific historical and cultural ideology is spread and then colonizes the world.[120] In this case, a neo-liberal

---

118 See BOBBIO, N., *Right and left.* Madrid, ed. Taurus, 1998, paper in which it is argued the realignment of the left does not render its difference with the right obsolete.

119 SKIDELSKY, R., "Keynes and social democracy," *La Vanguardia.* Barcelona, July 21, 2010.

120 BECK, U., *What is globalization? Fallacies of globalism, responses to globalization.* Barcelona, ed. Paidós, 1998, pages. 169 and 170,

ideology which earns its legitimacy from the thinking by which the progress of human beings is measured through the acquiring of more goods and services. Economic growth brings happiness and a market without restrictions will increase growth and happiness. Faith in indefinite growth and consumption is backed by the anthropocentric nature of humankind. From this perspective, the natural world is "at the service" of humankind and therefore is considered to be simply a source of consumables to be transformed into an increasing quantity of goods and services for the benefit of human use.

Regardless of whatever nuances we may wish to incorporate, and leaving other factors aside, we could conclude that the neo-liberal philosophy that shapes the world both economically and politically is the source and origin of a process which has accelerated over the last 25 years. This process has led us, with its unfulfilled promises of individual and universal liberties,[121] to a world in which

---

"Globalism is a mental virus which has become installed in the interior of every party, of every writing, of every institution. This is the sense in which neo-liberal globalism appears to its mortal enemy, Marxism. (...). Neo-liberal globalism is a highly political action which, contradictorily, presents itself in a totally apolitical way. Revolution portrayed with absence of politics! This ideology defends non-intervention and the following of the market laws which, unfortunately, require the reduction of the (social) State and democracy. It is wrong to think that globalization requires the application of world market laws in a certain way. Economic globalization is *not* a mechanism nor automatism, but is, increasingly, *a political project* whose transnational agents, institutions and followers in the argument (World Bank, WTO, OECD, multi-national companies, along with international organizations) promote neo-liberal economic policy."

121 FRIEDMAN, M., *Capitalism and Freedom*. Chicago: University of Chicago Press, 1982, pp. 2, 8 and 9 state: "Freedom is a rare and delicate plant. Our minds tell us, and history confirms that the great threat to freedom is the concentration of power. (...) There is an intimate relation between economics and politics, that only certain combinations of political arrangements are possible, and that in particular, a society which is socialist cannot be democratic, in the sense of guaranteeing individual freedom. (...) The kind of economic organization that provides economic freedom directly,

obsession with growth at any cost and consumption without limits has risked the very equilibrium of the planet, leaving the vestiges of social injustice and unhappiness entrenched in a significant part of society today. "Ill fares the land" in the words of Tony Judt.[122]

What Role Should Sub-states and Entities Take to Foster One Path or the Other?

"Small is beautiful" announced Schumacher in 1973.[123] Today, small is beautiful and also powerful in the "social network."[124]

---

namely competitive capitalism, also promotes political freedom because it separates economic power from political power".

[122] JUDT, T., *Ill Fares the Land.* London, ed. Allen Lane, 2010, pp. 1, 2, 3 and 4: "Something is profoundly wrong with the way we live today. For thirty years we have made a virtue out of the pursuit of material self-interest: indeed, this very pursuit now constitutes whatever remains of our sense of collective purpose. (…) The materialistic and selfish quality of contemporary life is not inherent in the human condition. (…) We cannot go on living like this. (…) Indeed, the rising generation is acutely worried about the world it is to inherit. But accompanying these fears there is a general sentiment of frustration: 'we' know something is wrong and there are many things we don't like. But what can we believe in? What should we do?"

[123] SCHUMACHER, E.F., *Small is beautiful: Economics as if people mattered.* New York: Perennial Library, 1973.

[124] CASTELLS, M., *The information era, v. II The Power of Identity.* Madrid, Alianza Editorial, 2003. Pages. 462 and 463 writes: "Thus, the dominant logic in the society network gives rise to its own challenges in the form of communal resistance identities and project identities which arise from these spaces, in conditions and by means of processes which are specific to each institutional and cultural context. (…) Power (…) is no longer concentrated in the institutions (the state), organizations (capitalist companies) or the symbolic controllers (mass media, churches). It is disseminated through global networks of wealth, power, information and images, which circulate and transform within a system of variable geometry and dematerialized geography. (…) For this reason identities are so important and, in short, so powerful in this structure of power under constant change, as they construct interest, values and projects based on experience and they refuse to go away,

If we continue to leave economic and political decision making to the school of neo-liberal thought we will continue riding the horse of capitalism without controls or regulation. If we succumb to the supremacy of the market and the totalitarianism of consumerism and marketing, then humanity will march inexorably to a point of no return.

We must recognize that the current economic system has broken through the barriers — or is on the point of doing so — and has led us to a perilously critical situation. It is necessary to substantially change the existing structures and demand equilibrium in the distribution of power, which cannot lie only with the protagonists of globalization and the capital markets, as is claimed by Federico Mayor Zaragoza.[125]

Taking advantage of precisely this reaction to the current crisis, it is necessary to initiate a change in the system on a world scale which would enable the reins of the future to be taken up by "the people," as is clearly established in the first paragraph of the introduction to the United Nations Charter.

States have not only substituted peoples, but they have also transferred part of their economic resources and even their political and social responsibilities to giant international corporations. These corporations have, in many cases, enjoyed complete impunity to do as they please, or as some authors have stated, "to act in the areas free from law."[126] Revealing, according to Gurutz Jáuregui, this

---

establishing a connection between nature, history, geography and culture."

[125] MAYOR ZARAGOZA, F., "The problems of sustainability in a globalized world." *Revista de educación,* special issue April 14, 2009.

[126] I find the thought on this question made by CABALLERO HARRIET, F.J. particularly interesting *Algunas claves para otra mundialización*, n. 78, p. 61, in which he states: "perhaps the expression 'law-free zone to refer to the area in which the multi-national companies operate is not especially well chosen, similarly unfortunate is the expression that we are dealing with an "area of legal pluralism" and, even worse, that they constitute a `zone in which the traditional categories of Private and Public law can be applied to them'. The legislative arsenal of the World Trade Organization and its conflict resolving mechanisms; The World Bank's and the International Monetary Fund's batteries of

"utilitarian thinning down of politics particularly with regard to individualism, to the problems of identity, multi-culturalism, etc."[127]

It is necessary to establish social and political limits to economic power and to the power of the media. Powers which advocate uniformity on a world scale with a single economic and cultural template, replacing cultural diversity of nations with their own identity, matters which liberal thinking, to quote Gurutz Jáuregui again, considers "far from rational principles."[128]

---

regulations concerning structural modifications; the complex regulations on bilateral treaties; the regional economic cooperation agreements; the regulations on negotiations between Countries and multi-nationals or between multi-nationals.... constitute a real judicial system, the judicial system of the market. It is a judicial system which, obeying economic rationality, transcends public or private categorisation, consecrates the law of the strongest, establishes a symbiosis between the political and the economic and lays down efficiency and competition as its fundamental principles."

[127] JAUREGUI, G., *La democracia en el siglo XXI: un nuevo mundo, unos nuevos valores*. IVAP (Herri Arduralaritzaren Euskal Erakundea), Oñati, 2004, p. 221.

[128] JAUREGUI, G., *La democracia en el siglo XXI: Un nuevo mundo, unos nuevos valores*, pages. 217 and 218: "Relations between the defenders of the liberal tradition and those who defend cultural diversity have often been very difficult. And this is understandable if we bear in mind that they are supported by a very different logic. The political theory of liberalism is traditionally rooted in three major characteristics, individualism, universalism and statism. On the other hand, defenders of the cultural tradition have defended a political organization which is of a more collective or organic nature than individual, and therefore, distant from the liberal individualism. Because of this liberalism has been traditionally considered as somewhat distant, perhaps even contrary, to its very essence, the existence of groups, collectives, nations, etc. within the same nation state. This has often brought about the liberal rejection to cultural diversity, considering those groups that promote it to be minorities and emotionally motivated, far from the rational principles upon which, supposedly, are founded the states of law with a liberal base. The proliferation of minority movements, (ethnic, religious, nationalist, etc) seen in the last thirty years and especially, since the collapse of the communist systems,

The time has come to begin a process of transition and recovery of self-government, the identity and self-determination of peoples and nations. In spite of its apparent complexity,[129] this is now possible due to the social networks and the institutional interrelations that promote a world which is increasingly less remote both physically and intellectually. Only in this way can true democracy and the dignity of people triumph, following once again the thoughts of Federico Mayor Zaragoza, particular spurious interests which powerfully influence the political decisions of many governments.[130]

In this process, the citizens, the peoples are not alone. They have the support of an academic, scientific, and political community,[131] which more and more resists out of

---

has brought into question many of the foundations of liberal theory. For liberalism, this type of antagonism belong to a past era, a pre-modern time in which passion had not yet been eliminated or substituted by the rational dominance of the interests and by the generalization of the rational identities. Thus, many liberal thinkers reveal their perplexity and their incapacity to understand the current proliferation and resurgence of these minorities."

[129] KYMLICKA, W., *States, Nations and Cultures.* Córdoba, ed. Almuzara, 2004, p. 74, reflects on the error of wondering why minorities are so attached to their national identity, as if this were only a characteristic of minority national groups and was not common to the majorities, and he says: "we have to be able to adapt our own perception of the facts to take on board this profound love that individuals feel for their national cultures. It may be a real headache to try and provide an answer as to why people in general value their national identity, but it is not at all surprising that *minority* groups do –they do so for the same reasons that inspire the members of other majority national groups"; FINKIELKRAUT, A., *Lost Humanity.* Barcelona, ed. Anagrama, 1998, p.13, also reflects on this, stating: "the idea that all the peoples of the world constitute a single humanity is not, in fact consubstantial to human beings. Indeed, what distinguished mankind from other animal species for much of time was precisely that *they did not recognize each other.*"

[130] MAYOR ZARAGOZA, F., "Los límites del crecimiento," *Temas para el debate*, nº 181. December 2009, pages. 10–16.

[131] STIGLITZ, J.E., *El malestar en la globalización.* Madrid, Santillana Ediciones Generales, 2002, p. 308, states: "Equally of concern is what globalization can do to democracy. Globalization, in the way

control neo-liberal capitalism that is seriously endangering the identity of nations, social justice, defence of the natural environment, and the happiness of people.

In this sense, the words of Pope Francis in the European Parliament in November 2014 are particularly gratifying and healing: "The European Union's motto is 'Unity in Diversity,' but unity does not mean political, economic, or cultural uniformity, nor the uniformity of thought. In reality, any authentic unity is based on the wealth of the diversity that makes it up…In this sense, I consider that Europe is a family of people that could feel the institutions of the Union close to them if they wisely combine the desired ideal of unity with the diversity inherent

---

that it has been defended, often appears to substitute the old dictatorships of the national elites for new dictatorships of international finances"; SOROS, G., *La crisis de capitalismo global. La sociedad abierta en peligro,* Madrid, ed. Debate, 1999, p. 21, points out that: "We live in a global economy, but the political organization of our society is deplorably insufficient. We are deprived of the capacity to maintain or to counteract the excesses of the financial markets. Without these controls, it is likely that the global economy will collapse"; BERGER, P.L. y HUNTINGTON, S.P., *Globalizaciones multiples: La diversidad cultural en el mundo contemporáneo.* Barcelona, Ediciones Paidós, 2002, p. 21, writes: "between the different sectors of cultural globalization tensions and agreements arise in equal number, both at an elite and a popular level. If there is one common subject it is individualization: all the sectors of the emerging global culture foster the independence of the individual above tradition and collectivism. (…) individuation as an empirical phenomenon must be differentiated from 'individualism' as an ideology (although, of course, they are frequently linked). This consideration is useful, as it helps to explain why the new global culture is so widely popular." ; KRUGMAN, P., *El gran engaño: Ineficacia y deshonestidad; Estados Unidos ante el siglo XXI.* Barcelona, ed. Crítica, 2004, p. 352, writing in homage to the economist James Tobin, he points out: "It seems to me that his death symbolizes the end of an era in which economic debate was, not only pleasant, but also more honourable than it is today.(…) he was also a public figure, for a period the most relevant defender of an ideology which we could call free market Keynesian: the belief that the markets are something marvellous, although they work better when the government is vigilant, in order to limits its excesses."

to each people, being aware of their history and their roots." He then addressed MEPs in the following terms: "Dear MEPs, the time has come for us to build Europe together, not a Europe based on the economy but on the sacredness of the human being, of inalienable values."[132]

"The Basque Case": A Successful Model in Sustainable Human Development

It is precisely self-government and identity which are the keys to involving a whole society in the successful application of a model of sustainable human development, as least this is what the Basque Country has shown. More self-government and greater responsibility for ones actions are the foundations for an increase in welfare for men and women in any kind of community.

The Basque Community has shown that in spite of having to confront an extreme situation—as is the process of economic restructuring within the context of political conflict and violence—it is possible to successfully apply a model of sustainable human development based on the endogenous capacity to make decisions, i.e. self-government.

As has already been mentioned, the defence of socio-economic, cultural, business, and language self-government is not only related to a legitimate political objective, such as the recognition of one's own personality in a globalized world, but it is also an essential tool with which to achieve sustainable human development.

The Basque Autonomous Community today ranks above countries such as Germany, France, Spain and Great Britain with regards to life expectancy, training, per capita income, and building a balanced society.

The period between 1980 and 2013 demonstrates that 'self-government' means 'welfare' in an empirical way. This is what I have partly dedicated my life to, and still do, initially from the Basque political institutions and now from the *Agirre Lehendakaria Center for Social and Political Studies,* in which the University of the Basque Country (UPV-EHU),

---

[132] HOLY FATHER FRANCIS. Speech to the European Parliament, Strasbourg, November 2014.

together with Columbia University (New York) and George Mason University (Washington), are working on several research projects. These all take *The Basque Case: A Comprehensive Model for Sustainable Human Development*,[133] a research project I led with the participation of these American academic institutions, as their intellectual starting point.

Indeed, the direct relationship between exploring self-government in greater depth and increasing the welfare of people in Basque society is one of the subjects studied by the *Agirre Lehendakaria Center*. When self-government was granted in 1980, the Basque Autonomous Community had a per capita income of 3,000 euros per year (89% of average European income). This figure reached 6,000 euros in 1986, the year we entered the European Union as it was then. The figure doubled in those six years, to 90% of average European income.

By 1998 our per capita income stood at 108%, meaning that we had achieved and surpassed the average European income figure. By 2008 we had a per capita income of 31,000 euros, i.e. 34% above the European average. According to the latest published data (2014),[134] the Basque Autonomous Community is currently 29% above the European average.

According to Eurostat and Eustat data, in 2001 we were in eighth position in the European ranking in terms of income per capita, with 120% of average European income. We jumped to fourth place in 2005 (129%), and by 2008 we were third with 134%. In 2013, with the economic crisis fully affecting Europe, the Basque Country was third in the Top 10, with 129% of average European income.[135]

According to the official statistics life expectancy in the Basque Country was 80.9 in 2007,[136] positioning it among the top three counties in the world together with Japan and

---

[133] IBARRETXE, J. J., *The Basque Case: A Comprehensive Model for Sustainable Human Development*. Virginia (USA), George Mason University, February 2012.

[134] Eurostat, Eustat, July 2014.

[135] Source: EUROSTAT (24/06/2014), EUSTAT (17/07/2014) and in-house data.

[136] Source: PNUD, EUROSTAT and own production, 2007.

Iceland. And according to the latest statistics life expectancy in the Basque Country is 82.7 as of 2013[137] while also occupying a privileged place in Europe in relation to education levels. More than 80% of our men and women aged between 20 and 24 have received secondary or further education.[138]

Furthermore, Basque society is increasingly more committed to the struggle for the principle of equality between men and women, a principle, which is in our opinion the most important political project of the 21st century.

And, finally, the Basque Society is demonstrating that it is possible to look the markets in the eye without having to avoid looking people in the eye. Thus, the poverty risk rate — which measures the proportion of a population below 60% of the average income of the country, therefore measuring if a society is socially balanced — ranks alongside countries such as the Netherlands, Sweden, Denmark, France, Luxembourg, the Czech Republic and Austria, the European countries which register below 20% in the index.[139]

This is all reflected in the last report (in which Basque Autonomous Community was measured) from the United Nations in 2007 on the Human Development Index, in which the Basque Autonomous Community was situated in third place, only below Iceland and Norway.

In fact we have to "look beyond GDP." I stand up for sustainable human development, which means not just taking the economic agenda into account but also the cultural and social agendas as well as the environmental agenda. In a nutshell, a triple agenda: economic, social and environmental.

Unfortunately, economists and international agencies have not been able to measure the welfare of people. It is well-known — and accepted — that what is not measured is not improved. We are now in a new phase: what is not

---

137 Source: HWO, EUSTAT and own production, 2013.

138 Source: EUROSTAT (2014.06.13), EUSTAT (2014.07.28) and own production, 2014.

139 Source: EUROSTAT (2014.05.21), EUSTAT 2014.05.25) and own production, 2014.

measured is not even part of the agenda. Professor Joseph Stiglitz expresses this very succinctly: "What we measure affects the decisions we take."[140]

Indeed, 'market' and 'economic growth' have been the key concepts handled along with GDP. It has become not only the main parameter but almost the only one measured. As Robert Kennedy said shortly before he was assassinated in 1968, GDP (or GNP) gives us excellent information about many things, but it does not tell us anything about why life is worth living.

> "Yet the gross national product does not allow for the health of our children, the quality of their education, or the joy of their play. It does not include the beauty of our poetry or the strength of our marriages; the intelligence of our public debate or the integrity of our public officials. It measures neither our wit nor our courage; neither our wisdom nor our learning; neither our compassion nor our devotion to our country; it measures everything, in short, except that which makes life worthwhile."[141]

Commitment to the people. Government must be for the people. Move from the concept of economic growth to the concept of sustainable human development. From the concept of economy to that of an ethical economy. In this sense, Prof. Rogowsky expresses a belief that "the Basque Model is a method of ensuring both solidarity and competitiveness." He also expresses a "belief in the importance to find a model of development that will allow businesses to compete on a global scale, but at the same time

---

140 STIGLITZ, J., Professor of Economics at the University of Columbia and Nobel Prize for Economics in 2001, presided the Commission to Measure Economic Development and Social Progress created on the initiative of French President Nicolas Sarkozy, 2009.

141 KENNEDY, R. F., Address, University of Kansas, Lawrence, Kansas, March 18, 1968.

ensuring that nobody is left behind".[142] And Prof. Mitchel states that the Basque case has been "guided by the coherent identity of the Basque people, the values that Basque society represents, the concept that growth has to be for a reason and trickle down does not happen unless directed. Within a context of a widening inequality gap, the Basque experience offers a good alternative model to neo-liberal."[143]

So, the Basque Country has been an excellent example of economic, industrial and social transformation over the last 35 years. In fact, it is for this reason, that the "Basque model" is studied at the Harvard Business School under the tutelage of Prof. Michael Porter,[144] and in many other Universities throughout the world. In fact, the improved research program that finally gives rise to this publication is a very good example of this.

Identity and Innovation: Roots and Wings

The Basques are an ancient people occupying a position of world leadership in sustainable human development. The future objective is to consolidate as a nation the strategy of sustainable human development and that will be possible if the project is supported by two pillars: identity and innovation. Roots and wings. Identity is needed to maintain survival as a people who are open to the world and

---

142 ROGOWSKY, R., contribution made in relation to the *Basque Case: A Comprehensive Model for Sustainable Human Development* research program at the bilateral meeting held at the School of Public Policy, George Mason University, Washington, January 24, 2011.

143 MITCHELL, C., contribution made in relation to the *Basque Case: A Comprehensive Model for Sustainable Human Development* research program at the bilateral meeting held at the School of Conflict Analysis and Resolution, George Mason University, Washington, January 24, 2011.

144 PORTER, M., in AZUA, J., *Clusterizar y globalizar la economía: "La magia del proceso."* Bogotá, ed. Oveja Negra, 2008, prologue, writes that: "The Basque Country is today at the vanguard of thought, of how the regions and the nations should formulate and implement cluster policies."

innovation in order to look creatively and with solidarity towards the future.[145]

Some of the most advanced countries in the world, especially the smaller northern European countries, have made innovation an essential part of their national identity and a way to project themselves to the world.[146] Deference and universality turn out to be complementary; they strengthen and accompany each other.[147] It is perfectly possible to enrich oneself with universal culture and add one's own and different cultures. As Prof. Cowen suggests: "co-existence between local and universal culture is possible, using the term 'piggy back' to describe the manner in which the local cultures can grow and expand by taking advantage of globalization."[148] To participate in global networks by

---

[145] It is precisely when solidarity is questioned or forgotten as evidenced by DOMÈNECH, A., *El eclipse de la fraternidad.* Barcelona, ed. Crítica, 2004, when we are most in need of it.

[146] CASTELLS, M., y HIMANEN, P., *El Estado de bienestar y la sociedad de la información: El modelo finlandés.* Madrid, Alianza Editorial, 2002, p. 186, writes: "The cultural identity and the strong national feeling would appear to be essential components of the Finnish model of the Information Society. They are legitimate sources for a government to use to adopt an active role, (…) Identity projects to the future, installing Finnish pride into the collective achievements of Finland as an advanced Information Society. Social homogeneity and national solidarity lend strength to inclusion programs and favour the emergence of a model of the use of technology driven by society. Therefore, instead of undermining global competitiveness, the strong national identity provides a platform on which to construct technological capacity and develop social experimentation. Local and national identities add value to the Finnish companies with their interaction with global economic and technological networks."

[147] JAUREGUI, G., *La democracia en el siglo XXI: Un nuevo mundo, unos nuevos valores.* p. 277 points out: "Universality and difference, therefore, do not have to be conflicting. (…) Against the influence of the community the support of logic and modernization is essential. But, in the same way, there is no possible resistance to the seduction of the market without the support of a sense of social and cultural belonging."

[148] COWEN, T., contribution made in relation to the *Basque Case: A Comprehensive Model for Sustainable Human Development* research

means of an intercultural dialogue[149] and in doing so strengthen one's identity as a people.[150] In fact, it would be easy to perish in the face of the political and economic

---

program at the bilateral meeting held at the Mercartus Center, George Mason University, Washington, January 24, 2011.

149 MUÑAGORRI, I., "Derecho penal intercultural y crisis del principio de soberanía." In PORTILLA, G., (coord.), *Mutaciones de Leviatán: Legitimación de los nuevos modelos penales.* Madrid, ed. Akal, 2005, pages. 183 and 184, writes: "Human rights must be regarded as multi-cultural, that is to say, from the plurality of the cultural conceptions of human dignity. …and faced with the competing notions of equality and difference to opt for understanding the right to be equal whenever difference creates inferiority and the right to be different whenever equality endangers identity. That is, to look for a cross-cultural dialogue on human dignity which may lead to mixed conception of human rights which, instead of restoring false universalism, organizes itself like a constellation of local, mutually intelligible meanings and of networks which can transfer the power of those meanings into a legislative framework."

150 CABALLERO HARRIET, F.J., *Algunas claves para otra mundializalización.* Pages 242 and 243 state: "Today, once again, in the face of the universalistic aspirations of neo-liberalism (in this case) that seek imposition as a social, political and economic model across the planet, as a sole ideology and world view, the cultures have begun to react defensively, emphasising identity. (…) Let's return to culture! It is not just a cry, it is now an attitude that proves that the era of universalisms has finished. That the time of the 'utopian dreams' of the 'false utopian universalists,' which were really masks obscuring the real identities, belong to the past. And far from being the end of utopias, it is now when the 'real utopia' begins. It is the utopia which will be created not from a dream but from reality; not from the ethereal universalism but from the dynamic reality of cultures. The return of cultures, this time, will not mean the defensive return of the cultural-refuge identity but a culture in which the individual can discover themselves (as a cultural subject, as a political subject, as a universal subject) and, from this point, to set out on the true route to liberty in as much as an authentic 'cultural-relational identity' is being constructed in permanent dialogue with every culture on earth. This is, from the reality of the culture of the peoples, the 'New Utopia.'"

onslaught of globalization without the foundation of a "sense of social and cultural."[151]

It is not necessary to imitate but to learn. For many years the Basques have been associated with an entrepreneurial spirit, which has been the basis for a long history of growth and development. Rooted in this tradition, it is now necessary to pin our hopes without fear on the global village and make social and technological innovation a part of the Basque identity and a way of relating to the world, thereby helping the Basque Country to become an open and attractive intersection point for the global networks.[152]

Identity can play a driving role in this transformation project for the Basque Country in this new stage. Today, adopting the positive vision of crisis held by Albert Einstein,[153] we can use the need to overcome a really severe

---

[151] GUIBERNAU, M., *Los nacionalismos.* Barcelona, ed. Ariel, 1996, p. 146, indicates: "Intrinsic to globalization is the dialect between 'the local' and 'the global' (…). Globalization is expressed through the tension between the efforts of the global community and those of cultural identities, between ethnic breakdown and homogenization. (…) The renewed strength and the attraction of `national identity' and of nationalism presents itself as a secular answer to the search for identity in a world threatened by growing homogenization."

[152] CASTELLS, M., y HIMANEN, P., *El Estado de bienestar y la sociedad de la información: El modelo finlandés.* Madrid, Alianza ed., 2002, p. 179, writes: "The new economy is a global economy in which the success of a nation depends on its capacity to convert itself into an attractive intersection point for the global capital and people networks. (…) we are not only talking about entering into a new economy, but into a new society which is characterized globally by multiculturalism and multi-ethnicity."

[153] EINSTEIN, A.: "We do not aim to change things; indeed we always do the same. Crisis is the best thing that can happen to people and to countries, because crisis brings progress. Creativity is born out of anguish just as day is born out of the dark night. It is in crisis that invention is born, discoveries and grand strategies. He, who overcomes a crisis, overcomes himself without being 'overcome.'" This phrase traditionally attributed to Einstein, is a non-literal transcription of his reference to the 1929 crisis in his essay *The World As I See It,* published in 1935. The phrase coincides

crisis as a spur, but society is more materialistic and comfortable, the nation project is endangered and requires a mechanism to promote it.

We have no alternative but to face up to an exercise of reflection: it is the capacity to collectively inspire ourselves with a shared vision of sustainable human development which can mobalize and motivate everyone and make possible the achievement of our goals, as experiences in the Basque Country and elsewhere have shown us.[154] Talking about these themes Prof. Whitfield suggests, "the success of public-private shared leadership may be dependent upon the organization of Basque society of all levels. This has created an *associative life* that reflects the cooperative and dynamic culture of the Basque people."[155]

---

with the profile of Einstein described by HOLTON, G., *Einstein: historias y otras pasiones.* Madrid, Taurus, 1998.

154 CASTELLS, M., y HIMANEN, P., *El Estado de bienestar y la sociedad de la información: El modelo finlandés.* Pages 183 and 184: "Finland has shown that a fully developed welfare state is not incompatible with innovation technology, with the development of the information society and with a new dynamic and competitive economy. On the contrary, it appears to be a factor which contributes decisively to the growth of this new economy from a stable base. It provides the human foundation for the necessary productivity for the model of information development, and also provides institutional and social stability which mitigates the damage to the economy and to the people during periods of potentially severe recessions. (…) Finland contrasts sharply with the Silicon Valley model, driven entirely by market mechanisms, the individual entrepreneurial spirit and the culture of risk, with considerable social costs, dramatic social inequality and a deteriorating base of locally generated human capital and economic infrastructure. (…) The Finnish state has used incentives and strategic planning to complement the market mechanisms, instead of substituting them. It has also used participatory mechanisms and has acted within the framework of a legitimate and democratic state, which contrasts with the experience of the developing Asian countries, which are characterized by social authoritarianism and a hierarchal relationship with respect to business."

155 WHITFIELD, T., Centre on Inernational Cooperation, New York University, contribution made in relation to "The Basque Case. A Comprehensive model for Sustainable Human

From this point of view, it can be seen that a country in which the humanism of its organizations and the social, scientific and technical innovation are imbued in its very identity, an identity which is open to the world, is in possession of a powerful lever of change.

Development" research program at the bilateral meeting held in New York, 13th May 2011.

2
The "Basque Experience": An Applied Model of Sustainable Human Development. Principles and Context

The industrial revolution at the beginning of the 19th century marked the basic principles for the orientation of public policies based on the enlightened belief in science and progress at the service of humankind, the obsession with economic growth as a synonym for progress and welfare and its quantification in terms of the annual increase in GDP, leaving aside other aspects related to social balance and environmental sustainability.

Later, pressure from trade union organizations and the heightened social awareness of governments led concern for the social environment to be included in the process of development. Thus, social development, as a comprehensively inclusive concept for all the factors relating to social progress and economic growth, gradually became the reference point for the public policies that gave shape to the framework of institutions that nowadays make the social state a feature of European society.

It was not until very recently, when in the 1970s the environmental aspect became one of the principal concerns of the public and of international organizations. One of the things that triggered this new awareness was a report published in 1972 by the Club of Rome,[156] according to which, to continue with the rate of growth of the previous 25 years humanity would head for an environmental collapse with disastrous consequences in the 21st century.

This first report was followed by various reflections from international organizations revealing the growing

---

156 MEADOWS, D., *The Limits of Growth.* Report commissioned by the Club of Rome to be drawn up by the MIT (Institute of Technology of Massachusetts) in 1972. The main thesis of the report is that in a limited planet exponential growth (population and GDP) are not sustainable.

concern for the problem of global sustainability and its compatibility with economic growth.[157]

But it is not until the relatively recent era when the concept of sustainable development became institutionalized, appearing for the first time in 1987 in an official document which was drawn up at the request of the Environmental Committee of the United Nations under the direction of G.H. Brundtland,[158] — Prime Minister of Norway — with the expressive title "Our common future." In this report, known as the *Brundtland report* sustainable development is defined as:

> "...development that satisfies the needs of the present without compromising the capacity of future generations to satisfy their own needs."

Human Development

This definition corresponds well to the concern surrounding the environment and its relation to economic progress, but it does not sufficiently take into account the "human character" of development, that is the need for economic growth to be related to the reduction of poverty and social inequalities. Hence the introduction of the concept of human development established and defined by the United Nations Development Program (UNDP) in 1990.

Human development is a comprehensive concept which entails "a process by which the opportunities of mankind are enhanced."[159]

With this focus it is possible to speak of development when people increase their capabilities through

---

[157] First Earth Summit Final Statement. Stockholm Conference, UN, 1972; World Strategy for the Conservation of Nature, International Union for the Conservation of Nature and the Natural Environment, 1980; The United Nations World Charter for Nature, 1982; Global Agenda for Change, World Convention on Environment and Development UN, 1983.

[158] BRUNDTLAND Report, United Nations Committee for Environment and Development, 1987.

[159] UNITED NATIONS, UNDP Report on Human Development, 1990.

education, improve their life expectancy, and increase their chances of achieving higher incomes.[160]

For this reason, in 1990 the UNDP proposed a more complete indicator than GDP, the Human Development Index as a synthesis of the education, health, and sanitary conditions of the population of different countries. Since then, the Human Development Index, albeit with its omissions and limitations,[161] is an international indicator which permits the comparison of the relative situation of all the countries throughout the world, with an ever more significant political and media impact.[162]

---

160 AGUADO, I., BARRUTIA, J.M., y ETXEBARRIA, C., "El desarrollo sostenible a lo largo de la historia del pensamiento económico." A paper presented at the *X Critical Economy Conference: Alternatives to capitalism?* Barcelona, March 23–25, 2006. The study is framed within a line of research into *Public policies in the area of sustainable development* led by the University of the Basque Country and another by UNESCO on Sustainable development and environmental awareness.

161 See KELLEY, A.C., "The Human Development Index: 'Handle with Care.' *Population and Development. Review* 17, n° 2, June 1991, pages. 315–324, points out how limited the index is in relation to its objectives; HICKS, D.A., "The Inequality-Adjusted Human Development Index: A Constructive Proposal." *World Development*, n° 8, 1997, pages. 1283–1298; NOORBAKHSH, F., "A Modified Human Development Index." *World Development*, vol. 26, n° 3, 1998, pages. 517–528; CHAKRAVARTY, S.R., "A Generalized Human Development Index." *Review of Development Economics*, Manuscript n° 9165, 23 August 2000; BLANCHFLOWER, D.G., OSWALD, A. J., "Happiness and the Human Development Index: The Paradox of Australia." *Australian Economic Review*, June 2005; GRIMM, M., HARTTGEN, K., KLASEN, S., and MISSELHORN, M., "A Human Development Index by Income Groups." *Instituto Ibero-Americano de Investigaciones Económicas*, University of Göttingen, n° 155, November 15, 2006; COSTANTINI, V., MONNI, S., "Environment, human development and economic growth." *Ecological Economics* 64, 2008, pages. 867–880; LOZANO, S., GUTIÉRREZ, E., "Human Development Index: A Non-Compensatory Assesment." *Cuadernos de Economía*, 28(50), 2009, pages. 223–235.

162 UNITED NATIONS, UNDP, *"Human Development Report,"* 1990. The HDI (human development indicator) appears for the first time in this report. From 1995 onwards two new indexes are

More recently, this report has added the concept of gender equality as a complementary variable giving rise to the GDI, Gender-related Development Index, which takes into account the perspective of gender equality as one of the great challenges of the 21st century.

Sustainable Human Development

The integration of the three aforementioned perspectives: economic, social, and environmental which were previously considered separately in human development and sustainable development, first took place at the international level at the United Nations Conference for the Environment and Development held in 1992 in Rio de Janeiro.[163]

In the aforementioned summit, 179 States approved the documents that represented the bases upon which to design all environmental and social development strategies.

- Rio Declaration for Environment and Development
- Agenda 21
- Agreement on biological diversity
- Agreement on climate change

The Rio declaration situated Sustainable Human Development on a tri-dimensional base. It put forward a new model of development that included an economic, a social and an environmental dimension.[164] This tri-dimensionality, later accepted in the academic world,[165] constitutes the pillar

---

incorporated: the GDI (Gender-related Development Index) and the GEI (Gender Empowerment Indicator).

163 UNITED NATIONS, Rio Summit, 1992. United Nations Conference for Environment and Development. (Second Earth Summit).

164 The term environment in its widest sense as a combination of the preservation of the natural environment and of cultural diversity — the UNESCO Universal Declaration on Cultural Diversity (2001) — Sustainable Development in a diverse World sponsored by the European Union.

165 See GOODLAND, R., "The Concept of Environmental Sustainability." *Annual Review of Ecology and Systematics*, v. 26, 1995, pages. 1–24; JIMENEZ HERRERO, L.M., *Desarrollo sostenible:*

on which the model for socially and environmentally balanced development is to be constructed, and has formed the fundamental axis of the sustainable human development policy promoted in the Basque Country.

The European Strategy for Sustainable Development

The European Union has raised sustainable development to the category of priority objective, situating sustainable growth, respectful to the environment and the integration of the environment with other policies at the center of the objectives of the Union in the 1977 Treaty of Amsterdam.[166]

In the various summits held since (Cardiff 1998, Cologne 1999, and Helsinki 1999) the environmental aspect and the transversal policies are dealt with more thoroughly.[167]

Transición a hacia la coevolución global. Madrid, ed. Pirámide, 2000; SIERRA LUDWIG, V., "Desarrollo sostenible: Acotaciones conceptuales y revisiones estratégicas." *Boletín Económico de ICE*, nº 2749, November 25 – December 1, 2002, pages 13–23; AGUADO, I., BARRUTIA, J.M., and ETXEBARRIA, C., "El desarrollo sostenible a lo largo de la historia del pensamiento económico." *X Jornadas de Economía Crítica: ¿Alternativas al capitalismo?* Barcelona, March 23–25, 2006.

166 EUROPEAN UNION, Treaty of Amsterdam, 1997, Art. 2: "The Community will have the mission to promote, through the setting up of a common market and a common economic and monetary unit and the carrying out of common policies or actions mentioned in Articles 3, 3ª, the harmonious, balanced and sustainable development of economic activities throughout all of the community, a high level of employment and social protection, equality between men and women, sustainable and non-inflationary growth, a high degree of competitiveness and the convergence of economic results, a high level of environmental protection and improvement, the raising of the quality of live, economic and social cohesion and solidarity between the member states"; and Art. 6: "The requirements of protecting the environment should be included into the definition and along with the carrying out of community policies and actions such as those referred to in Article 3, in particular those with the objective of promoting sustainable development."

167 EUROPEAN COUNCIL, CARDIFF Summit, 15th and 16th June 1998. In the Cardiff European Council the foundations were

But it is only in March 2000, in the Lisbon summit, when a strategy of sustainable development is first envisaged which includes both economic and social aspects.[168]

The fundamental milestone which definitively marked the incorporation of the three pillars — economic, social and environmental — within a comprehensive legislative framework can be found in the sustainable development strategy for the Union which was passed in June 2001 at the Gothenburg summit.

The "European strategy includes the following objectives and targets in the short term":[169]

- the need to act with a wide range of coordinated policies
- limit climate change and increase the use of clean energies
- respond to the threats of public health
- more responsible management of natural resources
- improve the system of transport and land planning

The result of this strategy is that various commitments in the area of sustainable development have been made at the highest levels of the different European institutions, both within the scope of the Committee and the Council as well as in European Parliament itself. Commitments which have affected the action of national

---

laid for coordinated action on a community scale in the areas of agriculture, transport and energy. The Cologne European Council June 3–4, 1999 urged for coordination and coherence in fishing areas. In the Helsinki summit of December 1999 in which the European heads of states reaffirmed their commitment to sustainable development, and extended the strategies which had already been approved relating to agriculture, transport, energy and continued with those relating to the Domestic Market, Development, Industry, General Affairs, Economy and Finance, and Fishing.

168 EUROPEAN COUNCIL, Lisbon Strategy, Conclusions of the Presidency. Lisbon, March 23–24, 2000.

169 EUROPEAN COUNCIL, Strategy of sustainable development for the EU: Conclusions of the Presidency. Gothenburg, June 2001.

governments and have guided the strategy action lines for human sustainable development in the Autonomous Community of the Basque Country.[170]

The Regional and Local Dimension in Sustainable Human Development

The regions and the communities constitute an essential element in implementing a strategy of "bottom up" sustainable human development.[171]

In the process of globalization in which we are immersed, the regional communities, the principle of subsidiarity, and the capacity of self-government promote relational social capital, the synergies of participation and citizen involvement, and the capacity to develop "home-

---

170 See among others: COMMISSION OF THE EUROPEAN COMMUNITIES, 2001. Communication: "Sustainable Development in Europe for a better world." European Union Strategy for sustainable development (Proposal to the European Council of Gothenburg); DECISION N° 1600/2002 of the European Parliament and Council, July 22, 2002. Sixth program of Community Action in Environmental matters; EUROPEAN COMMISSION, February 2005. Communication to the Council and the European Parliament: "Revision European Union Strategy for Sustainable Development 2005. First balance and future directions"; EUROPEAN COMMISSION, December 2005, Communication to the Council and Parliament, Platform of Action for Sustainable Development; EUROPEAN COUNCIL, 2006, Sustainable Development Strategy renewed in Europe which details the complementary strategies from Lisbon for growth and employment and the long term Sustainable Development Strategy (see EU Council document n° 19117/06 June 9, 2006; EUROPEAN COMMISSION, 2009 Report, Communication to European Parliament, to the Council, the European Economic and Social Committee and the Committee of the Regions on the assessment of the deployment of the European Union Strategy for Sustainable Development.

171 BARRUTIA, J.M., ECHEBARRIA, C., y AGUADO, I., "Una red de políticas para la difusión de la Agenda 21 Local en Euskadi." Rev. *Economiaz* n° 64, 2007, pages. 215–235.

grown" policies which become irreplaceable assets in the process of sustainable development at a world level.[172]

The importance and the implication of the local and regional dimension in the European scenario has gradually increased, giving rise to the holding of various "sustainable cities" conferences which began in 1994 with the Aalborg Charter;[173] as well as developing Agenda 21 on a local level and other initiatives at the international level where the Basque Country features prominently.[174]

---

[172] See BAIROCH, P., *Cities and Economic Development: From the Dawn of History to the Present.* Chicago, University of Chicago, 1991; SCOTT, A.J., *Regions and the World Economy. The Coming Shape of Global Production, Competition, and Political Order.* Oxford, Oxford University Press, 1998; STORPER, M., *The Regional World: Territorial Development in a Global Economy.* New York, The Guildford Press, 1997; SCOTT, A.J., STORPER, M., "Regions, Globalization, Development." This document was written by the working group Globalization, Regions, and Economic Development sponsored by the Center for Comparative and Global Research, International Institute, UCLA, published, 2003, Regional Studies, v. 37, pages. 579–593.

[173] *The Charter of European Cities towards sustainability,* known as the Aalborg Charter, was approved by 80 European local authorities and 253 representatives of international organizations, national governments, scientific centers, assessors and individuals, participants at the European Conference on sustainable cities held in Aalborg, Denmark, May 24–27, 1994. For the first time a commitment was made to participate in local Agenda 21 initiatives and to develop programsprograms for sustainable development and at the same time a campaign for sustainable European cities began.

[174] Gauteng Declaration, September 3, 2002, in which 23 regional government representatives, among them the Basque Country, and 4 Regional Government Associations subscribed to the founding document of the regional Government Network for Sustainable Development (nrg4SD). This document was signed at the World Summit on Sustainable Development which was held in Johannesburg (South Africa) August 26 – September 4, 2002. Since then the Basque Country has worked intensively in the Network for the promotion of sustainable development and the objectives of Agenda 21 as well as the Millennium Declaration, and in extending these commitments to other areas of the world, especially in the global south.

Application of a Slobal Strategy of SHD: "From Theory to Action"

Some of the principal problems in the effective development of a strategy of sustainable human development have already been pointed out by the International Institute for Environment and Development — IIED — and by the European institutions themselves.[175] Essentially they are related to two aspects:

- The difficulty in involving all the protagonists, public and private as well as citizens in the process, an involvement which requires a new, more participative, more accountable style of government.

---

[175] The EU plays an important role in the International Forums on the environment. In particular, it participates in the United Nations program for the environment and has contributed decisively to many of the most important agreements. For example, on the Ozone layer (signing of the Montreal Agreement), climate change (ratification of the Kyoto Protocol in May 2002), desertification (the EU supported the Forest Forum, the agreement to fight against desertification), protection of the sea (through Program 21, the UNEP regional program for the seas and the UN agreement on Law of the Sea), biodiversity (in February 2002 it began the European regulation on cross-border traffic, also the protocol on bio-safety was ratified in May 2002), waste products and dangerous chemical products. In the application of the Johannesburg agreements it has committed itself, especially in areas of basic sanitation infrastructures, biodiversity, fish populations and chemical products, which fulfil the development objectives of the millennium. In May 2007 it signed a document known as the Liepzig *Charter on Sustainable European Cities,* in which the member states committed themselves to certain common principles and strategies for urban development policy, to the modernization of infrastructure networks, and the improvement of energy efficiency, to innovation in education policies, to paying particular attention to the less well-off neighborhoods within the global context of the city, to the search for strategies to improve the physical environment, the strengthening at a local level of the economy and labor market policy, to the promotion of an efficient and sustainable urban transport system. The structural funds and the JESSICA and JEREMIE awards have the objective of creating strong European cities and regions that boast a high quality of life.

- The establishment of plans, programs and concrete objectives for action, bearing in mind the singularities of each territory and avoiding excessive levels of bureaucratization or the continuous production of reflections, documents and debates on long term global planning.

Bearing in mind these two references, the Autonomous Community of the Basque Country, since the recovery of the instruments of self-government with the Statute of Gernika in 1980, has applied pioneering but effective policy of sustainable human development, specifically in the period 1998–2008, in many cases at national and European level, sustained in a vision of a shared country and developed along three major action strategies:

- The axis of Economic Growth
- The axis of Equality and Social and Cultural Equilibrium
- The axis of Environmental Sustainability

Responding, thereby, to the tri-dimensional nature of sustainable human development:

- The area of Development
- The Human area
- The Sustainable area

With this objective a comprehensive strategy has been carried out using the public policies developed by the Basque Government which are expressed in a series of key strategic plans and specific action programs in the three areas of sustainable human development, under the criteria of shared leadership and participating with the rest of the Basque institutions and the business and social agents involved, and from a perspective of focus on the action with the establishment of around a hundred objectives and the getting underway of more than 400 specific actions with which to reach them.

Commitments to the objectives, actions and indicators that have been publicly presented, both to society and to the Basque Parliament[176] and which, furthermore, have been annually evaluated in order to measure the level of progression made.

A Vision for the Basque Country

First of all, it is extraordinarily important to underline that the group of initiatives for achieving sustainable human development make sense only if they are given a comprehensive vision, a "Vision for the Basque Country."

In the Basque case, this comprehensive yet shared vision was defined at the Foro Euskadi 2015[177]:

> A country…
> at peace,
> proud of its roots and its traditions,
> tolerant and respectful to diversity,
> highly productive,
> which competes using its people,
> who use their creativity and take responsibility for their work
> within the framework of shared projects,
> in an open and international setting,
> socially cohesive,

---

176 Government Program 1998, 2001, 2005 and Investiture Debates in 1998, 2001 and 2005.

177 THE BASQUE COUNTRY FORUM OF COMPETITIVENESS 2015 opened in 2004 with the idea of becoming a source of participation for the drawing up of a new strategy of competitiveness, an outlook of the Basque company for the future. Participation took the form of breakfasts and workshops from which a document entitled "Business Competitiveness and Social Innovation: Strategic Bases and Lines of Action" was drawn up and then presented on March 10, 2005 in the Palacio Euskalduna in Bilbao. The document later became the "Business Competitiveness and Social Innovation Plan 2006–2009." During this same period another participation process took place concerning the strategy for science and technology, including the drawing up of a white book and intensive group work, which, once aligned with the competitiveness strategy, became the "Science, Technology and Innovation Plan 2010." These are the two pillars upon which the vision for the Basque Country 2015 was built.

supportive to the world
and respectful to the environment.

Three Strategic Axes. Axis of Economic Growth

The axis of economic growth has been sustained on the engine of innovation and competitiveness. For this reason, throughout the period under consideration, strategic mainstay plans were put into action in order to improve the global competitiveness of the Basque economy, and specifically to promote technological development and innovation.[178]

Axis of Social Balance, Equality, and Cultural Development

An equitable growth, with faces and eyes, constructed by the people for the people. To advance towards equality, social equilibrium, and personal cultural development was the second pillar of the policies of human sustainable development in the Basque Country. With the aim of developing the social pillar strategic mainstay plans were set into motion, with the corresponding development into programs, objectives, and specific actions. In our analysis attention will be brought to the following:

- In the area of basic services: in order to guarantee people's future and their welfare the strategy to promote excellence in training and deployment of a quality health service stand out as the most important pillars of the welfare state of a society.
- In the area of social balance: the plan to combat poverty, developed through various commitments and actions and which culminated with the approval of the law against social exclusion.[179]

---

[178] Business Competitiveness and Social Innovation Plan (2001–2006 and 2006–2009). Science, Technology and Innovation Plan (PCTI 1997–2000) (2001-2004) and PCTI Horizon 2010.

[179] See Charter of Social Rights in the Basque Country. Parity of minimum pensions up to 100% of the minimum inter-professional salary. Minimum salary of insertion. Social emergency

- In the area of Equality: the "Positive Action Plan" for equality between men and women and its culmination in the Equality Act.[180]
- In the area of cultural development: "The Basque Culture Plan," as a strategic pillar for the promotion of different cultural activities in the Basque Country.[181]

Furthermore, within this second axis, various different strategic plans were passed in areas relating to health, employment, public housing promotion, integration of immigrants, family assistance and education.[182]

Axis of Environmental Sustainability

The third mainstay axis of the policies of sustainable human development in the Basque Country is formed by the defence of environmental sustainability and the struggle against climate change.

Hence, among other measures, three comprehensive intervention plans were drawn up:

- The Basque Environmental Strategy 2002–2020
- The Basque Energy Strategy 3E 2010
- The Sustainable Transport Director Plan

Supplementary benefits. Law 18/2008 December 23 for minimum wages and social inclusion.

[180] Positive Action Plans. I Plan (1991–1994). II Plan (1995–1998). III Plan (1999–2005). IV Plan (20052010). Law 4/2005 February 18, 2005 for equality between men and women.

[181] Department of Culture of the Basque Government. Basque Culture Plan 2004–2008. Directions for the Basque Culture Plan (2009–2012) (Basque Culture Council 19-2-2009).

[182] Health Plan 2002–2010. Inter-institutional Family Support Plan. Family Law 12-2-2008. Infant Schooling Plan 0–3 years. University Plans: I, II and III Basque Professional Training Plan. Land Use and Housing Law (June 30, 2006). Basque Immigration Plan. Basque Cooperation for Development Plan. Employment Plans 2003–2006 and 2007–2010. Labor Health and Safety Plan 2007–2010, etc.

Through these tools the objectives and specific actions were given shape for reducing pollution, fulfilling the Kyoto commitments, improving energy efficiency, and promoting sustainable mobility.

In the following sections we will consider in greater detail the development, the crucial axes and principal plans of action of the sustainable human development strategy in the Basque Country, since the beginnings of self-government in 1980, with the Statute of Autonomy of Gernika, examining with a closer focus, due to its relevance to the new paradigm of the 21st century, the period 1998–2008.

In short, we will offer a detailed analysis of "the Basque Case" as an applied model of sustainable human development.

3
Economic Strategy: "Social, Scientific, and Technical Innovation"

First Phase: 1980s, Our Own Distinct Strategy: "Learn to Compete"

From the experience of the Basque Country it can be confidently stated that solely because in the 1980s we learned to compete, and because later in the 90s we learned to compete and cooperate, by the end of the 90s and the beginning of the 21st century innovation in cooperation could be defined as the great lever of transformation of the new century, making it possible to achieve the objective of sustainable human development.

We are therefore talking about a process of comprehensive change of a country over a span of 30 years.

At the beginning of the 80s, when modem Basque self-government got underway with the State of Autonomy of Gernika (following the death of the dictator Franco in 1975) the Basque economy found itself immersed in a profound crisis, seriously harmed by the slowing down of the world economy and especially by the distortions of the previous decades. Iron and steel, shipbuilding, machine-tools, and capital were sectors in decline. The growth of GDP was negative,[183] unemployment rates were extremely high,[184] and the main industries of the country were seriously affected,

---

183 The importance of the Basque economy in relation to the state fell according to data from the Banco de Bilbao in GDP terms from 7.80% in 1975 to 6.54% in 1983. And according to EUSTAT and INE data from 6.42% in 1982 to 6.23% in 1983 and 6.04 % in 1984.

184 URIARTE, P.L., "Euskadi es la autonomía española más rica tras superar una grave crisis." Rev. *Fomento de la Production*, n. 1298, January, Barcelona, 2010, states: "the unemployment rate of the 80s reached 25%, with a strong industrial decline, collapse of basic industry and obsolete infrastructures, along with a brutal recession that went on into the 90s, obliging the first great economic and social transformation."

basically as a result of the limited attention, which is not to say neglect, which they had suffered for years, both by the public and private sectors.

The new Basque Government, created in 1980, established three major objectives: regain the people's trust, prepare the country for its integration into Europe, and above all, industrial restructuring, the main priority. An arduous task for a government which was in turn beginning the process of negotiation and transfer of competences, establishing a governmental structure and passing basic laws to govern the fate of this new Autonomous Community of the Basque Country, becoming actively involved in the day-to-day management of businesses in crisis, in intense strikes, and, moreover, in the midst of a brutal campaign of violence, assassinations and human rights abuses by ETA, which intimidated the whole of society, but especially the entrepreneurs, many of whom, despite the threats, carried on standing up for the country, in an attitude of bravery that we should acknowledge and show our gratitude for.

At this point, the "fledgling" Basque institutions took a courageous and risky decision, a "country-building decision": to make a commitment to the "real economy," to the productive economy, to Basque industry, to "grassroots competition." A commitment to doing what we knew best while bringing on board new knowledge, new technologies. The recognition of those institutions and the people behind them is even greater, if possible, given that they took their decision counter to the prevailing current of neo liberal socio-economic thought at that time in Europe and Spain, magnificently summed up in the phrase: "the best industrial policy is one that doesn't exist" to which the Spanish ministers of the sector subscribed.[185] The media were mercilessly critical of the policy.

---

[185] ETXEZARRETA, M., "Aquellos polvos y estos lodos", *Reggio´s*, 7 June 2010, says that: "the scorn for all industrial policy ("lthe best industrial poilcy is the one that doesn't exist") and the liberalising, privatisng enthusiasm of SOLCHAGA and BOYER, at that time (1982) held that the salvation of the economy lay with the market".

Contrary to the neo-liberal school of thought, which entrusted everything to macro-economic policies, the Basque people, opted for a separate, distinct policy of microeconomic orientation, the strategy of a country backed by social initiative and clear public involvement. Following the reflection of Karl Polanyi, the idea of a market that regulates itself is purely utopian; "such an institution could not exist in a lasting way without annihilating human substance and the nature of society, without destroying mankind and without turning its eco-system into a desert." [186] The aim was to foster a "kind-hearted economy" to the detriment of a "ruthless economy" in the words of Prof. Samuelson[187] and fight against something that, incredibly, John Maynard Keynes had warned us about in the 1930s,[188] the acceptance, for at least the coming 100 years, of a world in which fair is foul and foul is fair; since foul is useful and fair is not. "And in this future, which is now the present," as Joaquín Estefanía wisely puts it, "everything to do with the economy has grown dark."[189]

In fact, in a global economy, the lesser effectiveness of macroeconomic policies means that governments must devote greater efforts to microeconomic and institutional

---

186 POLANYI, K., *La gran transformation, crítica del liberalismo económico*, Madrid, ed. La Piqueta, 1989, p.26.

187 SAMUELSON, P. and NORDHAUS, W., *Economía,* (16 ed.), Madrid, ed. McGraw-Hill, 1999, p. 718, state: "Our econom is a "heartless economy". (...). This obstinate emphasis on effeiciency pays no attention to the income of laid-off workers, to the companies in crisis, to the crumbling cities or the countries or regions that are losing their comparative advantage. (...). The growing inequality of income in the United States is a serious reminder of the cruel inequalities in a market economy".

188 See KEYNES, J. M., *Economic Possibilities for Our Grandchildren,* London, ed. Macmillan, 1933.

189 ESTEFANÍA, J., *Contra el pensamiento único,* Madrid, ed. Santillana, 1997, p.108, says: "In 1930, John Maynard Keynes, the greatest economist of all time, came to Spain (...) to give a lecture (...), entitled "Posible economic situation of our grandchildren". (...). Well, we are the granndchildren of Keynes, the future he talked of. The true motive of Keynes' theoretical effort was fear of the future and in this future which is now present, all the economy has grown dark".

policies, since quality training, a good health system, social cohesion, a sound, supervised financial system, good infrastructures, etc. are decisive elements n this globalized world. As Guillermo de la Dehesa says, "the reform of the State to adapt to the new trends in globalization calls for a greater dedication to microeconomic policies and, at the same time, a growing collaboration between the State and civil society which will mean that the rules become more objective and more transparent and that they are fulfilled to a greater extent, leading, as a result, to a greater credibility."[190]

Thus, from this moment on, a whole set of innovative measures were put into action, pioneering as regards the Spanish state, enabling a "first economic and social transformation" in Basque society to be successfully tackled. This approach saw from 1981 onwards, the formation of: the Society for Industrial Promotion and Reconversion (SPRI); SOFAD, an institution specialising in the promotion and assessment of takeovers, mergers, and the acquisition of new technology; the Basque Energy Board (EVE) (1982) to establish the energy and regasification strategy; the Network of Protected Technology Centres; the Technology Park of Zamudio (1984); the Industrialdeak program; the program for the Introduction of Microelectronics (IMI); Basquexport for the promotion of exports and the internationalization of Basque companies; the Plan for Exceptional Relaunching in 1986 to promote the development of small and medium-sized enterprises; and the special plan Euskadi Europa 1993 to prepare the country at European level from the point of view of its infrastructures, health, or education and a complete array of instruments, incentives, and support that set out to rescue the social value of the "entrepreneurial spirit" that had fallen into such decline at that time. There was a total awareness, as stated Ricardo Aláez, Javier Bilbao, Vicente Camino, and Juan Carlos Longás, on analyzing a strategic sector, very specifically in the Basque case, such as the automotive one,

---

[190] DE LA DEHESA, G., *Comprender la globalization,* Madrid, Alianza ed., 2002, p. 121.

that the space, the territory, and its vitality in taking initiatives, play a key role in regional competitiveness.[191]

The paradigm of the 80s was the reconversion and the restructuring, a time of active industrial and social policies. We learned to compete. But we should not simplify, because although it is true that we must stress that this phase was devoted to "reconversion," it is also true that this was when the first steps were taken in the Basque network of science and technology, in advanced technologies, in diversifying the economic and industrial fabric, in the development of the education system and Basque occupational training, etc. Steps without which it would have been impossible to tackle the subsequent stages later on.

Second Phase: 1990s "Learning to Compete and Cooperate"

If the paradigm of the 80s was "learning to compete," that of the 90s was "learning to compete and cooperate." A new country-wide strategy was developed and accompanied by a greater level of self-government in key affairs such as healthcare, social services, infrastructures, public works, and the updating of the Economic Agreement,[192] the "well-spring" feeding the system of self-government.[193] Prof.

---

191 ALÁEZ, R., BILBAO, J., CAMINO, V. y LONGÁS, J. C., *El sector de automotion: Nuevas tendencias en la organization productiva.* Madrid, ed. Civitas, 1996, p. 205, writes: "the regions do not all compete equally. Companies need certain requirements with regard to labor, markets, raw materials, etc., which are not in the same supply in all places, (…). Space acts in the same way as a government structure of economic transactions and activities (…) Thus organizing spaces are formed which will have geographic pecularities to the extent that there are regions whose pecularities enables companies to generate a quasi-income without incurring the problems of rigidity and risk which are linked to the great integrated structures which are poorly adapted to uncertain and volatile environments."

192 Reform of the Economic Agreement 1997, which incorporates essential elements such as the collection of the Special Taxes and Income Tax legislation.

193 The Economic Agreement between the Basque Country and Spain must be seen as one of the most genuine, essential, unique, or even exclusive examples, if you like, of the Basque Country's

Hughes-Hallet suggests that "*Going Basque* describes the process of transition from a system of centralized governance and fiscal policy to a model of local government where taxation is controlled by the local community."[194]

In addition to all this, it was a time when there was an intense process of integration of the country, its people and its companies into the European marketplace and its society. However, it is also true that the European outlook of the Basque people enabled the dangers that integration implied to be transformed into opportunities. These were opportunities for the Basque economy and society, which saw in Europe a space for freedom, welfare, and safety, while the memories of the Franco dictatorship and, in particular, the attempted coup d'états which had done so much harm to the future development of self-government in Euskadi to the

---

model of self-government. In fact, it establishes that the Institutions of the Basque Historical Territories may maintain, establish, regulate, levy and inspect, within their territory, their taxation system.So, aside from being a legal instrument of bilateral relationship between the Basque Country and Spain in the area of taxation and finance it is a maximum exponent of recognition of the Historical Rights of the Basque people and a key factor in modernising these rights. The very etymology of the word used to describe this type of pact, "concertado" (agreed or harmonised), clearly illustrates the spirit with which this instrument was conceived. It is not the outcome of a process of competency decentralization or of transferring state taxes; instead, its genesis lies precisely in a reverse process in which a set of powers remains in the hands of the Basque Historical Territories after having ceded others to the State as a result of the abolition of the "fuero" system in place –by force- throughout the nineteenth century (1839 and 1876).It is also an instrument for economic progress, and to improve the quality of life and well-being of the Basque society as a whole.

194 HUGES-HALLE, A., contribution made in relation to "The Basque Case: A Comprehensive Model for Sustainable Human Development." Research program at the bilateral meeting held at the School of Public Policy, George Mason University, Washington, January 26, 2011.

extent of paralyzing[195] and holding back autonomy were still so fresh.

On the other hand, the challenge represented by the European Internal Market in 1993 and the "fear of displacement" as regards the axes of European growth,[196] was a catalyst to redefine the "country-making strategy" in a more comprehensive and cooperative way, going beyond the more sectoralized process of the 80s. It was a strategy which was envisaged as "a new competitive space in solidarity."[197] This new country-wide strategy meant reindustrialization policies linked to territorial and social policies, revitalizing the areas where the industrial dismantling was taking place (the Margen Izquierda, or Left Bank, of the Bilbao estuary, Ayala or Pasajes), or the "3-R" plan for extraordinary support of struggling industries, or the Plan for Extraordinary Investment to attract and retain investment or develop key investments to place Euskadi on the world stage, such as the Guggenheim Museum. It meant establishing a "welfare network" in the country, essential for constructing a supportive and prosperous society, forming the bedrock for competitive advantages. The country's commitment to quality,[198] to our own know-how,[199] to science and

---

[195] Of the 37 areas pending transfer in 1988, only 3 to date (justice administration personnel, Toll Motorways with private concessions and Scientific and Technical Research) have been transferred to the competence of the Autonomous Community of the Basque Country.

[196] In 1989 a study by a group of French geographers called RECLUS featured the concept of the *Blue Banana*, also known as the *European Megapolis* or the *European backbone,* a discontinuous urbanized corridor situated in Western Europe. It extends roughly from the North West of England, in the north to Milan in the south. It is the London-Milan axis.

[197] AZUA, J., *Clusterizar y globalizar la economía. "La magia del proceso".* Bogotá, Ed. Oveja Negra, 2008, pages. 218 and 229.

[198] In December 1992 the Basque Government set up EUSKALIT, the Basque Quality Foundation, initially in order to administer the first Basque Quality prize. It was promoted at the beginning by the Department of Industry and Energy of the Basque Government and included 21 different bodies, both public and private. Nowadays there are 23 bodies and EUSKALIT has provided support for the policy of promotion of quality, innovation and

technology policies,[200] and to internationalization[201] rounded off the country's strategy.

In short, the reflective and thoughtful use of self-government and the idea of the European challenge regarded as a catalyst let us redefine and adapt a project for the country based on a set of integrated policies linked to education, health, employment, and training of our men and women, to housing, equality, the environment, and financial and tax incentives, which allowed a new competitive context to be brought into being. This new competitive space in solidarity was also characterized by developing a new approach: cooperation.

In fact, the idea of cooperation forms part of the history and personality of the Basque people. To this effect,

---

excellence for all of Basque society. The mission of EUSKALIT is to boost innovation management through promoting a culture of quality in all areas of Basque society.

[199] A relevant example is the decision to continue producing steel. The closure of Altos Hornos de Vizcaya (4,000 workers used to produce 1.500.000 Tns/year) gave way to the installation of a mini-steel mill (600 workers producing 2,000,000 Tns/year).

[200] The Science, Technology and Innovation Plan 2001-2004 reflects in Chapter 3: pages. 40 and 41: "total expenditure in R&D in the Basque Country has grown continuously since 1990 (with the exception of 1994) at an inter-annual average rate of 7%. Considering that in 1979 expenditure in R&D as a percentage of the GDP in the BAC (Basque Autonomous Community) represented 0.069 % (compared to a national figure of 0.3%) and that in 1981 it only reached 0.097% (0.42% in Spain) it can be seen that the *effort in terms of innovation in the Basque Country in the last two decades has been spectacular*". In fact, by 1998 total expenditure on R&D in the Basque Country had risen to 396.2 m. Euros, accounting for 1.11% of the GDP. This level was already above the national average (0.87% in 1998) although still somewhat far from the European levels (1.8% in 1998).

[201] It was in 1994 when a boost was given to the international image with the setting up of the first Basque cooperation and development offices abroad, specifically in Argentina, (Basque-Argentinian Institute of Cooperation and Development), in Chile (Basque-Chilean Development Foundation), in Venezuela (Basque-Venezuelan Institute of Cooperation - Eguzki) and in Mexico (Basque- Mexican Development Institute), and followed later by many other initiatives.

Richard Wilkinson and Kate Pickett recognises that: "One of the best-known co-operative groups is the Mondragon Corporation in the Basque region (…). Mondragon co-operatives are twice as profitable as other Spanish firms and have the highest labor productivity in the country. It is hard to explain some of the successes unless a combination of ownership and participation does indeed have the potential to improve productivity by reducing the conflict of interests. (…) Employee-ownership has the advantage of increasing equality specifically by extending liberty and democracy. It is bottom-up rather than top-down. (…) As a way of creating more egalitarian society, employee-ownership and control have many advantages. (…) Rather than being compatible with just one system of management of work organization, employee-ownership is highly flexible. (…) As a means of transforming our societies, employee-ownership has the advantage that it can (and does) exist side by side with conventional business structures."[202] In addition, Prof. Clark underlines the role of social cooperation in Basque culture: "the significance of the Mondragon cooperatives confirms the Basque support for collective solutions to community-wide problems."[203] Futhermore, Mr McDonnell identifies "the culture of cooperation as a value of both ancient and modern Basque society, as the key to the success of the Basque Model" and states, "the study demonstrates that when people do not have a sense of belonging, they lack a sense of vision of purpose."[204] Finally, commenting on the idea of competition and cooperation, Prof. Melchin states that "Dr. Ibarretxe's research reveals that the important themes of the Mondragon cooperatives have been implemented throughout Basque society. Not only that it is

---

202 WILKINSON, R. and PICKETT, K., *The Spirit Level: Why Greater Equality Makes Societies Stronger.* New York, ed. Bloomsbury Press, 2010, ps. 251, 252, 253 and 254 .

203 CLARK, R., contribution made in relation to the "Basque Case: A Comprehensive Model for Sustainable Human Development" research program at the bilateral meeting held at the School of Public Policy, George Mason University, Washington, January 24, 2011.

204 MCDONNELL, A., Member of Parliament, Westminster, London, March 30, 2011.

possible to compete in cooperation, but also that the social sector makes a valuable contribution to the economic growth of the industrial sector."[205]

Learning to compete and cooperate was the change of paradigm in the 90s. A strategic public-private alliance to define a vision as a country and firm commitment to clusterising[206] the economy.

The clusterisation process of the Basque economy[207] has, over time, arranged itself into a profitable network of active relationships grouping together Clusters[208] which include representatives of companies, governments, universities, technology centers, and collaborating bodies. But at its outset things did not run so smoothly, there were many dissenting voices. We were coming from a high level of

---

205 MELCHIN, K., Director of the Lonergan Center, Saint Paul University, Ottowa-Canada. Contribution made in relation to "The Basque Case: A Comprehensive Model for Sustainable Human Development" research program at the bilateral meeting held in New York, May 13, 2011.

206 In contrast to the traditional forms of business association (Trust, cartels, etc.), a Cluster in the industrial world is a concentration of mutually related companies within a relatively defined geographic area, in such a way that they form a specialised productive pole with competitive advantages. The "cluster" concept was popularised by Professor PORTER, M., *The Competitive Advantages of Nations*. New York, ed. Free Press, 1990.

207 PORTER, M., in AZUA, J., *Clusterizar y globalizar la economía: "La magia del proceso."* Bogotá, ed. Oveja Negra, 2008, prologue, points out: "the Basque Country launched its strategy for competiveness based on clusters in 1990. The 'cluster' philosophy has favoured the design of successive Basque economic policies. The Basque Country has enjoyed considerable success, being one of the most prosperous regions in Spain, with a higher GDP than the EU average (…) The Basque Country is today at the vanguard of the way of thinking about how regions and nations should shape and implement clusterization policies."

208 Basque Clusters: Aeronautic (1997); Audiovisual (2004); Automotion (1993); Knowledge (1996); Electrodomestic (1992); Energy (1996); Machine Tool (1992); Environment (1995); Paper (1998); Maritime Forum (1997); Port of Bilbao (1994); Telecommunications (1996); Transport and Logistics (2005).

intervention from the Basque Government in industry, especially in the previous decade, and this, in many companies, had led to government dependence with regard to strategic decisions that they had to take. We needed time, effort, learning, resources, and a great drive from public leadership and company collaboration (public-private alliance); but there was a base, a breeding ground to tackle the change of paradigm.[209]

Whatever the case, at the end of the eighties and beginning of the nineties, Michael Porter marked a milestone on the history of economic thought and his model of competitiveness[210] has been applied in hundreds of socioeconomic settings around the world. The Basque Country was the subject of the first application of the theory of competitive advantage of nations in a non-State country in the world and acted as the basic methodology with which to progress towards the achievement of the structural changes needed in the Basque economy in the years to come.

This new competitive space in solidarity and cooperation meant that our own strategy, which enabled us in the 90s "to learn to compete and cooperate in solidarity," built upon a previous stage from the 80s, in which a strategy, also our own, let us "learn to compete." Solely because these two stages had been overcome previously could the new change of paradigm be tackled in order to achieve sustainable human development at the beginning of the 21st century: "innovate in cooperation."

---

209 PORTER, M., in AZUA, J., *Clusterizar y globalizar la economía: "La magia del proceso."* Bogotá, ed. Oveja Negra, 2008, prologue, warns: "A fair number of countries and regions have tried to set up clusters from scratch (…) the observed result from these efforts is disappointing, and have led to unjust criticisms of the concept of clusterization. Today no serious 'practitioner' would advocate clusters from scratch, but on the contrary would focus their attention on the best way to favour and promote collaboration, removing barriers for clusterized development."

210 See PORTER, M., *The Competitive Advantage of Nations.* New York, ed. Free Press, 1990.

Third phase: Change of Century; 'Learning to Innovate in Cooperation

By the final years of the 20th century, a "socio-economic welfare platform"[211] —fundamentally a product of self-government — training, and the public-private strategic alliance of the country, had been built in Euskadi. These act as the basis to improve competitiveness, attract investment, and achieve harmonious economic and social development in which territorial and social cohesion and the health and educational systems and the development of our own cultural roots were to play a decisive role. They became a differentiating factor of the competitiveness of the Basque Country in relation to the other countries of Europe and the world.

Over the length of this 30 year period, we can discern the clear, constant, and repeated commitment towards sustainable human development and the defence of the Basque identity; a Basque identity which is open to the world. The aim was a full-scale political demand and a similarly full-scale commitment to the social and political construction of the Basque Country. Behind the defence of identity, culture, and language there is not only a legitimate demand from the political point of view, but also a similarly legitimate defence of the economic, political, and social development. It is a demand for solidarity.

It was the ideal moment, when we were all making our reflections on the new century that would briefly be dawning, to put forward the development of a "project with both face and eyes": 'between Basques, from within, in which there is room for everyone. Today the debate is an economic one; the future will set out a cultural debate, with the sense of belonging and identity to the fore and as the key to defining areas of solidarity."[212]

It was to be a project where change would not be seen as a "necessary evil," but rather a great opportunity:

---

211 AZUA, J., *Clusterizar y globalizar la economía: "La magia del proceso."* Bogotá, ed. Oveja Negra, 2008, pages. 215 and 218.

212 IBARRETXE, J.J., Speech on being declared presidential candidate for the Basque Nationalist Party. Theatre Principal Vitoria-Gasteiz, Saturday, March 28, 1998.

> "The Basque Nation is a small nation that should abandon resignation and immobilism. Dynamism, vitality, enthusiasm and learning are the key factors of our development. We must construct an agreement from within; to define what we want to be; how we want to tackle the times ahead; how we want to solve our problems (Peace, employment, development, etc.) We must brace ourselves intellectually to accept change and intelligence to go into our identity in greater detail."

To tackle the new century "without fear of failure": "New times, new responses. The invention of the 21st century will be its people."[213]

The challenge of the 80s ("learning to compete") and that of the 90s ("learning to compete and cooperate"), the challenges of reconversion, of European integration, of competitiveness in solidarity, in order to succeed had a "lever of change," a social catalyst of huge potential, observed throughout history of Basque society: "the spirit of survival." However, as the 21st century began, Basque society little resembled the society which had entered into Europe in 1986.[214] It was a Country with more than an acceptable level of welfare and standard of living, which now had a level of per capita income considerably above the European average.[215] It was a more affluent society, indeed of a new social catalyst, a new lever of change for facing up to the "second economic and social change of the Basque Country": innovation.

---

213 IBARRETXE, J.J., Speech on being declared presidential candidate for the Basque Nationalist Party. Theatre Principal Vitoria-Gasteiz, Saturday, March 28, 1998.

214 The average income of the BAC was 90% of the European in 1986

215 According to EUROSTAT, EUSTAT and our own data the average income per capita of the BAC was 119% of the EU average. Ranking 8th in comparison with EU countries in income per capita.

The Second Great Economic and Social Transformation of the Basque Country": Innovation

In 2001, the Basque Parliament stated that, "constructing the Social state is to construct its economic bases via a competitive and innovative system, but always from the principle that people are above the marketplace."[216] The very social dimension of the individual bestows on them the right to a dignified existence and such a right is exercised through the access to work, education, health, housing and social protection.

It is precisely because the new Social State is based on the autonomy of the individual; it also recognizes the values and realities of business economics as the best alternative for tackling the economic problem in open society.

The overriding reflection made in the Basque Parliament on that day in 2001 was that:

> "A society which has attained the level of development that Basque society enjoys today, cannot now continue to approach the future in terms of adopting foreign technology and cost advantages; it must make a firm commitment to the challenge of innovation, quality and the creation of knowledge."[217]

The second great economic and social transformation of Euskadi was built upon three cornerstones: First, to construct the information and knowledge society; second, to make Euskadi a reference point in the European research and technology space; third to extend the principle of Total Quality as the means of organizational management.

---

216 IBARRETXE, J.J. Inaugeration Speech as Basque Country President. Basque Parliament, July 11, 2001. Session Diaries. VII Legislatura. N° 4: Page 20, paragraph 4.

217 IBARRETXE, J.J. Inaugeration Speech as Basque Country President. Basque Parliament, July 11, 2001. Session Diaries. VII Legislatura. N° 4: page 21.

The "so-called second transformation (program declaration of the President-Lehendakari of the Basque Government, Juan José Ibarretxe)," says Jon Azua, "sets out to move over towards the new knowledge economy reinforcing the commitment to: internationalization of our companies and economy by strengthening policies, programs and instruments for overseas promotion; a specific strategy to accelerate access to the Information Society; and the renewed and growing commitment to the Plan for Science and Technology which aims, through the achievements of its studies of factors and investments, to convert the Country into the new European space for innovation."[218]

The challenge of social, scientific and technical innovation was thus defined, and this was of enormous importance and significance, as a critical factor of economic development and a basic cornerstone to maintain and improve the social welfare system.

The "Basque Country Commitment" of the Twenty-first Century: Social, Scientific and Technical Innovation

The 21st century has already brought us a new way of seeing and understanding the world, "the global village," built upon a new setting, "the knowledge society," which enables instant transactions of information and knowledge and which forms the base of a new society. The significance of the new emerging model has been and will be, at the very least, equivalent to other revolutions that have arisen over the course of History (Neolithic, the Industrial Revolution, etc.) and which have also changed the established world order in all it touches.

In this new environment the implications go beyond society as a whole. It is, therefore, the responsibility of everyone and especially of the public institutions that all citizens in the community have access to and participate in this new model of society. As well as being a demand for competitiveness, it is a demand for solidarity. The most fortunate and privileged will have their opportunity one way

---

218 AZUA, J., *Clusterizar y globalizar la economía: "La magia del proceso."* ed. Oveja Negra, Bogota, 2008, p. 223.

or another. But other social groups and layers will go without if not offered preferential institutional support.

When the first "Science, Technology and Innovation Plan" for the new century was proposed and approved in 2001, it was constructed upon the following reflection:

> "Knowledge increasingly forms a source of competitiveness for a country and a true driving force behind the cultural, economic and intellectual progress of its people. Knowledge is generated following a critical and free reflection, fundamental in a democratic world, of natural and social phenomena. Scientific and technological breakthroughs, thus contribute to providing everyone with a deeper understanding of nature and society, to building a modern and competitive production fabric, as well as enjoying a greater quality of living and a healthy and sustainable environment."[219]

The "Science, Technology and Innovation Plan, 2001–2004" recognized and internalized these reflections, building upon them a coherent set of thematic programs and distinct actions geared towards empowering all the agents of the innovation system to bring the cultural process of innovation to life and to invent our future right now in the present.

In fact, this plan allowed us to reap the benefits of an ambition which had been renewed and reinforced every day for years: to place Euskadi on an increasingly higher rung on the international ladder in the field of innovation and scientific-technological development and aim to make us an outstanding reference point within the European research space.

This earlier desire was voiced among us through a profoundly innovative plan. Naturally, it was based on a defined background and clear references, making the most of

---

[219] IBARRETXE, J. J., Presentation of the Basque President at the "Science, Technology and Innovation Plan 2001–2004." San Sebastian, March 14, 2001.

the accumulated experience and therefore actions that had been seen to be effective and successful in previous initiatives. But at the same time it attempted to escape conventional approaches and defended a model of dynamic operation for the Basque innovation system, integrating social and business demands and incorporating the global dimension as a fundamental factor of competitiveness.

In this regard, the generalization of a new working philosophy in our Country was defended. A new philosophy into which the group of agents who made up the innovation system were gradually incorporated. There were essentially three basic principles upon which it was hoped the future would be built: competing, as the key to the continuous progress in the generation of knowledge and wealth; cooperating, as a formula valid for the generation of synergies and the strengthening of mutual capacities; sharing, as a strategy for the diffusion of knowledge, the generation of interdependencies, and connectivity between all the agents taking part in the innovation process.

In addition, the new strategy gave direction to the efforts and the development of capacities towards those areas considered as priority for the Country, thus establishing unmistakable commitments from the programming and financial point of view.[220]

But this "Science, Technology and Innovation Plan, 2001–2004" was, above all, a plan to integrate the various wills of the agents propelled by the new knowledge society to "discover and develop their own opportunities and advantages,"[221] and so be able, as proposed by Peter Drucker, follow a systematic analysis of the risks and the

---

220 See, "Science, Technology and Innovation Plan 2001–2004." the Basque Government.

221 BECK, U., *¿Qué es la globalization? Falacias del globalismo, respuestas a la globalization.* Barcelona, ed. Paidós, 1998, pages 198 and 199 warn about the "conception of old-fashioned innovation" and point out "What are the innovative contributions of the second modernity with regard to market and culture? The world market prizes *difference*. The idea is to develop and discover one's own opportunities and advantages (for example, regional characteristics)."

sources of innovation, in order to make the most of them.[222] The plan therefore ushered a process of reflection for its definition characterized by listening and building a consensus and a pioneering effort of inter-institutional coordination began which has subsequently turned out to be one of the keys of the new strategy.

New Instruments for the "New Commitment of the Basque Country"

It is in this new context where technological progress takes place at a breakneck pace and where knowledge emerges as a wealth-generating element. It is where the generation of knowledge and, more importantly, its effective exploitation is increasingly shaping itself as the single source of sustainable competitiveness at all levels. In this context from 2005 onwards, the next step was taken: the "Science, Technology and Innovation Plan 2010" (PCTI 2010).

Education was ratified as necessary for change as was the need for an education in modern conventions. Strengthening the concepts of high intelligence training, learning to learn, learning to solve or tackle complex problems, skills, know-how, attitudes, values, lifelong education, education for employability and not just for employment.

In this process, innovation should, therefore, be understood as a collective process involving the gradual and unanimous commitment of society, demanding the will to admit, tolerate, and use changes and permanent adjustments involved in the implementation of new ideas. These changes should also be perfectly assimilated for the sake of social cohesion and to avoid any process of social fragmentation and marginalization.

In the 2001–2004 legislature the objectives proposed for the convergence in income and convergence in

---

[222] See DRUCKER, P. F., *Innovation and Entrepreneurship: Practice and Principles.* New York, ed. Harper & Row, 1985. In this study it is proposed that innovators are successful whenever they define the risks and establish a limit, and if they systematically analyze the sources of innovation opportunities in order to take advantage of them when they appear.

employment with the European Union had been achieved. Undoubtedly, this was a joint achievement; it had not solely been the merit of the management by the Basque Institutions, but rather the joint, shared efforts of the whole of Basque society.

However, we were fully aware that successes achieved in the past are no guarantee of future welfare. The world was changing at a lightning pace. As is the case today, we were witnesses to a profound transformation, not only in the economic area, but also in the social one. Globally, we were dealing with a new information and knowledge society which not only affected the competition between companies and multi-nationals but also the relationships between people. Once more, the key to this new scenario was its people; people who were trained and people who were looked after and cared for.

Therefore, in 2005 the social convergence and technological convergence with Europe was put forward as the following joint objective. In a plenary session held in the Basque Parliament on May 22, 2005, it was expressed as follows:

> "Our next objectives for this legislature are clearly defined: to attain technological convergence and social convergence, projecting our international image as a supportive Country, standing among the top ten countries in the Human Development Index... We are committed to ethical progress which places the individual at the center of economic development. With this objective, we will promote all those social programs and policies that contribute to guaranteeing the right of each and every person in our society to enjoy a decent life, through their access to work, education, health, housing, social protection and cultural integration."[223]

---

[223] IBARRETXE, J. J., Inauguration Speech as Basque Country President. Basque Parliament, 11th July 2001. Sessions records. VII Legislature, n° 4, pp. 38 and 39.

A project was so defined to boost sustainable development in which technology and sustainability would be the axes of the policy to promote economic growth and to increase the welfare of Basque society as a whole.

Public commitment to research and innovation over the following years with the launch of a new institutional architecture to tackle the new objectives that had been set out. In other words, in 2005 the seeds were being planted of what would later give way to the creation in July of the Basque Science, Technology and Innovation Board,[224] the launch in June of the Foundation for Scientific Research of Euskadi (Ikerbasque), and the presentation in July of the Basque Innovation Agency (Innobasque) which brought together the agents of the system and whose objectives were making a reference model of innovation management, the promotion of patents, and the transfer of technology and the encouragement of participation in European projects and international relations.

The Basque Innovation System

Economic literature is emphatic when it comes to defending the concept of a system of innovation as the most efficient methodological approach for the study of the technological activities that take place in a territory.[225]

---

[224] Decree 1/2007 17th April by the Basque President to set up the Basque Council of Science, Technology and Innovation. Published in the BOPV 13th July 2007.

[225] For a general study of the literature on Innovation Systems refer, for example, to: BALZAT, M., *An economic analysis of innovation. Extending the concept of national innovation systems*, Cheltenham, ed. E.E. (Edward Elgar Pub), 2006; CARLSSON, B., JACOBSSON, S. HOLMEN, M., and RICKNE, A., "Innovation Systems: analytical and methodological issues", 2002, *Research Policy*, nº 31 (2), pp. 233-245; EDQUIST, C., *Systems of innovation: Technologies, Institutions and organizations,* London, Pinter, 1997, pages. 1-35; FAGERBERG, J. et al. (eds.), *Systems of Innovation. Perspectives and challenges,* Oxford, Oxford University Press, 2005; OLAZARÁN RODRÍGUEZ, M. y GÓMEZ URANGA, M. (ed.): *Sistemas regionales de innovation*, Leioa, Servicio editorial de la UPV/EHU, 2001; NAVARRO ARANCEGUI, M., "Los sistemas regionales de

It is an approach that arises from a concept that regards technological progress in an evolutionary way and which refers us to a process characterized by the following aspects[226]:

a) Technical change is a systematic phenomenon: to the extent that we say that the capacity to obtain technological responses in an economy is the consequence of the joint work of multiple institutions, working with the different objectives.
b) There will be several sources of cognitive enrichment liable to form the origin of a technical change for a country.
c) The phenomenon of technical progress is highly specific.

The first of the characteristics leads us to admit the need to bear in mind not only the behavior of each institution that works in the area of innovation, but also the content of the relationships that are established between them; the second of the characteristics makes us consider multiple sources of cognitive enrichment liable to form the origin of technical progress for a country, as well as bearing in mind the existence of multiple possibilities of inter-institutional interaction with technological interest. Finally, the specific nature of technical progress means that each economic context raises singular, distinct needs, the economic reality it describes is different in terms of available resources, of existing economic situation, of its geographical, demographic, educational, cultural characteristics, etc. and therefore, the technological solutions that it requires and can implement in order to improve its economic situation will be different.

---

innovation. Una revisión crítica", *Revista Ekonomiaz* nº 70, First quarter of 2009, pp. 24-59.

[226] See, for example: VENCE, X., *Economía de la innovation y del cambio tecnológico*, Madrid, Siglo XXI, 1995; FORAY, D. and FREEMAN, Ch. (ed), *Technology and the wealth of nations*, London, Pinter Pub, 1993; FORAY, D., *L'économie de la connaissance*, Paris, La Découverte, 2009.

However, this systematic concept, as we might expect, raises vague limitations as regards its practical identification if we turn to this need to take into account those institutions that may have an important role in the area of innovation. Depending on the emphasis that one or another author may place on the role of the different institutions, we will come across "broader visions" and "narrower visions" when it comes to outlining the institutional content that defines a system of innovation. In the most restrictive approaches, the main focus of the analysis will be aimed at the institutions and organizations which directly take part in the research and exploration processes,[227] while the broader visions will be advocating the relevance of the innovation processes of other elements such as education, training activities, and even the labor market and the financial system.[228]

Our analytical proposal, for the purposes of making the analysis that we set out to carry out operational, we rest upon a restricted concept of the system of innovation, otherwise a majority one in economic literature, which we will understand as the institutional framework that most directly supports the innovation process and which will take into account those agents and institutions that carry out tasks related to the creation, adaptation and diffusion of technological information.

If we make a brief historical reference that is useful as a starting point in order to introduce the description of the characteristics that present what we might call the Basque Innovation System, we could say that the creation of

---

[227] EDQUIST, C., *Systems of Innovation : Perspectives and Challenges.* FAGERBERG, J. et al. (eds), Oxford, Oxford University Press, 2005; FAGERBERG, J., MOWERY, D.C., and NELSON, R.R., *The Oxford Handbook of Innovation.* Oxford, Oxford University Press, 2005, pages 181–208; LUNDVALL, B-A, "National Innovation Systems-Analytical Concept and Development Tool," in *Industry and Innovation*, n. 14 (1), 2007, pages 95–119; NELSON, R.R. (ed), *National Innovation Systems: A Comparative Analysis.* Oxford, Oxford University Press, 1993.

[228] For example, COOKE, P; HEIDENREICH, M and BRACZYK, H., *Regional Innovation Systems.* London, Routledge, 2004.

technological capacities in the Basque economy has been a very recent phenomenon which got underway in the early 1980s coinciding with the passing of the Statute of Autonomy and the constitution of the first Basque Government, which found itself with a virtually non-existent innovation system. We can observe a significant change in the concept of the role of technical progress, which is given a leading part in economic development. A determined technological policy was put into action that, in those early moments, was to be based on the development of private technology centers, albeit with an important degree of public funding.[229] It was a change sustained over time and which was to be reflected in a considerable improvement in the position of the Basque economy in this area.[230] We should note that the deep-seated industrial tradition of the Basque economy, the sector in which technological dynamics are most intense, made the weakness of the scientific-technological system especially costly in competitive terms and made the need to take measures that would improve this situation more urgent.

To get an idea of the extent that this change of concept had for the importance of the technological component of the Basque economy during this period, in the 1970s the expenditure on R&D reached barely 0.063% of

---

229 NAVARRO, M y ZUBIAURRE, A., "Los centros tecnológicos y el sistema regional de innovation: El caso del Basque Country." Documeno de trabajo nº 38. Institute of Industrial and Financial Analysis, Madrid, Universidad Complutense Madrid, 2003. The same authors tell us that the model they propose coincides with the German Fraunhofer institutes, which had already guided the set up of Ikerlan in 1979 by the Mondragon cooperative group.

230 With regard to the Basque Innovation system, see also: DORRONSORO, G., "El sistema vasco de innovation ante los nuevos retos." *Revista Madrid + d.,* Monografía nº 22, 2008, pages 159–166; FERNANDEZ DE LUCIO, I.,"El sistema de innovation en Euskadi." *Ekonomiaz* nº 56, 2004, pages 296–305; MOSO, M. y OLAZARÁN, M., "Actores, ideas e instituciones: Políticas tecnológicas regionales y creation de un sistema de I+D en la Autonomous Community of the Basque Country," in OLAZARÁN, M. y GOMEZ URANGA, M. (ed.), *Sistemas regionales de innovation.* Leioa, editorial service of the UPV/EHU, 2001., pages. 405-432.

GDP, by the end of the 80s it had reached 1%, standing close to the Spanish average, to rise to 1.96% by 2008, according to the latest data of the INE,[231] placing us above the average of European countries, which we had already surpassed in 2007.[232] Turning to a closer reference in time, we could say that over the period 1998–2008 the volume of resources devoted to R&D has multiplied by 3.40, meaning that over this time, the percentage of expenditure on R&D in the Basque economy went from 1.11% to 1.96%.[233] However, despite the improvement undergone in this field, we should point out the efforts made are still inadequate and underline the need to maintain this upward trend in technological investment with the aim of closing the distance that separates us from the most developed countries such as the USA, where 2.67% of GDP is invested, and other reference countries such as Germany and France where the investment in GDP in 2008 came to 2.63% and 2.02% of GDP respectively.[234] In fact, in 2013, after being above the European average for the first time in 2008, we have lost the position, and the investment of the Basque Community is 1.99% of GDP, below the European average 2.02%[235]

Without aiming to be exhaustive and focusing attention on those aspects that are most significant to understand the technological problems of our system, we bring to the foreground the leading role played by the companies in this area, both as regards to funding and especially the execution of expenditure on R&D. This leading role, at first glance, indicates a high degree of commitment by the company to the innovation process, but that also shows that this company commitment can manifest itself because the Basque scientific-technical context forms an efficient support to make business innovation activities profitable. Basque business would be funding 56% of R&D

---

[231] INE, published December 18, 2009.

[232] INE, data % R&D / GDP, year 2007: BAC 1.88%, EU27 1.77%, Spain 1.27%.

[233] Total expenditure R&D BAC in millions of Euros: 1998= 396.2; 2008=1.345.5, INE, 2008.

[234] See webpages of EUSTAT and EUROSTAT.

[235] Source: EUROSTAT, EUSTAT and own production, 2014.11.19.

expenditure, placing business prominence in this area above that seen in Spain and the European Union and executing 81.1% of the R&D carried out, much higher than the standards registered among the developed countries. These execution figures demonstrate the high degree of commitment of the companies of our system to innovation but also that the system is working with an approach that is excessively applied to the type of R&D that is being carried out.

This basically applied nature reveals an interesting technological business dynamic but also shows a shortfall in basic research implemented in our context and which will act as a factor limiting medium-term progress.

These shortfalls are particularly significant if we bear in mind that the new emerging sectors are constructed along emphatically scientific technological lines which demand the availability of a very firm scientific context that acts as the basis for the development of the knowledge upon which the new practical applications are to be carried out. Areas such as biotechnology, biomedicine, or new materials demand this support of basic research from which the applied and developed tasks can be carried out resulting in the new products and processes.

We might explain this absence of basic research as a consequence of the lack of a tradition of base-level research that has existed in our Community until relatively recent times. If Universities and public research centers make up the institutions where basic scientific research is carried out, it should be born in mind that, on the one hand our University is a very young one[236] and, on the other, that the Spanish Administration Public Research Centers have not been present in our territory.[237]

---

[236] In the Autonomous Community of Euskadi there are four working universities: the University of the Basque Country/Euskal Herriko Unibertsitatea; Deusto University; Mondragon University and the University of (Tecnum). A university network in which the amount of research work of the UPV stands out among the others but that, overall, the amount is still rather limited research, below the levels of other European countries.

[237] NAVARRO, M y ZUBIAURRE, A: "Los centros tecnológicos y el sistema regional de innovación: El caso del País Vasco."

It was in this latest decade when there was an important growth in the channelling of public resources towards basic research, both in public centers and in the University, to reinforce the support of basic knowledge which is absolutely essential in order to participate in the technological dynamics of the new product areas which are, inevitably firmly science-based.

The UPV/EHU (the University of the Basque Country) represents a fundamental axis in promoting basic research of interest for innovation. Despite being, as we have stated, a relatively young University, the support of the Basque Government and an appropriate internal dynamic made it possible that in the 2002–2008 there was 62% growth in university research in the area of Experimental Science.[238] In certain fields, such as is the case with Health Sciences, considered a priority from an economic point of view, the limitations on human resources available that were offered at the University made it necessary to develop the basic support in this area through the promotion of public research centers, which are more flexible administratively and have the capacity to incorporate high-level research personnel from other countries.

Over the course of the last decade, the Basque Government has promoted a network of centers that will work at preferentially basic levels in areas of interest for the technical and economic development of the Basque Community. These centers were designed to seek excellence and answer to two distinct models: 1) Basic and Excellence

---

Documento de trabajo nº 38, Institute of Industrial and Financial Analysis, Madrid, Universidad Complutense de Madrid, 2003, page 6: "if during the Franco regime, the Public Research bodies made up the block of Institutional research bodies which carried out basic research, none of these centers, based largely in Madrid, were located in the Basque Country."

[238] UPV/EHU (2009), "La Universidad en cifras." Page. 147.

Research Centres[239] and 2) Cooperative Research Centres (C.I.C.).[240]

The former institutional group includes 6 centers of excellence that back up the support of basic skills in the fields of biology, material physics, applied mathematics, and neurosciences, while the latter would work in the same areas, in addition to others, but in a more applied field in an attempt to directly involve other agents, technology centers, and companies in their projects in the search for specific practical applications.

All this would also give rise to intensive training with the permanent presence of predoctoral fellows.

Finally, and with the aim of offering a general assessment of the situation in the Basque Country in the area of innovation, it may be especially significant to use the value of the European Innovation Index produced by the European Union as a benchmark to summarize numerically the technological capabilities of the European countries and regions. We should point out that this is an index that resumes in a single figure the measurements carried out in 29 areas corresponding to the most relevant demonstrations of innovation.[241] The data obtained in the index reveals that the

---

[239] Fundation Biofísica Bizkaia; Donostia International Phiysics Center; Materials Physics Center; Basque Centre for Climate Change; Basque Centre for Applied Mathematics; Basque Centre on Cognition, Brain and Langage.

[240] CIC biomaGUNE; CIC bioGUNE; CIC microGUNE; CIC nanoGUNE; CIC tourGUNE. CIC marGUNE; CIC energiGUNE.

[241] On 19th of March 2010 the Ninth Edition of the European Innovation Scoreboard (EIS) was released, this is the PANEL OF EUROPEAN INNOVATION INDICATORS (EIS 2009), which offers a comparative analysis of the innovation actions in the 27 member states of the European Union as well as in Croatia, Turkey, Iceland, Norway, Switzerland, and Serbia and has the objective of classifying these countries according to the degree in which their economies have innovation capacity and develop innovation activities.

According to the press release of EUSTAT 30th March 2010 the BAC ranks alongside the group of countries with high levels of innovation above the European average. The European Innovation Index (EIS) 2009 for Euskadi reached a value of 0.51, placing it in

Basque economy had a 3% higher technological level than the average European level and a significantly higher one —33%— than the average technological level of the Spanish economy.

Going into greater detail in this European perspective, we could also turn to anther community technological indicator, the Regional Innovation Index, designed to analyze the technological levels of the European regions, which qualified the Basque Country, in its 2009 publication, as a medium-high technological region in the context of European regions.[242]

An additional exceptional example that we could use to give a clearer view of the development of the technological capacity of the Basque economy in recent years, is offered by the choice of the Basque Country to host the sub-headquarters of the European Spallation Neutron Source (ESS) which will be situated in the Science Park of the UPV in Leioa.

The New Institutional Architecture, 2007

From 2007 onwards new institutional realities were put forward to give a greater impact to innovation in the Basque context. These new institutions set out to achieve a greater effectiveness with the resources employed so as to go into the main lines of action in greater detail and more efficiently. These lines of actions included:

10th position in the European Union-27 and above its average of 0.48. Euskadi stands out in three dimensions (Human Resources, Connections, Business Initiatives, and Economic Effects) with respect to the European average.

242 In December 2009 HOLLANDERS, H., University of Maastricht (MERIT: Maastricht Economic and social Research and training center on Innovation and Technology), TARANTOLA, S., and LOSCHKY, A., both from the Joint Research Centre, Institute for the Protection and Security of the Citizen 8IPSC), Econometrics and Applied Statistics (EAS) Unit, Ispra, Italy published the report *REGIONAL INNOVATION SCOREBOARD (RIS) 2009*, based on the methodology of the European Innovation Indicators (EIS) of the Program Pro Inno Europe of the European Commission.

- Actions aimed at sector diversification seeking movement from production activity towards high value added sectors, inevitably those with a high scientific basis. The application of biosciences, new materials, and technological approaches deriving from applications of nanotechnologies form the central axis of the new activities to be promoted.
- Actions aimed at improving the efficiency of the system. We should highlight the reorganization of the technological resources in the scope of the public sector, especially technology centers, through a policy of mergers whose objective was to obtain a size allowing a better use of resources, to find more effective specialities, to avoid duplicates, and to take part in more ambitious projects. We could also mention the actions geared towards reinforcing the degree of integration into the system, aiming to maximize the relationships, in both number and intensity, between the agents of the system. Programs such as those directed at the maintenance of the activities of Innobasque (the Basque Innovation Agency) and the Ikerbasque Foundation — bodies dedicated to coordinating and giving coherence to the scientific and technological activities of the Basque Innovation System — would work towards these objectives.
- Actions aimed at the internationalization of the Basque Innovation System. Funding university research programs, research personnel mobility programs, the merger of technology centers, the organization structure proposed for the basic and excellence research centers, and the Cooperative Research Centers also worked in the direction of further integrating the Basque Innovation System into the International System.

Let us highlight the launch of three basic institutions that set out the new strategy to "cultivate, care for, and attract talent":

Science, Technology, and Innovation Board

Created in July 2007 by the Lehendakari, it is the highest body of participation, assessment, and leadership on the policies that revolve around science, technology, research, and innovation in Euskadi. The Basque Science, Technology and Innovation Board is formed by the leading representatives of the Basque political institutions (Lehendakari; the Deputy Generals of Araba, Bizkaia and Gipuzkoa; the Ministers of the Treasury, Industry, Education and Health of the Basque Government), the rectors of the three universities of the Autonomous Community of Euskadi (EHU-UPV, Deusto and Mondragon) and the chairpersons of Ikerbasque and Innobasque.

Ikerbasque

Created in June 2007 by the Basque Government, the main function of the Foundation for Scientific Research in Euskadi, Ikerbasque, is to attract international experts to carry out their research work in centers located in Euskadi. Its aim is to help develop scientific research in Euskadi.

Innobasque

The Basque Government promoted the creation of the Basque Innovation Agency, Innobasque, which was presented publicly in July 2007. It was a non-profit making association whose mission was to coordinate and impel innovation in Euskadi in all areas, with the aim of fostering entrepreneurial spirit and creativity.
Innobasque is made up of the Basque public institutions, the agents of the Basque Science, Technology and Innovation Network, private companies, institutional representatives from the business world and organizations of all kinds related to innovation.

> Innobasque sets out to offer an effective platform and collaboration network for all these agents, through which they can develop activities that promote the values and attitudes associated with innovation in Basque society. Their actions reflect overseas the image of an innovative Euskadi, at the cutting edge of R&D&i, and all those who contribute to generating the dynamics of innovation in Basque companies and organizations.

Also in 2007 — a key year in understanding the "Basque country commitment" to social, scientific and technical innovation[243] — on October 22, 2007, following its approval by the recently created Basque Science, Technology and Innovation Board and the Basque Government, the "Science, Technology and Innovation Plan 2010" was presented in public.

The PCTI 2010 verifies the commitment of the public and private institutions of the Country to situating Euskadi as a reference point for innovation in Europe. The shared vision, passed over to Basque society in its presentation, was "to make Euskadi the reference point, not a reference point, but the reference point in the area of innovation in Europe."[244]

If the first economic transformation acted to strengthen the operational efficiency to place the Country on the European quality map, the second great economic transformation in which we are currently immersed must act to place us on the European innovation map, a map upon which the Regional (territorial) Systems shall have a greater and greater role, which is why the development of self-

---

243 In 2007, the Autonomous Community of Euskadi according to INE figures for convergence with Europe in R&D areas, (1.87% /GDP in the Basque Country; 1.27% /GDP in Spain), and the European Innovation Indicator (with 29 indicators which takes into account both capacities as well as activities and results), placed the Basque Country with a value of 0.51, compared to 0.48 of the EU-27.

244 IBARRETXE, J. J., Presentation of the Lehendakari of the "Science, Technology and Innovation Plan 2010." Bilbao, Palacio Euskalduna, October 22, 2007.

government would seem essential to carry on making progress. It is a huge challenge that requires a great amount of renewed energy and creative initiative to reach this new frontier.

Placing the accent thus far on technological development, especially on the process, enabled us to make progress towards competitiveness often based on costs and on the productive efficiency achieved. Without leaving this field, in which it continued and still does so, with margin for improvement, it became necessary to focus on a broader vision of innovation, in accordance with the guidelines of the Oslo Manual,[245] which placed greater emphasis on the products and companies with a technological content and which fully incorporated innovation in their marketing and organisation.

To develop these objectives, the PCTI 2010 included five major areas of work[246]:

a) Firstly, the required cultural change that must accompany and contribute to innovation being perceived, not just by companies, but by Basque

[245] The Oslo Manual refers to the publication of the OCDE (Organization for Cooperation and Economic Development) and EUROSTAT (the European Community Statistic Office) entitled "Measurement of Scientific and Technological Activities. Guidelines for collecting and interpreting innovation technology data: Oslo Manual". This Manual was published for the first time in 1997. It is an important reference for the analysis and recompilation of data in areas of innovation technology, as well as a source for studies related to any activities related to innovation technology, its achievements, the types of innovation and the impact of the innovation on the role of the organizations, thereby contributing to the implementation of a constantly developing technological culture. The third edition, in 2005, is the result of the experiences accumulated since 1997 and needs of governments to adapt their innovation policies. The Oslo Manual third edition (2005) was passed by the CSTP (Committee for Science and Technology Policy), CSTAT (Committee for Statistics for the OCDE) and by the WPSTI (the EUROSTAT work group on Science, Technology and Innovation Statistics).

[246] See Science, Technology and Innovation Plan 2010 of the Basque Government.

society as a whole as the essential medium upon which our future welfare will be based.

b) Secondly, the recognition of the significance of science in the new paradigm and its importance not only in the field of basic excellence research, but also for the potential as a source to generate new initiatives that generate wealth for our country. (Science must progress via solid scientific projects which are able to attract research talent from outside our frontiers.)
c) Thirdly, the conviction that the future competitiveness of our country has its roots in the reality of the present productive fabric, both in industry and in services (to support the present is the base upon which to construct new challenges, which are not simply concentrated in "made in Euskadi" but also in "thought of in Euskadi").
d) In fourth place is the need to create new sectors which tomorrow will form the productive reality of our country and which must go through a greater technological intensity, enabling a qualitative leap in the value added generated in our country.
e) Finally, in fifth place, the firm support of entrepreneurial activities through encouraging the creation of innovative companies with a view to growth and global projection. This field of action is a paradigmatic example of the desired cross-fertilisation that must occur given the multiplicity and density of the relationships between the different agents of the Basque Innovation System, whose collaboration guarantees the existence of factors of specialization running from the generation of technology, business capacity, and the supply of different types of capital (seed capital, risk capital, investment capital, etc.), all factors necessary in the construction of solid proposals for value creation.

Basque Innovation System

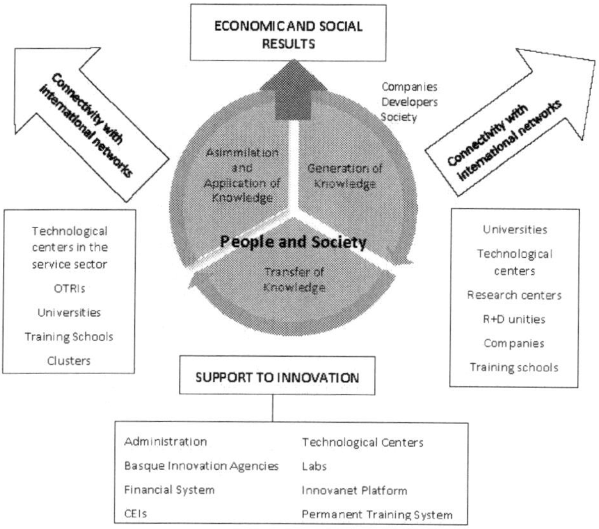

All this demands a richer, more varied and committed Basque Innovation System as defined in the PCTI 2010 itself, "a system which in short has knowledge at its heart, whose origin is found in the people who today make up Basque society and who are characterized by the economic basis and the context in which we move. A knowledge which has its own life and is constructed in an accumulative and synergic process — as can be seen in the diagram of the Basque Innovation System, — in which education, research and innovation all intervene. Knowledge that flows and evolves with the different agents of the Basque Innovation System represented by the companies, the agents of the Basque Science, Technology and Innovation Network and the Basque Government itself together with the Provincial Councils, as well as the General State Administration and the European Union. In short, it is about the blades of the motor of the second economic and social transformation of Euskadi, whose aim is the sustainable development of our country from a triple aspect; economic, environmental and social."[247] Therefore, the active involvement of all the agents of the Basque system of Science, Technology, and Innovation as well as Basque society as a whole is needed.

Involvement of the Whole of Basque Society

In order to achieve a system of advanced innovation, the PCTI 2010 refers to the concept of open innovation, making reference on the one hand to the inclusion of non-technology (organization and marketing) and the plurality of sources of innovation which are based on networks of collaboration with customers and users, distributors, suppliers, technology centers, etc. In the same way that there is a plurality of sources, there is also a plurality of areas where innovation cannot be limited to the world of business, but must pervade all society, reaching culture, art and creative industries, education, health, territory, and naturally the governance and public administration.

In a country which has seen how a single cultural infrastructure — the Guggenheim Museum — has placed it on the world stage, it seems to me that not many more examples are needed to demonstrate the huge contribution that a social innovation can make not only to the cultural wealth enjoyed by the community but to the creation of economic value itself.

The Basque people, "what is Basque," has long been associated with an entrepreneurial spirit, which has been the basis of a long history of growth and development. Now rooted into this tradition it is possible to unreservedly become involved with the global village and make innovation part of the Basque identity and the way that "what is Basque" relates itself to the world.

Using this vision, "identity" may play the role of the driving force behind the project to transform Euskadi in this new phase that opened in 2001. The "spirit of survival" that was the motivating lever of transformation in the 80s and 90s is now behind us. Today what is Basque is a more materialist

---

[247] See the "Science, Technology and Innovation Plan 2010" of the Basque Government.

and comfortable society, but we have the same need as then to find a joint stimulus with a shared vision. This is the only instrument that could mobilize and motivate the behavior of everyone and make the achievement of objectives a reality.

From this point of view, a Country which incorporates innovation and humanism of its organizations into its very identity has a powerful lever for transformation.

For this reason, 2007 and also 2008 were dedicated to provoke an "act of social mobilization" in Euskadi for knowledge and innovation. Even today, this dimension remains essential. In order to materialize this commitment, in the presentation before Basque society of the PCTI 2010,[248] it was announced that on the one hand 2008 would be the "Year of Innovation in Euskadi,"[249] and on the other adherence was proposed to the whole of Basque society to a "Manifesto for Innovation in Euskadi,"[250] which as an

---

248 IBARRETXE, J. J., Presentation by the Lehendakari of the "Science, Technology and Innovation Plan 2010," Bilbao, Palacio Euskalduna, October 22, 2007.

249 With the approval of a detailed program on behalf of the Basque Council for Science, Technology and Innovation and under the enthusiastic direction of Innobasque, Euskadi 2008 hosted "social mobilization" events for knowledge and innovation (Europe would declare the following year 2009 to be the year of innovation).

250 The *Manifesto for Innovation in Euskadi* is a commitment of the people and organizations involved to actively participate in the transformation process of Euskadi into an innovative society in all aspects of life, with the objective of raising levels of competitiveness, social cohesion, and the quality of life of its citizens. This commitment takes shape in the following principles:

1. To contribute to the promotion of the values and attitudes related to innovation and entrepreneurs (creativity, responsibility, risk taking, passion for knowledge, commitment with the surroundings, cooperation, networking, differentiating…) as a key element for the conversion of Euskadi into a country of innovation.
2. To continuously adapt the education model so that the country can respond to the changing needs of the international competitive scene, promoting values, attitudes, abilities and the necessary knowledge for people to develop all the potential innovation in society.

3. To construct a system of life-long learning aimed at enabling the people to be the principle driving force in the transformation change of our society towards innovation and knowledge, situating them at the center of the organizations so that they can freely participate and become identified with shared projects for which they can make full use of their abilities.
4. To promote critical and free thinking in a society which promotes scientific spirit and the development of public reason in order to enable change in organizations and institutions in our territory and which contributes to the construction of a modern, open and innovative country which reflects solidarity in all its actions.
5. To promote a practice of permanent innovation in organizations through the spreading of a culture of cooperation, networking and the deployment of tools and methods aimed at creating in them the dynamic capacities which enables them to evolve, to generate leading research projects as well as visible results in terms of competiveness and value creation for society.
6. To promote the Basque system of Science, Technology and Innovation as one of the basic assets for leading the transition of Euskadi towards an innovation society, creating permanent collaboration areas between institutions and organizations from different social, economic and cultural arenas, for learning, carrying out shared projects and exchanging knowledge.
7. To favor a concept of open innovation, based not only on internal capacities but incorporating from all possible sources (users, suppliers, networks,….) and going beyond the product and the technology contemplates the intangible elements and the multiple dimensions which lead to the creation of added value.
8. To take innovation to all spheres, to all organizations and public and private organizations, profit or non-profit making, and in all aspects of life and especially to promote social innovation and innovation at the service of environmental sustainability.
9. To increase international awareness of our citizenship and organizations, their connection to the world networks, in particular in the field of science, technology, innovation and knowledge, promoting international ties and the capacity to incorporate new ways of thinking into our lives.

example and in order to bear witness to the commitment, many people, institutions, political parties, and economic and social organizations ratified that very same day.

---

10. Make innovation part of the very identity of the Basque Country, projecting an image of a society in which innovation is a component linked to the singularity of the Country, to its competitive model and its unique value proposal.

4
Social Cohesion Strategy: Commitment towards Equality

One of the keys for tackling an economic and social transformation to foster sustainable human development is to define the challenge of social, scientific, and technical innovation as a critical factor of economic development and a basic cornerstone to maintain and improve the system of social welfare.[251] However, it is vital to promote an innovation with "values," innovation with "roots," innovation with "a face and eyes." Because innovation should be at the service of people, because beyond the policies and the budgets, the fundamental key to make that second economic and social transformation of Euskadi a reality and to continue achieving human development were, as is the case today, the people. The people, and as Humboldt, Rousseau, and all the authors from the school of natural rational law would say, its basic attribute: freedom.[252]

---

[251] SAMUELSON, P. y NORDHAUS, W., Economía, (16 ed.). Madrid, ed. McGraw-Hill, 1999, pages 36, 717 and 718 state: "Equity (…) The markets do not necessarily produce a fair distribution of income. A market economy may produce unacceptably high levels of inequality of income and of consumption," and in finishing (p. 717) they pose the question: "the markets may be powerful engines of prosperity, but they can also generate great inequalities (…) how should we use the best materials to improve our personal and civic lives?" concluding (p. 718): "Our economy is a 'ruthless economy.'"

[252] Liberty is a fundamental attribute for all writers from the school of rationalist natural law. Following this very tradition, HUMBOLDT VON, W., *Los límites de la action del Estado*, first study, translation and notes by Joaquín Abellán, Madrid, ed. Tecnos, 1988, p. 30, writes that "liberty is, undoubtedly, the only necessary condition without which not even the most plethoric of spirits can produce healthy results. Whatever man does not embrace with his own will, whenever he considers himself directed or restricted by others, he cannot identify with his being, he is always apart from himself and

The people are the basic invention of the 21st century. People and their education are the basic capital of a nation.

Based on this background reflection, the social construction of Euskadi would be the true backbone of the management of the Basque Institutions from 2001 onwards, representing the institutional response, from the statement values of an open society, to the changes that are felt. Mr. Murdoch identifies "two dimensions of social capital in the Basque Case: first, bonding social capital, that enables those already connected within a community to become closer and second, bridging social capital that brings people together who do not identify themselves as being part of a shared community."[253]

The aim is to bring about the individual right of all people to carry out a project of an independent life, with hiding behind the charity of passive policies that invite the situations of social marginalization to become chronic, but developing an active strategy which enables each person to exercise their right to effective integration into society.

Therefore, alongside an economic strategy, it is essential to tackle, in all modern, committed Governance programs a social cohesion strategy. This is, as put forward in the Basque Government program for 2001, a second axis: cohesion, equality, and social integration.

Because education is the most important asset for individual fulfilment and the basis for a country's success and therefore, it was a priority to guarantee the maximum quality of the levels of compulsory education and that occupational and university training also had sufficient resources. From there on, the specific challenge was to make it possible for everyone to enjoy life-long learning, both in relation to their working position and in general.

On the other hand, the advanced Social State that we wish to develop was committed to the existence of basic

---

does not function rigorously, with human strength, but with mechanical ability."

[253] MURDOCK, A., Head of Centre for Govenment and Charity, London South Bank University, London. A contribution made in relation to "The Basque Case: A Comprehensive Model for Sustainable Human Development" research program at the bilateral meeting held in London, March 31, 2011.

universal services, such as the guarantee that the best expression of equality is the inclusion of all citizens. This was the case of the health system, which had reached high standards of quality and whose reform set out to continue principles of universality, solidarity and equality as the central axis of the system. In this respect, the new "Health Plan 2002–2010"[254] would promote total quality, in an attempt to reduce waiting lists, improvement in training and the treatment of patients, and increased satisfaction with the service.

In addition the social protection policies were to be not only aimed at the situations of exclusion, but also at the specific problems of particular groups, placing special emphasis on the care of elderly dependent people, on the family support policies (Inter-institutional Plan for Support for Families[255]), on the equality between men and women to share the chores and functions of life (Basque Law of Equality[256]), on Youth (Gazte Plana[257]), and on the immigrant population (Specific Plan for Immigration[258]).

Culture was also presented as the final link in the chain of policies that must make up the Social State. Its importance is extraordinary, both for its contribution to individual enrichment and for its role of encouraging economic development in the advanced societies. Commitment to culture through open participation in the

---

254 BASQUE GOVERNMENT, *Basque Health Plan 2002–2010*. Government Council July 9, 2002, BOPV nº 149 of July 15.

255 BASQUE GOVERNMENT, I Inter-institutional Plan to Support Families with children, Government Council, session 3rd July 2001. BASQUE GOVERNMENT, II Inter-institutional Plan to Support Families, Government Council, session September 26, 2006.

256 Law 4/2005, February 18, for Equality between Men and Women, BOPV 42, March 2, 2005.

257 IBARRETXE, J.J. Inauguration Speech as Basque Country President. Basque Parliament, July 11, 2001. Diary of sessions. VII Legislature. Nº 4: page 27.

258 BASQUE GOVERNMENT, I Basque Immigration Plan 2003–2005, Government Council 9th December 2003. BASQUE GOVERNMENT, II Basque Immigration Plan 2007–2009, Government Council June 12, 2007.

Basque Culture Plan,[259] and Euskera, as the heritage of Basque Culture, forming a millenary legacy which arrived to us from generation to generation, which belongs to and requires all of us, without a doubt been behind the level of socio-economic development that this country has reached in the last three decades.

Also in 2001 two key questions were put forward in the Basque Parliament in order to tackle the change of paradigm: innovation in cooperation. The first was the Exterior Projection of Euskadi, because the social construction of Euskadi does not only have an internal dimension, but also an external one. Euskadi cannot become a closed-in country, self-isolated, but must be open to the world. And it proclaimed:

> "We wish to integrate ourselves into a globalized world, increasingly interdependent, accepting relationships and ideas of others, but providing our own identity."[260]

Then, as now, it was necessary to develop an exterior policy which would give Euskadi a "face in the world," promoting the defence of its interests and the positive image of its traditional values. To achieve this, the development of a comprehensive Basque exterior policy was needed including all the institutions and the different areas of responsibility. In short, the aim was to go from awareness to international recognition of Euskadi as a country of the future, with its own personality and identity, not at conflict but coexisting, friendly, welcoming, enriched by other identities and cultures.

To undertake this objective, it was proposed to promote the presence of Euskadi in those European Union decision forums where Basque interests came into play. The approach was not a nationalist one, but rather one of a

---

259 BASQUE GOVERNMENT, Basque Culture Plan, Government Council September 21, 2004.

260 IBARRETXE, J.J. Inauguration Speech as Basque Country President. Basque Parliament, July 11, 2001. Diary of sessions. VII Legislature. N° 4: pages 28 and 29.

Country, because, as other States of the European Union have demonstrated, it is absolutely normal that regional or national realities with their own identity may directly participate in the community organs or even preside over the European Councils.[261]

The second question put forward was that a serious, efficient and rational management of public resources is an essential instrument in attaining sustainable human development. Today, this is obvious, when we look at the socio-economic predicament of the European Union as a whole and many of its countries for having done the complete opposite of what Confucius wisely advised in the sense that when prosperity arrives, do not use all of it.[262]

Without a doubt, 2001 saw the opening up of a new era in the Basque Parliament and in the Basque Country; the door was opened to the debates of the 21st century.

An ethical commitment was put forward in defence of life and Human Rights to banish violence. A commitment to dialogue as an instrument, the only formula of a non-dogmatic use of reason.[263] A commitment to respect the decisions of the Basque citizens was proposed, the greatest democratic expression of impartiality and reasonable commitment. And a commitment was made for the

[261] The cases of Scotland, Flanders and Wallonia.

[262] It is interesting here to remember, in broad terms, some of the timeless fundaments of the Confucian philosophy. For Confucius, the noble man (in moral terms) must govern and if a prince does not match this ideal, he should surround himself with virtuous ministers. If the governing prince is virtuous, his subjects will imitate his example: governor/subject, husband/wife, father/son. He advocated the value of the power of example, governors, he said, can only be great if they lead exemplary lives and are guided by moral principles. In this way, the citizens of their states would have the necessary stimulus to achieve prosperity and happiness.

[263] See POPPER, K.R., *La sociedad abierta y sus enemigos.* Barcelona, ed. Paidós, 1994. The author insists that faced with a conflict, after scrutinizing the possibilities, there is only room for two solutions, one is emotionally inspired and eventually turns into violence, the other is inspired by reason and requires rationality, and therefore impartiality and reasoned commitment.

construction of sustainable human development in Euskadi, as a model in the state and in Europe.

Below, we will go into each of these basic policies of social and cultural balance in greater detail, fundamental to achieve a society which is not only more prosperous but also happier.

Excellence Training: Adapting People to a Globalized World

Today it is generally accepted that the new era is one of the knowledge and learning society and economy. The first refers to knowledge as the basic input of the production process, the second, coined by Lundwall,[264] stresses that what is really important is the ability with which workers, organized and countries acquire new skills, which is to say, knowledge as a flow.

We have seen that the socio-economic development strategy of the Basque institutions from 2001 onwards was a strategy designed to encourage the transition from the cost-based, low cost model of competitiveness to one based on innovation and differentiation. In this new model, the importance of innovation in companies and in society as a key concept to transform the production fabric and company development that has a bearing on the importance of the entrepreneurial spirit and on the sizing and internationalization of companies, the "increase and improvement of human capital," in short, support for the adaptation of people to the globalized world. This latter concept, the "increase and improvement of human capital" is the basis of the model and the key to influence the other two, innovation and company development.

It is exactly because, in this new context, a constant process of learning is required, general education has, from its outset, a unique importance,[265] in that it forms the basis

---

264 See LUNDWALL, B.A., *Innovation, Growth and Social Cohesión: The Danish Model.* Edward Elgar, 2002.

265 See for sake of interest the Document *Curriculum Vasco: Itinerario Cultural.* Proposed by the experts, San Sebastián, Mitxelena Artes Graficas, 2004, in which, in its three sections, the fifty knowledges can be found through which the four aims of education can be

upon which all later educational routes are laid out. Within this, most crucial are firstly the skills instrumental in learning itself: language, writing, foreign languages, and mathematics. As we find ourselves immersed in a new technological revolution and technical progress is at the roots of economic progress, technological and scientific skills are often added to the above ones, relegated those linked to social sciences and humanities. But it is true that the humanities — as our history has demonstrated — also have a highly important role in the knowledge society, skills aimed at improving relationship and communication abilities being decisive in helping to build bridges between key people in knowledge creation.

The long-term implementation of the economies will be conditioned by the way that this basic challenge of general education is dealt with, by the capacity of the education system to promote independence and ability to collaborate, by the domain over the instrumental subjects and by its approach to activities related to practical questions and the resolution of problems.

Having placed the emphasis on basic education, we must raise the level of analysis still further, because not only is it suggested that training is important, but that a radical change is needed in the concept with which people, companies and administrations understand training and adaptation of the organizational structures needed for the creation of knowledge.

The economic analysis concluded that knowledge possessed by employees increasingly accounted for a greater proportion of production capacity (compared to traditional factors of fixed capital, inputs, or management techniques), thus creating the modern concept of human capital:

> "Knowledge that individuals acquire during their lives used for the production of goods, services or ideas in market and non-market conditions."[266]

---

achieved, those being: learn to know, learn to do, learn to live with others, and learn to be.

[266] ORGANIZATION FOR ECONOMIC CO-OPERATION AND DEVELOPMENT (OECD), 'Measuring What People

Recognition of the central role of human capital as a production factor has deep implications for the reaction of public agents and policies. Let us briefly go over some of the most important ones.

From the point of view of people it could be said that training has always been considered as an investment. The confirmation of the clear relation between years of training and levels of income demonstrated the existence of a positive return on the investment in education. In reality, this relation is complex and often not automatic at all. Labor segmentation and the firm dependence on a demand linked to structural change revealed that the return on education effort has not been as expected and that it is not only the years of education that matter, but rather the adaptation of specific specialities to the labor demands of the market.

There can never be too much knowledge and so it is very hard to talk about over- investment in training. But it is true that the qualification structure of our population is heavily biased towards higher education. Perhaps with better information more people would have taken other decisions regarding their educational efforts. Information is always a key in decision making and in the case of human capital, public policies should enable all the required information, including forecasts, to guide personal decisions, achieving a greater adaptation to the changing demands of the labor market over one's life: lifelong learning.

Lifelong learning, or permanent training has a general purpose and covers all life skills, but is especially important in professional life to adapt to the acceleration of innovation characterized by today's economy and to tackle the corresponding obsolescence of what we know[267].

As a result of the above, the flexible combinations of workers with different skills will be more and more common;

Know: Human Capital Accounting for the Knowledge Economy," 1996.

[267] In recent times we have discovered a subject the importance of which has proven to be decisive: the adaptation of people and organizations to the new information technologies, which the majority of the people have had to discover after finishing their "period of studies."

fluent communication with clients will be increasingly important; long-term worker positions and functions will be seen less and less.

As regards companies, the concept of human capital or training costs have never been clear as an investment. In those where estimation of a return is difficult, then logically the consideration of the cost dominates and training activities are only considered vital when they are dictated by a pressing need. Here too, public policies need to contribute towards making a radical change on this perspective. This change should rest not solely on information and subsidies, but on reviewing tax concepts and accountancy rules in order to take effective steps in the concept of investment.

We should also remember that the change of concept does not only affect the recognition of learning and education as an investment, but also the way the organizations work. In Basque society, there are companies who are very much attached to the Taylorist hierarchical and pyramidal industrial paradigm. In some places this may sound still far off, but in a country of cooperatives it should be easier to recognize that the appearance of human capital points towards a change in organizational rules, because knowledge is personified in individuals and they are not going to deploy their skills in a framework of alienating work.

We must also stress that the commitment towards innovation and knowledge requires a growing quantity of creative people, entrepreneurs able to work in a globalized world. In this sense it is useful to incorporate into the reflection that demographic projections that state that from 2006 onwards[268] the potentially active population begins to diminish for two diverging evolutions of the population pyramid: the generations arriving at retirement age are great in number and those that are joining the labor market are much smaller. As can be seen from the decrease of people in those age brackets in the demographic projections, we are therefore faced with a downward evolution of skilled people that the system of occupational training or the university

---

268 Demographic projections of the potentially active population, EUSTAT, 2005.

system will be able to supply over the coming decade to Basque society.

We must therefore pay special attention to the "increase and improvement of human capital," both from a qualitative and quantitative perspective, because it is also important that the training of people adapts to the present and future needs of the production fabric.

To summarize, it is clear that the first factor of competitiveness of the new economic and social model for Euskadi in the 21st century will be people and their skills. The public authorities will also have the huge responsibility to avoid new inequalities that those who "don't have" are also those who "don't know."

In this undertaking the whole educational system has a crucial role in that it must be able to respond to the new requirements and progress towards a new educational and training model that promotes the knowledge and skills that the new context demands.[269] In addition, not only does the knowledge of people count; it is also important to transmit new values: an entrepreneurial and creative spirit, the acceptance of risks, non-conformism, solidarity, and attitudes that are demanded by the new innovation-based society.

Thus the main objectives and lines of action of the Basque Government were implemented through regulatory changes in education, in the "First Basque Plan for Occupational Training"[270] passed in 1997, and in the "Second Basque Plan for Occupational Training 2004–2007,"[271] which meant a drastic break with the defunct

---

[269] BECK, U., *¿Qué es la globalization? Falacias del globalismo, respuestas a la globalization,* Barcelona, ed. Paidós, 1998, p. 191, points out: "If work is to be substituted by knowledge and capital, then another political consequence may be that work has to be valued or shaped by *knowledge*. But this means that is necessary to *invest in training and research*. (…). One of the most important responses to globalization consists of *constructing and reconstructing the knowledge society and the cultural society*; to prolong and not reduce, training, separating it from specific trades or professions".

[270] BASQUE GOVERNMENT, First Basque Plan Occupational Training, Government Council 22nd April 1997.

[271] BASQUE GOVERNMENT, Second Basque Plan of Occupational Training, Government Council 9th November 2004.

concept of the training ends and procedures unique to the professional environment, to seek the integration and linking of different training offers and activities in order to satisfy the different qualifications needs of our human resources. In turn, this fits the need for a preferential attention towards detection of training needs with the coordinated action of the different agents who come together in the training and production areas and with the generation of flexible and diversifiable structures able to coordinate and integrate the efforts carried out in different spheres.

With regard to university education, these objectives were deployed in the "Law on University Planning from 1998"[272] and in the "University Plan 2000–2003" passed using this law,[273] which only referred to the University of the Basque Country. Subsequently, in the "Law on the Basque University System,"[274] passed in 2004, and its development through the new "University Plan 2007–2010"[275] which will develop the strategic process of adaptation of the universities of the Basque University System to the requirements of the Bologna process.[276] The time frame for the full implementation of the European Higher Education Area, known also as the Bologna process, runs until 2010, coinciding with the enforcement of the plan.

---

272 LAW 19/1998, 29th June, Ordenación Universitaria de la Autonomous Community of the Basque Country, BOPV 16th July 1998.

273 BASQUE GOVERNMENT, University Plan 2000-2003, Government Council 14th November 2000.

274 LAW 3/2004, 25th February, of the Basque University System, BOPV 12th March 2004.

275 BASQUE GOVERNMENT, II University Plan 2007-2010, Government Council 4th December 2007.

276 The universities of the Basque Country are connected to the European Area of Further Education, so they are committed to promote the objectives featured in the Bolonia Declaration: 1. Adaptation to an easily readable and comparable system of qualifications; 2. Creation of three main cycles: the Graduates Degree, Masters Degree and Doctorate; 3. Creation of a system of credits eligible for all countries; 4. Promotion of European cooperation in the field of further education; 5. Promoting students and teachers mobility within a common area; 6. Emphasis of curricular development to complete student training.

As well as trying to shape quality and innovation as reference points of the educational policy, innovation projects were promoted in the centers around the priority lines of innovation: schools for everyone (attention to the educational needs of the students in the inclusive school; cultural and social diversity; gender equality); better schools (leadership and management process, co-existence and educational community, program of education for coexistence, peace and Human Rights, quality of learning and a program of success for all); schools in the society of the 21st century (new curriculum and key skills, information and communication technologies, social and European frameworks, integrated treatment of languages, scientific education, and sustainable development). The innovation and quality of occupational training was also promoted, adapting it to the possibilities and demands of the information society. The development of innovative practices in the areas of education and occupational training were also encouraged and their transfer, even between different participating countries, within the program of actions included in the "lifelong learning program" and the "Sub-programs: Leonardo Da Vinci and Erasmus."

The improvement of quality has thus formed the basic objective of the Basque education system; this objective is linked to the principal challenges faced by education in these early years of the 21st century. To tackle such challenges, it is precisely the processes of educational innovation in their widest sense that should provide the improvement needed in the areas of training and management of the education system.

In the knowledge society, the intensive use and updating of material and human resources forms a decisive factor in achieving sufficient levels of competitiveness and employability, levels that on the other hand would be constantly reviewed and checked. To a certain extent, due to the pressure of continuous social and economic changes, a new way of seeing education and training has emerged in recent decades, among whose characteristic features we should emphasize the passage from a concept of the training and learning process geared towards results and success to a vision of this process based on the acquisition of skills and the increase in qualifications; and the development of a training environment where the mechanisms of formal learning are complemented and not substituted by other non-formal or informal ones.

By way of conclusion, we could state that the systems of training and learning should adapt themselves to a scenario where the means of access to knowledge will multiply and also the type of people interested will broaden. Educators and trainers will become guides, mentors or mediators for learning. Their role will be rather to support the student so they can develop their own learning. As well as motivation, active learning should include the development of a critical mentality, the ability to identify different learning possibilities.

Training centers will not only be accountable for their degree of organization and specialization but also depending on their capacity to form part of the broadest networks through which they can guide people in the best way to satisfy their demands. The services must be accessible and respond to exacting standards of quality. Finally, training centers should have firm roots in their local environment, broad connections with their surroundings while maintaining and enabling connections with other learning communities with which they are associated. The local relations will provide trust while the participation of wider networks will be essential to guide the activity and the awareness of individuals and groups.

Improvement of Health and the Coordination of the Socio-health Area

The Basque Health System (Osakidetza) geared all its activities in the first years of the 21st century towards its ultimate objective of increasing the years of living free from incapacity of the Basque citizenry. To do so, it has pursued two specific objectives: the permanent improvement of the quality of healthcare and the guarantee of the sustainable economic-financial state of the system.

In order to achieve these objectives, six major strategic guidelines were developed:

1. The first line consisted of developing the objectives and strategies of the "Health Plan 2002–2010"[277] at an individual, community, and inter-sectorial level defined in 2002 for the whole decade. This plan set five objectives: 1) to consolidate a position of leadership in health promotion through encouraging health education, fostering health lifestyles and other means 2) to develop disease prevention programs 3) to evaluate and control physical, chemical, and biological risks 4) to have the training systems that would allow greater awareness of the health needs and evaluation mechanisms of sanitary operations 5) to make progress in the knowledge and monitoring of the social inequalities in health and health care.
2. The second strategic line set out to guarantee accessibility to a quality healthcare through contracting officially approved health services. It involved making sure all the public and private health devices were adapted to their care purpose; determining the quantity and quality of the health provisions financed with public funds, or carrying out actions that contributed to enabling the physical and temporal access to health provisions.
3. The third line was the contribution to the development of the Socio-Health Area in co-ordination with the Social Services, the Provincial Councils and the Town Councils. All as a result of the fact that in recent years an increasingly evident need has arisen for co-ordination between the Health System and Social Services to deal with people who, due to health problems, to functional limitations or to their situation of social marginalisation, require the simultaneous, coordinated and stable attention of both of these networks.[278]

---

[277] BASQUE GOVERNMENT, *Basque Health Plan 2002–2010*, Government Council July 9, 2002, BOPV nº 149 July 15.

[278] The development of this socio-health area and the coordination between both networks was defined in the "*Strategic Plan for Socio-Health Care 2005–2008*" which encompasses and coordinates the

4. The fourth line of action was to improve the care infrastructures in order to cover the demand for healthcare through the modernization and adaptation of Osakidetza to the needs of healthcare. This line, which was laid down in a "Plan for the Modernisation and Adaptation of the Infrastructures and Equipment of the Basque Health System"[279] included the following partial objectives: 1) increase of the number of beds available in public health 2) refurbishment and expansion of different services and the launch of new health centers 3) providing Osakidetza with the necessary technology and equipment.
5. The fifth strategic line was to actively participate in the "Euskadi Plan for the Information Society"[280] by means of developing objectives and actions in the field of technology and training systems.

---

competences in this area for the government, the provincial councils and the Town Councils. The plan pursues four general objectives:

a) To increase the number of people cared for who have socio-health needs which means forecasting an increase in the supply of services personell or increasing support actions for carers. b) To achieve quality care providing maximum satisfaction for users and families. This means improving and developing services; offering personalized and quality care; improving efficiency; and inter-disciplinary involvement of the intervening professionals. c) To achieve a single system of care which is shared between the service networks: social and health, to be achieved through a single access system; a single portfolio of services and joint planning. d) To maintain the level of excellence in the future. This objective responds to the question of how it is possible to learn, innovate and grow.

279 BASQUE GOVERNMENT, "Modernization and Adaptability Plan of Infrastructures and Equipment of the Basque Health System 2007–2012," Government Council October 9, 2007.

280 From June 23, 2000 when the updating of the Information Society (CIT's) was passed, a working strategy was launched in order to complete the Second Great Economic Transformation of the Basque Country and which Euskadi in the Information Age *(PESI 2010)* stands out: *La agenda Digital de Euskadi.* Government Council October 9, 2007.

6. The sixth strategic line was to contribute to the generation and application of knowledge through R&D&i in the Basque Public Health System within the framework of the new "Plan for Science, Technology and Innovation 2010,"[281] which was the Objective of the Basque Health System, but was common to the whole economy and all Basque society.

From the perspective of budgetary resources it was predictable that there would be rising tensions. The increase of provisions per person, resulting partly from the development of new therapies, diagnoses and technologies; the demographic change — which had not been anticipated when the Health Plan was drawn up in the early 2000s[282] —

[281] BASQUE GOVERNMENT, "Science, Technology and Innovation Plan 2010" (PCTI 2010). Government Council October 19, 2007.

[282] New tendencies and new demographic forecasts: Aging in the population is a phenomenon which has been prevalent in the Autonomous Community of the Basque Country for several decades and has important repercussions on the job market and on social expenditure. Along with this since the eighties there has been a tendency to a falling population determined by very low birth rates and by a slightly negative migratory balance. The novelty of this last fifteen years has been the unexpected reverse of this population trend. The new movement is explained by an upwards inflection in the birth rates, but also by another phenomenon related to globalization which is the significant flow of immigrants, mainly from outside the EU, and the subsequent reverse in the net migratory balance. Neither of these phenomena had been foreseen by the 1995 population projections by Eustat which forecast a continuous fall in the population on the horizon of 2010. (Population Projections 2010. Eustat). At the start of the decade, Eustat drew up six demographic scenarios (Demographic Scenarios 2050, Eustat) based on different hypotheses for birth rates and migratory balances. In only two of those scenarios were an increase in population considered. The most optimistic of the six estimations for 2015 had the population of the Basque Country rising to 2,101,000. However, the next projection carried out by the same statistics body in July 2005, predicted an increase in population to 2,194,000 people, almost one hundred thousand

the increase of immigration, the process of ageing and the ever more costly medical innovations provoked, a growing demand for services which challenge a limited capacity of resources, and also, as in other sectors, a lack of professionals. To guarantee the financial feasibility of the system it will be necessary to find the maximum possible effectiveness and efficiency in the allocation of resources.

Social Inclusion and the Fight against Poverty

On December 23, 2008 the Basque Parliament passed the Law for the Guarantee of Income and for Social Inclusion.[283] The basic objective consisted in tackling the fight against poverty and exclusion in the Autonomous Community of

---

more than the most optimistic forecast. The trend reversal is supported by real data from the "Municipal Population Update" (Update of the municipal census. Eustat) which reveals significant increases in the population in recent years, produced by two phenomena: by natural movement, which changes direction and starts to be positive due to a gradual increase in the number of births which equals the number of deaths (According to the statistics of Births and Deaths of Eustat, in 2004 for the first time since 1989 the number of births was greater than the number of deaths), and by the migratory balance which also changed to positive and explains all the population increase. It is estimated that the new trend towards population growth will appreciably change the population pyramid. In the period 2000-2015 the cohorts between 0 and 15 years increase; the population between 15 and 40 falls considerably and the population aged over 45 also increases notably. The resulting net increase is the balance of these changes in directions. This change, which is being confirmed by real data, places serious challenges to the education system, to the business economy and the sustainability of public health expenditure.

[283] Previously in the same year LAW 8/2008 June 25, was passed, modifying the Law Against Social Exclusion and the Social Rights Charter Law, increasing basic income to 88% of the SMI (minimum inter-professional salary) and, furthermore, and this is, in our opinion, the most important, the lowest pensions were subsidised, increasing these to a 100% of the SMI when the unit of coexistence is a contributing pensioner or not. A percentage which would be maintained after the passing of the Law for the Guarantee of Income and Social Inclusion which took place in December.

Euskadi, guaranteeing, from a single legislative framework,[284] both the right to a minimum income or economic resources as the right to insertion.

The main objective of the broad body of regulations, developed from 1998 onwards using the advances undergone in the Autonomous Community of Euskadi since the launch of the Integrated Plan for the Fight against Poverty in 1989, was the struggle against social exclusion, which towards the end of the 90s had become, given the structural nature of the phenomenon, multidimensional and the process of social dualisation that it represented, one of the essential challenges of Western society.[285]

---

284 The legal framework in the Autonomous Community of Euskadi in the area of guaranteed income and social inclusion had been previously determined by Law 10/2000, December 27, on the Charter of Social Rights — modified by Law 4/2007, June 22 — and still, to a significant extent, given the lack of legislation changes, by Law 12/1998, May 22, against Social Exclusion — modified by Laws 8/2000 and 9/2000, both from November 10 and by Law 4/2003, June 25, and by the previously mentioned Law Lay 4/2007, June 22 —, as well as by its development regulations, in particular, Decree 198/1999, April 20, which governs the Minimum Inclusion Income, Decree 199/1999, April 20, which regulates the Social Emergency Benefits, Decree 1/2000, January 11, under which the inclusion agreements are regulated and the Order of February 14, 2001 under which the Employment Incentives for the Beneficiaries of Basic Income and the beneficiaries of Social Emergency Aid are established.

285 Since 1974 the European Commission has been promoting dialogue, action, and research into the areas concerning poverty. It was in 1975 when the "First Poverty Program," in which the Commission defined poor people as "those individuals or families whose resources are so limited that they are excluded from a minimum standard of living which is considered acceptable in the member state in which they live." In the decade of the 80s, the focus on poverty dominated European academic, social and political thought, based on income levels as criteria for determining if people were in poverty or at risk of falling into poverty. And the struggle against poverty became a target in the EU at the end of the 1980s and during the 1990s with the experimental programs Poverty I, II and III. The lack of legal bases in the treaties for the EU to act in this area, coupled with the resistance from some member states, and the evident limitations of these programs led

The Basque Public Administrations were aware that it was not enough to simply tackle the phenomenon of poverty and insecurity in its most classic sense — despite these being the most visible signs — but rather a more complex reality which, returning to the statements of purpose of the 1998 law, was defined as "the impossibility or the incapacity of exercising social rights, fundamentally the right to work, but also access to education, training, culture, health, proper housing and social protection." This text had already influenced, in line with European guidelines, the role of work as an element of inclusion by showing that, to a great extent, the break with the link that existed between the individual and society ended in their non-participation in the productive process and in stating that, "in our modern society, work makes up the principal means of acquiring rights and duties as regards society and that society acquires them as regards the individual."[286]

The right to work thus becomes a "sine qua non" of full citizenship and acquires its full meaning as a political right. Non-participation or residual participation in the labor market almost necessarily determines the start of an

---

the European Union to extend the concept of poverty and to include the concept of SOCIAL EXCLUSION, in which the concept of poverty is taken beyond its economic dimension to include social aspects (situation of being an immigrant, lack of housing, lack of resources, insecure employment situation, prostitution, lack of social networks, racism…) life experiences (in which the personal environment is visualized) — academic failure, addictions, illnesses, prison…) and the family situation (normally disorientation, violence, abuse…), which occur in situations of exclusion. Social Exclusion and the fight against poverty are now an integral part of the aims of the EU. In fact, it is from the Lisbon Strategy (2000) when these were linked to growth factors and employment, as decisive factors for the eradication of poverty and fight against exclusion, and it is when the term SOCIAL INCLUSION became to the fore and the European Strategy of Social Inclusion which determines all the social policies of the member states and acquired greater and greater relevance in the community agenda to the point when 2010 was named the European year of the Fight Against Poverty And Social Exclusion.

[286] LAW 12/1998, May 22, against Social Exclusion, BOPV n° 105 June 8, 1998, paragraph 4 of the exposition of motives of the law.

exclusion process with direst consequences on the exercise of other social rights.

Seen from 2008, the balance is positive and we could state that undoubtedly the contention of poverty rates and the fall seen in the data referring to its most serious forms are a result of public policies which have received a new boost in recent years, allowing the prevention, with relative efficiency, of the more extreme forms of the phenomenon. However, it became necessary, in order to redirect the efforts of the public policies, to be aware of certain trends which determine the qualitative nature of this evolution: feminization of poverty, single parenthood, job insecurity, immigration, and access to an independent life for young people.

So defined the Basque System for the Guarantee of Income and Social Inclusion, and two essential innovations were incorporated into its structure. The first was the arrangement, in a single provision called Income Guarantee, of three different modes of income:

- Basic Income for Social Inclusion: aimed at people and coexisting units lacking their own economic resources from pensions or work and whose monthly level does not reach the amount of Basic Income for Social Inclusion. This provision would always be accompanied by the application of specific support geared towards social and/or labor inclusion in the framework of the inclusion agreement.
- Complementary Pensions Income: aimed at people receiving contributory or non-contributory pensions, whose monthly income level does not reach the Minimum Inter-Professional Salary.
- Complementary Work Income: aimed at people with income from work whose monthly amount does not reach the Basic Income for Social Inclusion. This provision will be associated with the application of specific support aimed at the improvement of the labor situation through the intervention of the Employment Services or, whenever deemed appropriate or necessary by the Social Services, the

application of alternative support orientated towards social inclusion.

The second innovation was the introduction of Complementary Housing Provision, whose purpose was to provide the neediest people — which is to say those benefiting from Income Guarantee — access to housing.[287]
To summarize, the Law on the Guarantee of Income and Social Inclusion from December 2008, reaffirmed and consolidated principles such as public responsibility, universality, transversality of the policies for social inclusion, equality as regards access to and application of services and provisions, personalized and comprehensive attention, the continuity of this attention, the quality and optimization of resources, the coordination and involvement of all the Basque Public Administrations, the participation and integration of the gender perspective as well as the priority of female labor inclusion. It also influenced some new and highly significant principles regarding the nature of the model:

- Consolidation of the principle of double rights: the principle of double rights recognizes both the right to have economic means to deal with life's basic necessities if they cannot be obtained from employment or the various systems of protection and social care, and also the right to receive personalized support for labor and social inclusion, by means of obligatory participation in an inclusion agreement, so putting into practice the principle of reciprocity between the Administration and the citizen in a situation of exclusion, along the lines laid out by the European guidelines of Lisbon, Nice and

[287] This service thus covered many of the needs which were previously covered by the social emergency benefits (AES); with the substantial difference that now it became a right for the future. Furthermore, the introduction of this service would mean that the AES became once again an emergency service.

Aalborg[288] which make a close link between the economic provisions of basic income and the right to work.

- The central role of employment as an instrument of social inclusion. The model is based on the recognition of employment as a basic tool for inclusion within our society and the need to reduce both unemployment rates registered among the least privileged groups as well as the high rates of inactivity in certain other groups. Therefore and notwithstanding the need to recognize that for some the aim of labor inclusion is quite remote, there is an underlying general objective of enabling the greatest possible number of people to incorporate into the labor market and, in keeping with this objective, returning the labor market its capacity as a factor of social inclusion.
- Activation of social policies and making employment profitable. The social policies applied in the Autonomous Community of Euskadi — in particular the policies against Social Exclusion — have taken on the challenge of activation since they were created, as shown by the recognition of a specific right to receive the support needed for socio-labor inclusion from the Administration.

It could even be said that the development of these policies have made up the main innovation in the development of the social policies of Western countries in recent years — confirmed by the fact that since 2003, in the framework of the European Employment Policy, the EU

---

288 AALBORG CHARTER (1994), Lisbon Summit and Strategy (March 2000 with the objectives for the 2000-2010 period). In December 2000 the Council of Nice met and later ratified the Treaty of Nice on February 26, 2001, in which the Charter of Basic Rights of the Union was left unsigned, due to the opposition of the United Kingdom, but did remain as a point of reference for the member states. In the annex to the conclusion of the Presidency of the European Council of Nice in 2000 strongly underlined the will to fight against all forms of exclusion and discrimination, as well as a commitment to seek full employment.

Council recommends the introduction of tax and financial rewards to make the work more attractive — implying a change in paradigm, away from 'welfare to work' towards 'welfare in work,' through the development of economic provisions linked to labor participation in work benefits. The development of these policies may have a positive impact in terms of stimulating labor inclusion and, above all, in terms of income redistribution and protection of those workers with low wages, so providing employment with its former capacity as a mechanism of protection against poverty and as a magnificent tool for social integration.

Finally, the development of these measures would seem to be especially appropriate in a context such as the Basque one where the difference is increasingly smaller between Basic Income and the Minimum Inter-Professional Salary[289] which might cause distortions in the demand for these provisions and in the workings of the labor market.

Quality of Employment

Employment is the main mechanism by which the population can achieve social inclusion and the acquisition of rights.[290] The employment strategy was expressed in its most

---

289 It should be born in mind that the December 2008 Law for the Guarantee of Income and for Social Insertion establishes the types of economic benefits and their characteristics: in terms of quantity, the maximum amount of benefit, in its modalities of Basic Income for Social Inclusion and the Supplementary Benefit to Earned Income, is fixed at 88% of the Minimum Interprofessional Salary (SMI) for single persons living alone and may rise to 125% of the SMI for family units made up of four or more persons. For the modality of Supplementary Income to Pensions — aimed at people receiving contributory or non-contributory pensions, whose monthly income does not reach the Minimum Interprofessional Salary — a maximum of 100% of the SMI is established for single persons living alone and up to 135% in the case of family units made up of 3 or more persons.

290 RIFKIN, J., *The aim of work: New technologies against jobs; The birth of a new era.* Barcelona, ed. Paidós, 1996, p. 201: "Almost all the most prestigious company directors and economists continue to claim that the spectacular technological advances of the third industrial revolution will be slow to take effect: reduction in the

advanced form in the "Third Interinstitutional Employment Plan 2007–2010," passed in 2007,[291] which was inspired in *Employment Guidelines* of the revised Lisbon Strategy.[292]

The numerical targets of the European strategy for 2010 translated to the Basque Country were reachable targets with regard to total employment and female employment rates, after a decade of spectacular growth as we will see when we analyze the results of the strategy in section two of chapter 6. For this reason, in contrast to the second 2003/2006 plan and to previous initiatives in this field, the 2007–2010 Employment Plan was thought of and conceived for a different situation and emphasized the qualitative aspects, the quality of employment.

The aim was to pay special attention to the observed weaknesses and failures in dealing with sexual inequality with specific measures to promote the entrance of women into the labor market (the real reason for the recovery of the employment in the Basque Country in recent years); the measures to reconcile family and employment; the earlier

---

costs of products, increase in consumer demand, creation of new markets and an increasing number of people who will be working high technology jobs and earning higher salaries. However, this concept of 'slow to take effect' will not serve as consolation to the increasing number of workers who find themselves unemployed or underemployed."

291 BASQUE GOVERNMENT, "Third Inter-institutional Employment Plan 2007–2010." July 17, 2007.

292 The European Lisbon Strategy was defined in 2000 (Conclusions of the Presidency. European Council of Lisbon, 23rd and 24th of March 2000), and was revised in 2005 (Conclusions of the Presidency. European Council of Brussels, 22nd and 23rd of March 2005). During the Council of Lisbon in March 2000, the heads of state and of government put into action a policy named "*of Lisbon*" with the aim of making the European Union the most competitive in the world and of reaching full employment before 2010. Developed in several European Councils after Lisbon, this strategy is bases in three pillars: economic, social and environmental. Win Kok, ex-prime minister of The Netherlands revealed in the review of 2005 that the results reached were mediocre and that it was necessary to redirect the efforts to generate stronger and longer-lasting growth in the creation of more and better quality jobs.

incorporation of youth into the employment market — still lagging behind the most advanced countries in Europe; the improved employability of elder unemployed persons; mitigating the consequences of the outcome of the likely decline in the active population with an active immigration policy to attract qualified and unqualified people: tackling the uncertainty of the job market, with measures to promote job stability and quality, principally for women, youth and immigrants; and safety in the workplace in order bring down the still high accident rate.

This meant, in line with the employment directives from the revised Lisbon strategy, giving utmost importance to extending and improving the level of human capital[293]; to adapting the education and training systems to meet the new demands of the labor market[294]; to promoting flexibility combined with job safety, and to reducing segmentation of the job market paying due attention to the role of the social interlocutors[295]; to improving working conditions as far as safety and hygiene are concerned so that in 2007 the "Second Safety and Health at Work Plan 2007–2010"[296] was implemented; to ensuring inclusive employment markets, increasing job attraction and offering financially worthwhile posts for all job seekers, including marginalized segments of the population and the chronically unemployed.[297]

---

293 EUROPEAN COUNCIL, Conclusions of the Presidency, employment guidelines from the revised Lisbon Strategy, Guideline 23, Brussels, March 22–23, 2005.

294 EUROPEAN COUNCIL, Conclusions of the Presidency, employment guidelines from the revised Lisbon Strategy, Guideline 24, Brussels, March 22–23, 2005.

295 EUROPEAN COUNCIL, Conclusions of the Presidency, employment guidelines from the revised Lisbon Strategy, Guideline 21, Brussels, March 22–23, 2005.

296 BASQUE GOVERNMENT, II. "Second Safety and Health at Work Plan 2007–2010." Government Council July 3, 2007.

297 EUROPEAN COUNCIL, Conclusions of the Presidency, employment guidelines from the revised Lisbon Strategy, Guideline 19, Brussels, March 22–23, 2005.

Integration of the Immigrant Population

One of the most unprecedented situations of the last decade has been the arrival to our society of a significant number of immigrants. In order to tackle this complex and global phenomena,[298] the Basque institutions decided to establish a coordinated and coherent immigration policy with the central objective of fully integrating the immigration population residing in the Basque Country.

The exclusive competence in the area of foreign affairs correspond to the Spanish state. Nevertheless the Autonomous Community of the Basque Country are able to attend this sector of the population through social services, housing, health, education, etc. The implementation of these very policies enabled care to be provided for a collective which is in a particularly disadvantaged situation, as is the immigrant population. Thus, the development of Basque immigration policy filled a gap in the Spanish legislation governing immigration,[299] which left immigrants in our community in a vulnerable situation.

Throughout history the Basque people, like other peoples, have been strongly identified with emigration both for economic and political reasons. We may often pause to

---

[298] A wide body of literature exists which serves to draw attention to the complexity of the phenomena of immigration, nevertheless it is worthwhile mentioning in particular: DE LUCAS, J., "Nuevas estrategias de estigmatización. El Derecho frente a los inmigrantes," in PORTILLA CONTRERAS, G., *Mutaciones del Leviatan: Legitimación de los nuevos modelos penales.* Madrid, ed. Akal, 2005; Doctoral thesis of BARBERO, I., *Hacia modelos alternativos de ciudadanía: Un análisis socio-jurídico del movimiento sinpapeles,* defended at the University of the Basque Country in 2010; Doctoral thesis of DIEZ INOA, S. A., *La globalización neoliberal y el fenómeno migratorio: Análisis del modelo hispano-dominicano,* defended at the University of the Basque Country in 2008.

[299] ORGANIC LAW 2/2009, December 11, reform of the Organic Law 4/2000 from January 11 on the liberties and rights of the foreigners in Spain and their social integration. This Organic Law 4/2000 has been reformed on three occasions since it was passed, by the Organic Laws: Organic Law8/2000 December 22, Organic Law 11/2003 September 29, and Organic Law 14/2003, November 20.

think where the Basque emigrants would have gone to over the centuries if the term "immigrants without documentation" had existed. We are indebted to many countries in the world which received us with open arms, and as a grateful people we must react against the ever-increasing European immigration laws and regulations which treat people like "cattle."[300] We must do this for the sake of justice, and also for the sake of intelligence, as in contrast to Europe which regards immigration with suspicion. We see in the United States that there is a powerful tendency to link immigration with achievement, progress, and innovation,[301] although, evidently this is not the only argument and there are also other very qualified points of view on the issue, such as that of Samuel Huntington.[302]

The Basque immigration policy was articulated through the immigration plans. The "First Basque Immigration Plan,"[303] in effect between 2003 and 2005, was an early effort to introduce the reality of immigration into the day to day tasks of the public administration and from this beginning the first steps were taken to improve access to the

---

300 See STORA, B. and TEMIME, E., *Immigrances. L`immgration en France au XXe siècle*. Paris, ed. Hachette, 2007; Doctoral thesis of BARBERO, I., "Hacia modelos alternativos de ciudadanía: A social-legal analysis of the movement of immigrants without documentation," defended at the University of the Basque Country in 2010; Doctoral thesis of DIEZ INOA, S. A., "La globalización neoliberal y el fenómeno migratorio: Analysis of the Hispanic-Dominican model," defended at the University of the Basque Country in 2008.

301 See CHUA, A., *Day of Empire: How Hyperpowers Rise Dominance and Why They Fall.* New York, Anchor Books, 2009, pages XXV, 305, 326 and ss.; and ZAKARIA, F., *El mundo después de USA.* Madrid, Espasa Calpe, 2009.

302 As a point of interest, see HUNTINGTON, S. P., *Who are We? The Challenges to America´s National Identity.* New York, ed. Simon and Schuster, 2004, which puts forward the argument that the Hispanic immigration, in particular from Mexico, is threatening national identity in the United States by failing to assimilate and by pronouncing its connection with its country of origin.

303 BASQUE GOVERNMENT, "First Basque Immigration Plan 2003–2005," Government Council, December 9, 2003.

public services (health, education, etc.) to reach the same level as for the native population.

With the aim of giving continuity to policy management and to the situation of the immigration in the Basque Country, the "Second Basque Immigration Plan" was passed in 2007.[304] A plan which, based on the principles of equality, public responsibility, and social co-responsibility, no gender discrimination and the participation in achieving the objective of integration at all levels of the Basque Public Administration: Basque Government, Provincial Councils and Local Authorities.

Support for Families

The family constitutes a fundamental element of society due to the importance of the social functions which it carries out. But the family, just like other institutions in advanced industrial societies — like Basque society — has been subjected to great changes and transformations.

It is evident that the family undergoes changes in parallel to the changes which take place in society, and also that kinds of families vary, changing with time. In order to understand these changes in the situation of the family and understand the processes which are taking place and the factors which are causing them, it is necessary to carry out a thorough analysis. The family has to be analyzed as an open social system — not closed — which reflects the changes taking place in society.

This influence which the change in other systems, such as the economic or the political, have on the family cause it to continuously adapt to the shifting social situation, thus requiring public institutions to adopt and put initiatives underway which will protect, support, and contribute to the promotion of the welfare of the family as a whole and of each of its members.[305]

---

304 BASQUE GOVERNMENT, "Second Basque Immigration Plan 2007–2009, Government Council June 12, 2007.

305 Recommended by EU Institutions, benefits for dependent children are the main examples of the family benefits aimed at supporting parents. They constitute the central element of the

The changes and transformations which have affected the Basque family, both its models and its behavior patterns, have a close relationship with three kinds of factors: the demographic tendencies influenced by low birth rates and population ageing; negative changes due to the instability of the labor market and the housing factor characterized by its high cost, placing a barrier to youth independence; and the cultural mix of values, aspirations, aims, and life projects.

In the Basque society, in recent years, the governing framework of the family policy made a decisive step with the passing of, on one hand, the Common-law Spouse Act in 2003, the main objective of which, as outlined in its Exposition of Motives was:

> "To contribute and progress to overcoming any lingering legislative discrimination against personal or social conditions or the circumstances of family members, understood in the diversity of ways of expressing affection and sexuality culturally admitted in our social environment, and to perfect the legislative development of the constitutional principles of non-discrimination and free development of the social, economic, and legal personality of the family, adapting the legislation to the social reality of the current time."[306]

And, on the other hand, in 2005, of the Care and Protection of Infancy and Adolescence Act.[307]

As far as family protection is concerned, the Interinstitutional Support Plan for Families with Children,[308]

---

family policies in all European countries, although considerable differences exist between them, in particular among the northern countries — Denmark, Sweden, Norway — along with France which have a more universal tendency, and the southern countries such as Greece, Italy or Portugal, in which the scope of the benefits is, generally speaking, notably less ambitious.

306 BASQUE PARLIAMENT, LAW 2/2003, May 7, Regulatory Law for Common-Law Spouses.

307 BASQUE PARLIAMENT, LAW 3/2005, February 18, Care and Protection of Infancy and Adolescence.

active between 2002 and 2005, involved the start of a road to a universal, comprehensive and coordinated family protection system. This plan had the overall objective of the removal of the economic and socio-labor obstacles which impede or make it difficult for families to have the number of children they want.

Later the Second Institutional Plan of Family Support[309] was passed and was in force from 2006 to 2010. This Second Family Plan aimed to respond to the emerging phenomena which were outlined in the diagnosis of the situation carried out when the plan was passed, attempting to consolidate the achievements of the previous plan by improving the existing measures and services and setting underway new family support programs.

It was clear that new ways of living together existed, and consequently the plan was inspired by the principle of respect for the diversity of the family. The aim was to remove any kind of discrimination based upon the kind of family origins. To this end the first objective was to promote and protect the rights of the different kinds of families and their children, ensuring the same rights for all, and the same access to financial benefits and available services. At the same time, compensation measures were promoted for large as well as for single-parent families taking into account their special characteristics and their level of need.

Furthermore, the Government faced with the evidence of conflict in the family decided that the best way to face up to this conflict was from the perspective of prevention. That is with education and training in abilities and strategies for the resolution of conflictive situations. All in line with the European recommendation in this field,[310] with the aim of preventing and resolving certain symptoms of the conflict, correcting inappropriate habits and behavior,

---

308 BASQUE GOVERNMENT, "First Interinstitutional Families with Children Support Plan," session July 3, 2001.

309 BASQUE GOVERNMENT, "Second Interinstitutional Families Support Plan," Government Council, session September 26, 2006.

310 The setting underway of initiatives in the area of family mediation has been boosted in recent years by the Recommendation on January 21, 1998 of the European Council, which called on Governments to set up family counselling.

counselling in problem solving and managing problematic situations, setting up mediation devices for spouses, meeting points for child visits, and introducing measures for the use of restraining orders for abusers and protecting the victims of domestic violence.

This Second Plan was also declared tributary to the previous one in the area of reconciling work and family life and proposed the continuation of the path taken with the setting underway of new measures.

Reconciling Work and Family Life

The First Interinstitutional Family Support Plan,[311] in 2001, set underway a series of measures to reconcile work and family life with the aim of removing barriers to employment arising from maternity or paternity, and to correct some of the limitations that the working life imposes on family life.[312] Thereby, attempting to foster the reconciliation between these areas, and eventually the equality of opportunities for men and women, both with regard to employment access, security, and to their possibilities of caring for their children at a time when this care is most needed.[313]

The experience proved to be a positive one, and the Basque Government took the decision to continue developing and improving the system of family protection, lending more importance to its reconciliation policy, and in 2006 with the "Second Interinstitutional Family Support

---

[311] BASQUE GOVERNMENT, "First Interinstitutional Family Support Plan," Government Council, session July 3, 2001.

[312] Among these measures the backing for the setting up of a network of education centers for infants under the ages of three and the granting of financial help for those, within the framework established by the Workers Statute took advantage of leave or reduced working hours for the purposes of childcare.

[313] Within the framework of the 1st Plan, Decree 177/2002 was passed first on July 16, regulating family and work reconciliation measures, secondly Decree 329/2003 was passed on December 23, in which employment aid was regulated and in which Chapter VI restructured the family and work reconciliation measures

Plan,"[314] a strategic line was established, incorporating a new subsidy program for parental leave and flexible employment hours for family care duties.[315]

Thus from 2007[316] onwards measures to reconcile work and family were established and were structured along four lines of action:

- Benefits for workers who take leave or reductions in their working hours for the purposes of childcare.
- Benefits for workers who take leave or reductions in their working hours for the purposes of looking after dependents in need of care.
- Benefits for substituting workers who take leave or reductions in their working hours for the purposes of childcare or to look after dependents in need of care.
- Benefits for contracting workers for the purposes of childcare.[317]

Social Focus of the Housing Policy

It is true that the current situation calls for a serious rethink on housing strategy given the structural changes we are witnessing. It would appear that the extended property boom with high price growth making it difficult for young people to buy property is finally coming to an end. There is an

---

314 BASQUE GOVERNMENT, 2nd Interinstitutional Family Support Plan, Government Council, session September 26, 2006.

315 Among the objectives of this strategy line are those of making it easier for women to enter into employment and to progress in their career, to foster co-responsibility between men and women in the care and education of their children, and to facilitate the reconciliation between family and work.

316 DECREE 118/2007, July 17, in which the family and work reconciliation measures were regulated. Basque Country Official Bulletin, n. 2007144, July 27, 2007.

317 The introduction of this new initiative, featured in the "Family Support Plan II," was based on the type of benefits available in Europe, where countries as different as France, Norway, Finland or the United Kingdom, have one or several benefit models for employing carers.

excess of supply at current prices and these have begun to fall so that the problem that the Basque institutions have been faced with is likely to change both in kind and in quantity. On the other hand the population changes and forecasts for future households and their sizes are data which should be taken into account in order to design the strategy for the future.

Nevertheless, the housing problem is a factor which has considerably affected young people and families in situations of relative and acute poverty, accommodation being a basic need. In fact, between 2000 and 2005 the price of m^2 of housing in the free market increased in the Basque Country by 51% and monthly rates rose by 34%.[318] The "Basque Housing Needs and Requirements Survey 2005" revealed that the percentage of households with young people who expressed the desire to enter the property ladder stood at 12.2%. The housing and accommodation problem also affects that sector of the population at risk of relative or acute poverty, which now features a relatively high proportion of immigrants thereby having the consequence of exacerbating their often already precariousness situation.

The housing policy of the Government was established through several director plans. Over the last decade the "Director Plan, 1998–2001" was put into action, enabling the construction of 13,599 social dwellings along with the "Housing Director Plan, 2002–2005," under which more than 20 million price-controlled social dwellings were constructed in this period with the emphasis on promoting rented housing. It is worth pointing out that between 2002 and 2005 the quota of price-controlled social housing accounted for 30.6% of all new construction,[319] more than the quota of 20.7% for the period 1998–2001.

---

[318] Department of Housing and Social Affairs, Real Estate Market Survey, Eustat.

[319] This quota of 30.6% for the proportion of price controlled social housing of total construction (20,731 price-controlled dwellings / 67,830 total of constructed dwellings between 2002-2005), was four times greater than the national average, according to data published by the Department of Housing and Social Affairs, Basque Government, Housing Director Plan 2006-2009, October 3, 2006.

Later, in 2006, the Land and Urban Planning Act was passed[320] as well as the "Director Housing Plan, 2006–2009."[321] From this point the housing policy featured in this plan comprehensively tackled the housing requirements, especially for the neediest, through measures which were adapted to different situations and counting on the participation of all the agents involved in housing. The following policies were featured:

- to increase the supply of price-controlled housing
- to intensify rent promotion policies
- to increase the amount of empty housing placed on the rent market
- to promote urban rehabilitation and renovation
- to promote quality construction, sustainability, safety, innovation and industrialization
- to intensify the struggle against fraud linked to price-controlled housing
- to seek ways which enable complementary actions and coordination between the different Basque public institutions

These specific actions were framed within four strategic lines:

1. Social and environmental development of the "new city." The promotion of price-controlled housing was framed within this line; the favoring of rented accommodation in the promotion of price-controlled housing; the cooperation between all promoting agencies for this housing and support for quality, sustainability and innovation.
2. Support for the "constructed city." In this axis, urban rehabilitation and renovation and the mobilization of uninhabited housing for the rent-controlled rent market of housing were featured.

---

320 LAW 2/2006 LAND AND URBAN PLANNING, June 30, 2006, published in the BOPV July 20, 2006.
321 BASQUE GOVERNMENT, "Housing Director Plan 2006–2009," Government Council October 3, 2006.

3. A personal and convenient service for people requiring, owning or renting housing, especially focussed on people using Etxebide, the collectives with special requirements and to boost the involvement of citizens.
4. Finally, a fourth strategic line instigated a study on behalf of the rest of the public administrations on the aspects which affect access to housing such as tax situation, family debt or urban planning.

Thus the "Housing Director Plan" following the approval of the Land Law in June 2006 and the "Housing Director Plan, 2006–2009," passed in October 2006, defined the strategic planning of housing policy for the whole of the eighth legislature, which was based on the following main objectives:

1. Promote price-controlled housing, both in terms of quantity and variability, with decisive actions in land purchase and promoting new price-controlled housing. Increasing the supply of price-controlled housing, mainly for rented accommodation. Thus, renting was promoted as the principal route of access to housing to attend the needs of those collectives in need of housing who did not have sufficient funds for purchase, among which single-parent families with women as the head of the household feature prominently.
2. Decisive support was lent to urban rehabilitation and renovation with the objective of making the best use of existing buildings and urban development. Aiming to maintain existing buildings in use and adapted to current circumstances while ensuring efficient use of public funds.
3. Measures to make use of uninhabited housing were continuously adapted as a formula to boost the housing supply in price-controlled rented accommodation. In this line, in the case of price-controlled housing, monitoring was carried out of effective housing occupation, and the legislation regarding sanctions applied for non-occupation and

repossession on the part of the administration were reviewed. The number of government and council owned housing flats and houses for rent was increased. In the case of free market housing, in order to foster their supply on the market a double edged, carrot and stick policy was carried out. On the one hand financial incentives were awarded to attract this housing to price-controlled renting for a minimum of five years, grants were awarded for housing rehabilitation, and tax incentives were introduced in collaboration with the Provincial Councils. On the other hand, formulas were introduced to deter the existence of unoccupied housing through financial and fiscal measures.

4. The level of services available in housing matters was improved so as to provide a quality service to the users of ETXEBIDE, the Basque Housing Service.
5. The overriding philosophy of the housing policy is to attend the social needs using public services in an efficient way. Logically, the level of care must be proportional to the level of need, so the neediest receive proportionally more intensive attention. Thus, the public sector focused its priorities in those actions which have a greater social content, aimed at the less-favored collectives, the more marginalized and those at greater risk, such as the handicapped, those under 35, single parent families, large families, and people on basic income. In order to achieve this general objective of accentuating the social aims of the housing policy, price-controlled renting was promoted, the actions of all protagonists were focussed according to their social content, the criteria of access to price-controlled housing were revised, actions were coordinated with social insertion policies, and the pricing policy of housing was reviewed.
6. More detailed attention was given to quality, sustainability, safety and innovation in construction.

Furthermore, the legislation affecting housing was adapted and regulated, both with regard to price-controlling and urban planning. Law 2/2006 June 30, on land and urban planning, was put into effect and remains so and towards the end of the legislature a law was being put underway with which to regulate price-controlled housing, to define the housing need, taking into account the changing patterns of households which were being observed in our society, which regulated the typology of controlling actions and established new areas of protection, regulated the operating agents, the array of infractions and sanctions, the Administration's favorable purchase options in the cases of price-controlled housing sales, the mechanisms enforcing information supply from notaries in the case of price-controlled housing sales, as well as the obligatory information to be supplied to house-buyers and renters.

Equality between Men and Women: The Political Project of the Twenty-first Century

The Equality Institution, Emakunde — Basque Women's Institute[322] — reporting to the Presidency of the Government, has been responsible for designing, planning, and assessing action and activities aimed at achieving real equality between men and women. Positive Action Plans for women in the Basque Country have been the tools and backbone of equality policies, carried out by the Basque Administration, at all levels during each legislature.

The "Second Equality Plan" was assessed in 1998 and this showed greater involvement by Government departments, Provincial Councils and a large number of Town Councils working in favor of gender equality. Over double the number of actions carried out in the previous period corresponding to the first plan were identified and analyzed.[323]

---

322 The Basque Women's Institute – EMAKUNDE, was created by Law 2/ 1988 of February 5 by the Basque Parliament.

323 Since the creation de Emakunde, three plans were developed in the Basque Country until Law 4/2005, of 18 February on Equality between Men and Women. The First Plan (legislature 1991- 1994)

From the quality point of view, we saw a trend to develop specific measures and resistance or greater difficulties in advancing the incorporation of equality between men and women in all policies.

This was therefore the central objective that would mark the content of the "Third Plan" approved in 1999 and which incorporated mainstreaming into general policy. Emphasis was therefore placed on a new process, a new strategy, adopted in the Fourth World Conference on Women, held in Beijing and defined as "a political and technical process that involved new ways of thinking and focused on policies...that envisaged full participation of women in all aspects of life and the analysis of all the proposals concerning general or sectorial policies and programs from a gender perspective."[324] From that moment on, reflections and literature about the gender question, fortunately, have become more common. It would be very long winded to list them all, but we do find it interesting, due

---

responded mainly to the philosophy of equal opportunities and focused its efforts on the rights and promotion of women, the objective was to correct the discrimination situation. The Second Plan (1995 – 1998) had the equal opportunity objectives of the first plan, but introduced a substantial change, a new perspective on equality. In the introduction it says that equality between men and women is not only a democratic right, but a strategic necessity for the political, social and economic construction of the Basque Country, in keeping with the most significant quality advances for women that were achieved at the Beijing World Conference (1995), where awareness was raised on the fact that future society and full economic and social development could not occur without the full participation of women and thus the need for the empowerment of women. In the assessment of the second plan 2,840 activities were identified and analyzed, much more than double those carried out in the period corresponding to the first plan. The third Plan (1999–2005) approved in 1999, introduced in its title the expression "focus on gender in public policies," in order to stress this new vision in all public policies.

324 IV WORLD CONFERENCE ON WOMEN, World Platform on women, Beijing, 1995.

to the suggestive opinion presented by the author, to refer to a paper by María Ángeles Barrere.[325]

During the execution of the new Plan, some fundamental questions arose, among others, with regard to programs and projects introduced and which had great repercussions on the consolidation of equality policies:

- Social awareness campaigns referring to the interest and social benefit of equality between men and women, with special impact on the need to eradicate violence against women.
- Creation of employment networks, like the network of Basque municipalities for equality or the Consultative Committee, a body for the participation of women's associations in the Basque Country.
- Intervention programs in education with the involvement of teachers, pupils and families in the preparation of material and development of activities that question gender stereotypes and propose new frameworks of relations between peers.
- Programs in business, together with the non-discriminatory selection and promotion of women in jobs of responsibility.
- Boost training for professionals through postgraduate masters courses at Basque universities.[326].
- General and specific studies on the situation of men and women in the Basque Country.
- Forums to promote Equality where institutions, organizations, and different groups show their commitment and work to advance in the development of women's rights.

---

325 See BARRERE, M. A., *Discriminación: derecho antidiscriminatorio y acción positiva en favor de las mujeres*. Madrid, Civitas, 1997.

326 Master on intervention on violence against women at the University of Deusto, and Master on Equality between men and women at the University of the Basque Country.

- Protocols of inter-institutional action in the area of violence against women.
- Training plans in the area of gender for professionals in the Basque Administrations.
- Action directed at men to promote their involvement in work for Equality between men and women.

The latter was a new, innovative program and was presented publically by the Basque Government through the International Congress "Men facing the new social order,"[327] held in the Basque Country in 2001. This was followed by a special Program entitled Gizonduz, "equality makes you more of a man," in November 2007, and the presentation in April 2008 of the Charter by Basque men in favor of equality and against violence against women.[328]

In 2005 the Basque Government promoted a qualitative leap in favor of equality by presenting the Bill on Equality between Men and Women, which was later approved by the Basque Parliament.

The objective of the Law was to establish the principles that would preside over action taken by public powers with regard to equality, and to regulate a set of measures directed at promoting and guaranteeing equal opportunities and the treatment of men and women in all areas of life, and in particular to promote autonomy and strengthen the social, economic, and political position of women.

This is in line with the United Nations regulation that adopts the Declaration and Action Program, approved at the end of the World Conference on Human Rights held in Vienna June 14–25, 1993,[329] which, based on the Preamble of

[327] Congress Publication, "Men facing the new social order." Emakunde, 2002.

[328] Both the Gizonduz Initiative in November 2007 and the Charter of Basque Men in favor of equality and against violence against women in April 2008 were presented with the conviction that only active and keen involvement of men will make it possible to progress towards real equality between men and women.

[329] GENERAL ASSEMBLY OF THE UNITED NATIONS, Declaration and Action Program of Vienna, A/CONF.157/23, July

the United Nations Charter, incorporates the actions and recommendations that originated in the concern for different forms of discrimination and violence to which women continue to be exposed all around the world. It is also in line with international legislation that commits to "ensuring by Law the practical realization of the principle of equality" [330] or by "incorporating the aim to eliminate inequalities between men and women in all policies."[331] This last aspect is

---

12, 1993, among others point 18 states: "The human rights of women and girls are inalienable, integrant and indivisible from universal human rights. Full participation, on equal terms, of women in political, civil, economic, social and cultural life on national, regional and international levels and the eradication of all forms of discrimination based on sex are priority objectives of the international community. Violence and all forms of sexual harassment and exploitation, in particular those derived from cultural prejudices and the international trade of persons are incompatible with dignity and the worth of the human person and must be eliminated. This may be achieved with legislative measures and national activities and international cooperation in spheres such as economic and social development, education, attention to maternity and to health and social support. The question of women's human rights must form an integral part of the human rights activities of the United Nations, particularly the promotion of all human rights instruments related to women. The World Conference on Human Rights urges Governments, intergovernmental institutions and non-governmental organizations to intensify their efforts in favour of the protection and promotion of human rights for women and girls."

[330] Article 2 of the Convention on the elimination of all forms of discrimination against women, adopted by the GENERAL ASSEMBLY OF THE DE UNITED NATIONS in Resolution 34/180 December 18, 1979, which came into effect on September 3, 1981, in accordance with article 27 (1) United Nations Treaty no. 20378, vol. 1246, p. 14.

[331] The third EMAKUNDE Equality Plan "focused on gender in public policies," (1999) i.e. gender "mainstreaming" has been included in the community law in two articles of the Amsterdam Treaty, three Community Action Programs and a growing number of non binding regulations. The Amsterdam Treaty of 1997 recognized gender "mainstreaming" as having a prominent role through the introduction of a new article 2 that establishes the promotion of equality between men and women as one of the

furthermore expanded by the Council of Europe when it speaks of the need to adopt measures to integrate the gender perspective in public actions: in planning, improving statistics and studies, recruiting staff, and establishing a procedure to incorporate the principle of equality in administrative regulations and action.[332]

The Law on Equality between men and women of 2005 establishes the areas for intervention, including a set of measures in each area aimed at eradicating the multiple forms of discrimination against women:

- Socio-political participation
- Culture and media
- Education
- Employment
- Other basic social rights
- Conciliation of personal, family, and professional life
- Violence against women[333]

"Positive Action" and "mainstreaming gender" are defined as the two inseparable strategies for the definition and execution of public policies. In this sense, and serving as an example, we should mention the contents of two parts of the Law on Equality, each developing the two strategies, which have also represented important changes in the situation of Basque women and general political planning.

> Article 19: "Before undertaking the preparation of a regulation or administrative act, the administrative body promoting it must assess the potential impact

---

objectives of the Union (together with economic convergence and the promotion of employment). However, the article that most embodies the spirit of the new strategy is the new article number 3.2 which obliges the EU in "all the activities" it carries out to fulfill its objectives of trying to eliminate inequalities and promote equality between men and women.

[332] Report on gender mainstreaming of the European Commission. Strasbourg 1998.

[333] See Law 4/2005, February 18, for Equality between Men and Women, BOPV 42, March 2, 2005.

of the proposal on the situation of men and women as a group. To do so, it must be assessed if the projected activity in the regulation or administrative act might have positive or adverse repercussions on the overall objective of eliminating inequalities between men and women and promoting equality."
Final Provisions 4 and 5: "Candidatures presented by political parties, federations, coalitions or groups of electors will be made up of at least 50% women. This proportion will be maintained for the whole of the list of candidates and for each set of six names. The election boards of the competent province will only admit those candidatures that fulfil the conditions expressed in this article."

Another important aspect covered by the Law is the creation of the Equality Ombudsman. This is an independent body to ensure the fulfilment of the principle of equality and defend citizens from possible discriminatory situations or practices for reasons of gender that might arise in the private sector.

This initiative is aimed at developing community mandates on the existence of independent organizations that provide independent help to victims when processing claims for discrimination based on gender, carrying out independent studies and reports and formulating recommendations on any question related to this kind of discrimination.

In short, over the period 1998–2008 fundamental keys were defined to advance in the exercise of the principle of equality between men and women:

- Prepare legislation to accelerate changes.
- Create structures to enable operational capacity in policies.
- Increase awareness in society about the need for equality.
- Train people to promote personal changes.
- Create mechanisms for coordination to enable the optimization of work in the administration.
- Planning with citizen participation.
- Generate the political will to advance.

In conclusion, the Basque Country is a benchmark with regard to equality policies in the region,[334] but there is still a lot to be done.[335] However, we are nearer to understanding people. Like birds we have two wings: the "male wing" and the "female wing." And just like birds we can "survive" with one wing, but we need both if we want to "fly."

Cultural Identity Open to the World. Basque Language: An Element for Integration, Cohesion, and Development

Basque is one of the main signs of identity of our society, it is the language of the Basque people, it is our own language, not because it is the only one we Basques own, but because our people are the only ones who own it. A positive sign of identity, an element for integration and cohesion. From the point of view of the Country, it is true that Basque is not our only language, we also have Spanish and French. As Koldo

---

334 The representation of women in public life has increased substantially: the Basque Parliament had 24% female MPs 1997 in and 53% in 2008; the Provincial Councils had 17% female members in 1995 and 41% in 2007; Councils in the BAC had 22% mayoresses and female councillors in 1995 and 35% in 2007.

335 The work we have to do is immense… but wonderful: the female-male salary gap, according to Basque Ombudsman data was 15.9% in 2006 in the Basque Autonomous Community (from 16.6% in 2002 according to the same source); according to the Budgetary Time Survey, Eustat 2008, the time that men and women dedicate per day in the Community to personal care (women 2hrs and 18m, men 1hr and 41m.) and to household tasks (women 3 hrs and 33 minutes, men 1 hr and 29 minutes) is substantially different, according to 2009 report data by the Economic and Social Council of the Basque Autonomous Community (CES), women in top management of Basque companies account for 4.9%, the report adds, and this is also important, that the effects of the current crisis have affected women that occupy management posts more (19.6% reduction), than male managers (13.4% reduction).

Mitxelena, the great Basque linguist and intellectual said, "erdera"[336] (foreign languages) are also ours.

We know that the main field for the development of Basque language and culture is Basque society itself. Here we build, day by day, the present and the future; but, in this 21st century, for us and for humanity as a whole, the world is a global village. We must open up and contribute with our work here.

This is nothing new. Basque society has always been open to the world. Bernat Etxepare, in his work *Linguae vasconum primitiae,*[337] the first book to be printed in Basque, wrote, "jalgi adi kanpora, jalgi adi plazara, jalgi adi mundura," "Basque go out! Go to the square! Open your doors to the world!"

Some fifty years later, Miguel de Cervantes, in his masterpiece, *Don Quijote*, put these words in the mouth of the Ingenious Hidalgo:

> "...and with regard to what you say, señor, of your son having no great opinion of Spanish poetry, I am inclined to think that he is not quite right there, and for this reason: the great poet Homer did not write in Latin, because he was a Greek, nor did Virgil write in Greek, because he was a Latin; in short, all the ancient poets wrote in the language they imbibed with their mother's milk, and never went in quest of foreign ones to express their sublime conceptions; and that being so, the usage should in justice extend to all nations, and the German poet should not be undervalued because he writes in his own language, nor the Castilian, nor even the Biscayan, for writing in his."[338]

---

[336] Erdera: in Basque, is any Language other than Basque. It is used to refer to Spanish and French in the Basque Country.

[337] ETXEPARE, B., *Linguae vasconum primitiae*. Bordele, François Morpain, maitre imprimateur, 1545.

[338] CERVANTES SAAVEDRA, M., *El ingenioso hidalgo Don Quijote de la Mancha*. Ed. from the IV Centenary. Real Academia Española. Association of Spanish Language Academies. Alfaguara, Basque Government, 2005, p. 667.

The 19th century, in the middle of the Romanticism Era and when Basque society lost its ancient laws and liberties by force, José María Iparraguirre (1820–1881), Basque poet and musician, and author of the song "Gernikako Arbola," a popular Basque anthem, sang to the Tree of Gernika as a tree representing freedom, wishing it to "give and spread your fruit around the world."[339]

In the 20th century, the great master Koldo Mitxelena claimed a place for Basque language and culture in the world:

> "Just as our people need to find a place among other peoples, so too must our Language find its place among other languages: a suitable place to ensure its continuity and development, without maximalist adventures."[340]

In the case of Basque, legal recognition was achieved with the recovery of democracy and self-government. The first recognition occurred with the establishment of the Government of the Basque Country in 1936, presided over by Lehendakari (President) Aguirre; the institution of self-government and recognition of the official nature of Basque language in the Statute of Autonomy of the Republic were cut short by the Franquist victory. Subsequently, legal recognition was recovered with the Spanish Constitution of 1978 and the Statute of Autonomy of 1979.

The Statute of Autonomy of Gernika (1979), in article six established that Basque is the language of the Basque People and that together with Spanish is an official language; and that its citizens are entitled to know and use both languages. It corresponds to the Basque institutions to create the conditions that enable the use of both language and regulate the necessary measures to guarantee the application of this official nature. This obligation,

---

[339] *Eman eta zabal ezazu munduan fruitua.* Verse from the Gernikako Arbola and current motto of the UPV-EHU University of the Basque Country.

[340] MITXELENA, K., "*El largo and difícil camino del euskera*": *The White Paper on Basque language.* Bilbao, Euskaltzaindia 1977.

corresponding to the institutions, is the origin of the need for an exhaustive knowledge of the reality of the country, and the application of measures to guarantee the use of the languages in different social spheres (administration, education, health, the media, publishing, cultural creation, etc.).

From a comparison between the Constitution (article 3) and the Statute of Gernika (article 6), we can see an asymmetry between the "duty to know" and the "right" to use Spanish established by the Constitution, compared to the "right" to know and to use Basque as established by the Statute. This asymmetry also exists in the case of Catalan and Galician, between the Constitution and the respective Statutes of Autonomy, reiterated further still by the Constitutional Court in its sentence on the Statute of Catalonia.

In developing article 6 of the Statute of Gernika in 1982, the Law on the normalization of the use of Basque[341] defined the system of double official nature established in the Statute and based on the following principles:

- It is a law for the normalization and promotion of the use of Basque, i.e. to open the doors to positive action in support of a minority and minimized language.
- It is a law that recognizes citizens' linguistic rights (right of use and choice of language), and assigns to public powers the resulting obligation to adopt all the necessary measures to guarantee an effective exercise of said rights. It is, therefore, a law that is respectful with citizens' freedom — who are under no imposition — but is demanding with the administration.
- It is a law to be applied not only to the administration of the Autonomous Community of

[341] LAW 10/1982, November 24, BASIC LAW ON THE NORMALIZATION OF THE USE OF BASQUE, Basque Parliament, BOPV no 160 of 1982.

the Basque Country but to any administration in the Autonomous Community. It is, therefore, a law that must be complied with by the administration of the State located in the Basque Country.

- It is a law that pursues social equality between the two official languages, real and effective bilingualism based on the principles of progressiveness and gradualism, bearing in mind the diversity of the sociolinguistic reality.
- It is a law of consensus, made possible by a general agreement on a favorable linguistic policy for the normalization of Basque as a factor of social integration and vertebration.

In the words of the renowned Basque physician Pedro Miguel Etxenike, the Minister for Education and Culture of the Basque Government who promoted the Law:

> "The agreement we reached at that time was based on three pillars:
> First: normalization and promotion. The primordial objective of the Law on Basque was the normalization of use, i.e. channel the right of citizens to know and use both official languages in everyday life (…)
> Second: nothing is possible against people's will (…). Certainly, no one will be obliged to speak a language they do not wish to speak, but the administration cannot act in the same way, as it is obliged to respond in the language chosen by the citizen.
> Third: strengthen the bilingual society (…)
> Fourth: social cohesion. Language policy must integrate, it must promote social cohesion. (…) Given that we propose to build a democratic society, it is necessary to build the foundations of language policy on social agreement. We Basqueophiles must be able to continually feed and strengthen the adhesion of citizens to Basque.
> As I understand it, the policy carried out over these last thirty years, bearing in mind the that the path

> supported by these fundamental pillars has born spectacular fruit. (…) Why has all this occurred? In my opinion, despite it being true that language policy promoted by public powers has been efficient (…), there is another more decisive reason: the will of society. It has been society itself that has decided to drive Basque on."[342]

Without doubt, together with the policies applied, the fundamental key for the survival and development of a language is to be found among its speakers. Laws and decrees are necessary, but no one should expect miraculous results from them. What is decisive is the attitude and language behavior of speakers. Therefore it is always necessary for public institutions and civil society to work together. Public institutions alone cannot ensure the full development of Basque as a normalized language of communication, which means it is and will be necessary to have the support of men and women who speak Basque and the effort of social groups committed to the social use of Basque.

Over the thirty five years from the approval of the Statute of Gernika, abundant energy and tools have been placed at the service of Basque and to a greater degree than ever: among others, political institutions, legal provisions, public budgets, planning and specific structures, without forgetting the important contribution of the social initiative. Thanks to all of the aforementioned, an enormous effort has been made and it is clear that hand in hand with this effort profound changes in the linguistic reality of our society have taken place.

The balance, because there have been ups and downs, is positive. Basque society has real reasons to feel proud of the effort carried out and the journey covered over the past three decades:

---

[342] ETXENIKE, P.M., "Cerca de treinta años de Ley del euskera," prologue in BAZTARRIKA, P., *Babel or barbarism*. Irun, Ed. Alberdania, 2009.

> "Clearly the recovery of Basque in the Autonomous Community of the Basque Country is the most important development in the world. It does sound pompous, but really (...) it is the only known recovery that has continued over more than 20 years with an average annual gain of a half a percent in knowledge and continues to be so. (...) In Navarre, however, Basque is being recovered at a much slower speed. It is clear that the help of the provincial authority enables recovery. And we all know that the problem in Navarre is that social support for Basque is much wider than institutional support."[343]

This must be recognized, without falling into self-complacency, because past success in this field does not guarantee or ensure the future of the language. This will be the case, if cutbacks take place or public policies that have been applied are curtailed by certain public powers.

Not in vain, the country of the Basque language, the three political-territorial areas of Euskal Herria (the Basque Country), are a reflection of three different policies and modes of action with regard to the language. With different results too, as can be observed in the results of the fourth and fifth Sociolinguistic Survey in Euskal Herria.[344] These results show how the process to revitalize Basque has advanced firmly in the Basque Autonomous Community (BAC) and more slowly in Navarre when seen from the perspective of the last fifteen years. In Iparralde (French Basque Country), however, the loss in Basque speakers continues, although this trend is decreasing and, with the

---

343 GROS i LLADÓS, M., interview held on News in Gipuzkoa, January 22, 2010. The Catalan lawyer and sociolinguist had established in 2009: "we are facing one of the best examples of known language recovery, one which arouses greater social unanimity, greater speed of recovery, higher percentage of language recovery, deeper bilingualism at an early age."

344 IV Sociolinguistic Survey 2006. Central Publications Service of the Basque Government. Vitoria-Gasteiz, 2008 and V Sociolinguistic Survey 2011. Central Publications Service of the Basque Government. Vitoria-Gasteiz, 2013.

contribution of young generations, new opportunities are being created for the recovery of Basque.

The different situation the Basque language is experiencing in its three territories is certainly clear. It is enough to mention, as an example, data referring to language ability by territories,[345] as we can see in the tables 1 and 2:

[345] IV Sociolinguistic Survey 2006. Central Publications Service of the Basque Government. Vitoria-Gasteiz, 2008 and V Sociolinguistic Survey 2011. Central Publications Service of the Basque Government. Vitoria-Gasteiz, 2013.

Table 1. Basque Language. Evolution of Language Competence 1991–2011 (%)

	1991			2011		
	Bilingual	Passive bilinguals	Spa/French speakers	Bilinguals	Passive bilinguals	Spa/French speakers
Basque Country	22.3	7.7	70	27	14.7	58.4
BAC	24.1	8.5	67.4	32	17.7	50.6
CCN	9.5	4.6	85.9	11.7	7.5	80.8
French Basque Country	26.4	9.3	64.2	21.4	9.1	69.5

Source: Department of Education, Linguistic Policy and Culture, V Encuesta Sociolingüística, Vitoria — Gasteiz, 2013 and own production.

Table 2. Basque Language. Evolution of the Use of Euskera 1991–2011 (%)

	1991			2011		
	As much/more than Spanish or French	Less than Spanish or French	(Almost) always in Spanish or French	As much/more than Spanish or French	Less than Spanish or French	(Almost) always in Spanish or French
Basque Country	13.7	6.8	79.5	16.1	8.1	75.7
BAC	15.6	6.8	77.7	20	8.9	71.7
CCN	6	3.1	90.9	5.5	4.6	89.8
French Basque C.	13.3	9.8	76.9	9.6	9.3	81.2

Source: Department of Education, Linguistic Policy and Culture, V Encuesta Sociolingüística, Vitoria — Gasteiz, 2013 and own production.

This clearly shows the boost that a suitable legal framework can give to a language. Basque, in effect, has total legal protection in the BAC and the greatest advances have been found in this Community. This is true, but it is also true that the development of Basque in the BAC shows us that neither better laws nor more efficient language policies can guarantee a complete spread in the use of Basque.

The key to the future of the language is social adhesion. It is therefore essential to know how to recognize and consider the limitations of society itself. New opportunities for the use of Basque must be created and promoted so that, day by day, citizens will take advantage and make use of existing opportunities; as Patxi Baztarrika quite rightly said:

> "Opportunities to use Basque must be created and guaranteed. But these opportunities must be used. In the first task, in which opportunities are created, an important role is played by laws, planning and institutions –although not only these, as the responsibility of generating attractive opportunities concerns, in some way, everyone who creates, produces and provides services in Basque-. In the latter, however, in which use is made of opportunities, responsibility corresponds, firstly, to citizens, and especially and above all to those who are capable of using Basque. It is a case of citizens wanting to do what they can do. Willpower and involvement, that is all."[346]

Having seen the results, we can say, without fear of error, that the Law on the Normalization of the use of Basque was ten years ahead of the European Charter for Regional or Minority Languages, a treaty ratified in Strasbourg November 5, 1992 by the European Council, in favor of defending and promoting the languages of Europe.

As a result of the common work in June 1998 between public institutions and civil society, to which we

346 BAZTARRIKA, P. *Babel or barbarism: A legitimate and efficient language policy*. Irun, Ed. Alberdania, 2009.

have referred previously and which constitutes a fundamental factor in the process to recover a language, is that the Advisory Council for Basque unanimously approved the "General Plan to Promote the Use of Basque," better known by its Basque name, "Euskara Biziberritzeko Plan Nagusia" (EBPN), which the Basque Government approved and adopted July 28, 1998. This plan was implemented over the decade 1998–2008, focused on the use of Basque and the development of new spheres for bilingualism in public and social life, with the main axis of action centred on the individual.

From the point of view of Language Policy and the normalization of the use of Basque, we can consider that the "General Plan to Promote the Use of Basque" represented a leap in quality of enormous transcendence in 1998.

Seven years after the approval and implementation of the Euskara Biziberritzeko Plan Nagusia, the Basque Government Department of Culture launched a broad process of reflection and debate in 2005 on the development of the "General Plan for the Normalization of the Use of Basque," on the road travelled and on what was still to be done.[347] A social debate developed in the heart of the Advisory Council for Basque whose first fruit was the approval of a basic proposal on April 29, 2008, entitled "Bases for a language policy for the 21st century," which was analyzed and debated over the summer and autumn of that

---

[347] On the proposal by the Culture Minister Miren Azkarate, in October 2007 the Special Commission *"Bases for language policy at the start of the 21st century"* was created. Subsequently, during the first months of 2008, the debate started with the following landmarks:

- January 2008: at the heart of the Special Commission, the Commission Permanent was created to draw up the Basic Proposal and Final Document. Commission made up of Aurelia Arkotxa, Lore Erriondo, Alberto Lopez Basaguren, Eneko Oregi, Pello Salaburu, Erramun Osa (secretary) and Patxi Baztarrika (president).
- April 2008: Basic Proposal was drafted.
- January 2009: Permanent Commission wrote and presented the Final Document of the open reflection.
- The Advisory Council for Basque approved it at the plenary session on February 9, 2009.

year. With regard to this debate, the Minister for Culture, Miren Azkarate stated in her presentation:

> "The Basque Government is leading the advance in the area of language policy and brought about this open and sincere debate, which would be important on its own, but is even more so bearing in mind its cause, reason and objective. It is a question of debating and agreeing on the subject of language policy, whose subject and field of action is society itself. In this sense, the best guarantee for success in the ongoing process to revitalize Basque is social involvement and for this it is fundamental to widen and strengthen existing consensus and this is the subject of this wide and fruitful debate. We are trying to consolidate the leap forwards in which Basque society is playing the lead role, based on strengthening and consolidating existing agreements and weaving new ones. Knowing that this is a social process, and therefore long in time, we are aware that much progress has been made, a lot has been achieved, but we also know that there is a lot more to do."[348]

All this led to the Advisory Council for Basque approving the document "Euskera 21"[349] at a plenary session held February 9, 2009. This strategic document, a consequence of many hours of debate, was only possible after listening to and comparing multiple sensitivities and opinions. In this sense, the document is the fruit of the agreement, and represented a step towards a renewed pact. In fact, at the start of the 21st century, a language policy based on consensus, persuasion, and democratic strength is indispensable. Here, in short, are the priorities of the Final Document:

---

348 AZKARATE, M., Presentation of the document from the debate, Bilbao, December 24, 2008.

349 ADVISORY COUNCIL FOR BASQUE, *Bases for Language Policy at the turn of the 21st century: Towards a renewed pact*. Vitoria-Gasteiz, Central Publications Service, Basque Government, 2009.

1. Guarantee knowledge and the use of Basque among new generations.
2. Look after, strengthen, and extend the vital niches and functions in which Basque is the usual language, in order to guarantee the inter-generational transmission of Basque and strengthen its character as a social reference. All in all, the objective is not only to extend the knowledge of Basque, but to produce Basque speakers.
3. Guarantee family transmission, attending especially to young bilinguals who in 25 years will be under thirty and will use Basque also as a family language. This is the main key to the future.
4. Strengthen the Basque speaking community, extending and strengthening presential and virtual networks for the use of Basque.
5. Increase opportunities to use Basque in large cities, giving priority to Basque speaking families, young people, and children.
6. Promote and enhance its prestige among adults — and as a minimum aim — passive bilingualism.
7. Promote cultural consumption in Basque, from an emancipating perspective for Basque cultural industries, producers, and creators.
8. Bring Basque and its universe closer to immigrants, in order to facilitate its wide and enriching integration, as well as bring Basque closer to demographically dynamic areas.
9. Make Basque more flexible and enrich communicative standards in Basque, as a method to favor the expressiveness of new speakers. Avoid formal accuracy as the sole criterion for communicative and expressive quality.
10. Guarantee opportunities to use Basque, leading to the respect for language rights, beyond mere recognition.
11. Make Basque attractive and project it suitably: Basque contains many universes, and has enough space to welcome inside the universes of those who come to Basque. The universe of Basque is more plural than the image we project would have one

believe, and we must make it even more plural, such that it reaches the same degree of plurality as society.

12. Make the image of Basque prestigious, clearly projecting cultural and communicative achievements on the one hand and, on the other, expressing and joining in the discourse that Basque constitutes an essential component of Basque social cohesion.
13. Use language technologies as well as, in general, information and communication technologies to develop Basque. Create contents for the web and suitably exploit virtual communication networks to the benefit of the normalization of Basque and thus increase the possibilities of its use. Indeed, Basque must use information and communication technologies as an indispensable requisite to achieve its full development as a language.
14. Nurture and permanently strengthen the widest possible consensus on language policy, in pursuit of a renewed pact that intimately links the revitalization of Basque and social cohesion.

The Advisory Council for Basque concluded its reflection on the final document with the following statement:

> "The Final Document does not aim to replace anything. It is the fruit of the effort carried out to group together multiple points of view. Consequently, as we said before, it aims to be the starting point for a renewed pact. Precisely, through the process of debate Euskara 21, the bases for this new pact have been placed on the table. Therefore, a task must be carried out over the coming months: revise the General Plan to Revitalize Basque (PGRE), a Plan which has been valid for the last ten years, in order to polish this valuable tool and adapt it to the start of the 21st century. In agreement, as

ever, with the bases that we're agreed in the process Euskara 21."[350]

As in the present and in the past, Basque people and Basque culture will also exist in the future and will be the protagonists of the future. Over recent years Basque institutions, legitimate representatives of the popular will, have led, through the use of the tools of self government — once again self government — a process that is enabling Basque to be situated on the path to normalization. It has been the collective work of the immense majority of our people, of the men and women of this country who have collaborated in the achievement of sustainable human development.

Most Basque men and women aspire to a bilingual Basque society, to real and effective bilingualism, to truly equal opportunities that enable Basque also to be used in all spheres of social life and enable whoever wishes to live in Basque to do so. To aspire to live not only, but also in Basque. To be politically active not in monolingualism, nor in Basque monolingualism, nor in Spanish monolingualism. We are not in the trenches of imposition, lack of communication, or exclusion. Nor are we working against anything or anybody, because we love and respect Spanish, which is also a language of the Basque people, because we love and respect French, which is also a language of this people.

We are working in favor of bilingualism, which considers Basque and Spanish to be common heritage, to be developed by everyone, which, bearing in mind the current situation of imbalance, involves an active and positive policy to support this minority and minimized language, Basque. A policy conceived and put into practice from a position of respect for Spanish and with the firm conviction that bilingualism is a value and linguistic coexistence an asset for cohesion and sustainable human development in Basque society.

For most Basque people, Basque and Spanish are languages that unite them and not languages that separate

---

[350] ADVISORY COUNCIL FOR BASQUE, plenary session held on February 9, 2009, Vitoria-Gasteiz.

them. The only thing that generates exclusion and division, the only sparks from that imaginary fire that some seem to wish to stoke, come from poor and reactionary attitudes and discourse, contrary to coexistence and equality, and which fortunately have very few followers in Basque society.

I believe, furthermore, that this social effort to give a future to the Basque language is work in favor of world culture. To develop what is ours and offer it to the world, that is the challenge. When we hear that of the 5000 languages that are spoken at present in the world only 500 may survive by the end of the 21st century — as feared by Merritt Rhulen[351] — this must be a motive for reflection for everyone. If Basque society continues to uphold the importance of its language, we are convinced that the Basque language will not be among the languages that disappear.

But, in any case, would universal culture be richer with 500 languages rather than 5000? No, it would be poorer. In fact, in the 21st century we are witnessing as mere impassive spectators what Baudrillard calls the "irreducible otherness of cultures,"[352] a process of "standardizing acculturation."

In the final analysis, if the Basque people and Basque Culture do not have a place in the world, this would be a problem for European and world culture.

Culture Open to the World

In this 21st century Basque society lives more integrated in the world and in global society than ever. We have built this relationship, we see ourselves open to the world and to interrelations; what is more, we know that it is a fact of life and a reason for the enrichment of our Country. We have a lot to contribute; we can show, at the same time, that we are

351 On this subject, see RHULEN, M., *A Guide to Worlds Languages: Classification*. Stanford, Stanford University Press, 1987; and *On the Origin of Languages*. Stanford, Stanford University Press, 1994.
352 BAUDRILLARD, J., "From antiterrorism to war. The violence of globalization", *Le Monde diplomatique*, Madrid, Spanish edition, November 2002, p. 17.

aware that we have a lot to learn and that our society has much to gain from this interaction.

Basque society wishes to be in the world, and to do what is in its power, without dependence or subordination. It is no more or no less than anybody. And on the other hand, the Basque community must also be projected to the outside world with its own cultural identity in all its expressions and manifestations. The future will mark relations between cultures, more than relations between States.[353] The future will be described by people.

Therefore, Basque people want to contribute what is theirs and is different to the global village; the language and culture that the men and women of this society use and develop. In the knowledge that doors and windows that open can be used equally to enter and to exit, to see and to be seen. Adopting as their own Gandhi's wish not to live in a house walled in on all sides, with the windows blocked up. He wanted the breeze from cultures from all over the world to blow on his home, as freely as possible, but he refused to be swept away by any of them.

Thus, while Basque, Spanish, and French are languages of the people, each day brings more languages, such as English, which is also among us, maybe not languages "from here" but they are also the languages of our people.[354]

---

[353] HUNTINGTON, S.P., *Clash of Civilizations and the reconfiguration of the world order.* Barcelona, ed. Paidós, 1997, p. 147 states: "Spurred on by modernization, global politics is being reconfigured in accordance with cultural criteria. Peoples and countries with similar cultures are uniting. Peoples and countries with different cultures are separating. Alignments defined by ideology and relations with superpowers are giving way to alignments defined by culture and civilization. Political frontiers are remade more and more to coincide with cultural frontiers: ethnic, religious and civilizing."

[354] SAID, E.W., *Culture and imperialism.* Barcelona, ed. Anagrama, 1996, pp. 515 and 516 says: "survival means establishing connections between things: in Eliot's words, you cannot deprive from reality the 'other echoes (that) live in the garden'. It is much more satisfactory and more difficult, to think with kindness specifically and in counterpoint about others, and not to do so solely about 'us'. But this also means that we must try not to

In this sense the Etxepare Basque Institute was promoted and created by a law[355] which regulated the development of the cultural institute under the name of the writer Bernat Etxepare. It adopted the motto "jalgi hadi mundura" (open to the world).

The mission of the Etxepare Basque Institute, as stated in law, is to open the Basque language and culture to the world with the following aims:

a) Universally promote the teaching, study, and use of Basque, respecting contributions by communities that share, favor and strengthen the international recognition of the Basque language, and promote whatever measures and actions contribute to disseminating and improving the quality of these activities.
b) Contribute to disseminating Basque culture abroad in all its forms and languages.
c) Bring the reality of our country nearer to Basque speaking groups around the world and to those places where the existence of Basque communities or historic cultural or commercial relations make this recommendable.[356]

Along the same lines as "making Basque culture, the culture of Basque men and women, fit to face the great cultural challenges of the 21st century,"[357] the Basque Government[358] took on the commitment to prepare a comprehensive plan for Basque culture at the investiture session on July 11, 2001. This was the start of a debate that

---

dominate others, nor try to classify them or put them in hierarchical moulds."

355 LAW 3/2007 of April 20, On the creation and development of the Etxepare Basque Institute, Basque Parliament, EHAA-BOPV no 2007089 of May 10, 2007, p. 10704.

356 Law 3/2007 of April 20 on the Creation and Development of the Etxepare Basque Institute.

357 Basque Culture Plan. Vitoria-Gasteiz, Central Publications Service, Basque Government. September 2004, p. 53.

358 IBARRETXE, J.J., Presidential Investiture Speech, Basque Parliament, Diary of Sessions. June 11, 2001, VII Legislature, no 4.

culminated on September 21, 2004 with the approval of the Basque Culture Plan[359] by the Basque Government Council. A strategic plan with work indicators up to 2015, defining four year actions and executed through an annual operating plan with the following budgets:

> This strategic plan is the tool that aims to reflect the agreement between different public and private agents in the Autonomous Community the Basque Country on the strategic vision, priorities for the whole of Basque culture, criteria for action and public actions with strategic effects. A tool at the service of Basque citizens, oblivious both to neoliberal conceptions —unsuitable for minority cultures — and interventionist conceptions of cultural management.[360]

Preparation of the Basque Culture Plan responded to one of the fundamental promises: participation. Plural work groups — social and private agents from Euskal Herria and public agents and institutions of the Basque Autonomous Community — were responsible for the first diagnoses, the detection of lines of future action and the definition of future action.

The Basque Culture Council, constituted as a meeting place for public and private agents of Basque culture in 2000,[361] has been responsible since its renewal in 2002 and especially since the approval of the preliminary document in 2003[362] for the preparation of the strategic plan for Basque culture.

In a process where opinions had to be conciliated and consensus sought in conceptual aspects — the area of action of the plan or even the idea of "culture" — as well as

---

359 BASQUE GOVERNMENT, "Basque Culture Plan," Government Council September 21, 2004.

360 Basque Culture Plan. Vitoria-Gasteiz, Central Publications Service, Basque Government. September 2004, p. 87.

361 BASQUE GOVERNMENT, creation of the Basque Culture Council, Government Council November 6, 2000.

362 Approved at the plenary meeting of the Basque Culture Council held at the Palacio de Villasuso, May 28, 2003.

future actions and technical questions, it was necessary to establish a work plan and a line of procedure to draft the final document.

One of the most interesting and new aspects in all this process, was without doubt the work methodology carried out which enabled not only an agile, but creative participation. In each of the phases of the process, two successive stages were opened: one a diagnosis and the other lines of action. At the same time, two types of participation were established: a presential work group and a "virtual" work group, through a debate webpage that started with coded access. This second type enabled wider participation to be conciliated with operative capacity in the size of the groups. Altogether 19 work groups were set up with the participation of over 300 people.

To culminate this process, the "Basque Culture Plan" was debated and approved by the Plenary Session of the Basque Culture Council on May 20, 2004, and was subsequently presented to the Basque Parliament on November 3, 2004.

The BCP takes into consideration both important questions to be tackled and actions to be carried out and the means to carry them out, guaranteed by knowledge, coordination, and public policies. In any case, the plan was set out as an unfinished document, a living document under permanent construction and reflection, in a dialogue with what is real and active. The plan requires constant updating of analyses and agreements. In short, it is a means to respond more efficiently to the cultural needs and challenges of Basque society.

To do so, the conceptual framework sought to raise awareness on the importance of culture. Valuing culture by conserving, creating, producing and disseminating it, has the double virtue of enabling the integration, adaptation, and development of our society and uncovering the very economic potential of culture in our times.[363]

---

363 IBARRETXE, J. J., in the presentation of the "Basque Culture Plan," September 29, 2004: "The text presented today to Basque society is a rich, mature, agreed and promising document that will have great importance for the Basque Country -Euskal Herria- to

The change in paradigm shows that if the 80s represented an industrial reconversion, with an enormous budget that lasted well into the 21st century, and the 90s led to the emergence of new productive areas based on public support with an unequivocal commitment to technology, the first decade of the new century was defined as the decade of knowledge and culture, for which information and communications were obviously indispensable. This commitment meant developing the following priorities:

- the primacy of the creation and production of contents
- the cultural integration effort
- reinforcement of identity
- modernization
- projection abroad

a) The new decade must be one of contents with the double elements of creativity and production. This means that the priority effort is in human resources, in ourselves; in knowledge and its application; in training and learning; in specialization; in creativity and in the productive means to bring it to public attention; in the emergence and collective esteem of creativity both in general and in authorship in particular, as it is a question of testing new authorship in the search for new values, or projecting consolidated authorship. In this sense it is

---

be able to face the cultural challenges of the coming decade. A tool at the service of Basque citizens, and oblivious to neoliberal conceptions — unsuitable for minority cultures — such as the interventionist conceptions of cultural management. The document in its philosophical and indicative part, understands Basque culture as the result of three central vectors, which are inherited nuclear culture — in which Basque plays a central role — cultures assimilated as one's own and the culture of current Basque citizens. In plural and open societies such as ours, collective culture is an amalgam of inheritance, contributions and recreation. It must be said out loud to banish both the concept that Basque culture is narrow and also the discourses that negate our identity."

also going to be a decade of creativity. The characteristics of the post-industrial economy and its consideration as a strategic sector emerging both from the cultural and economic sides can be applied to the cultural sector more clearly than to any other.

b) The effort to gain cultural integration based on a wide concept of Basque culture. Accepting that Basque culture presents different expressions in the different territories of Euskal Herria — this being understood as a historic-cultural reality with different versions of Basqueness — and favoring cultural links in this cultural and communicative space regardless of political and administrative considerations, beyond administrative-political compartmentalization between the BAC, the Foral Community of Navarre and the French Basque Country (Iparralde).

c) The reinforcement of identity has many meanings which refer both to received patrimony and social esteem which is undergoing a process of collective generation, together making up the identification and differentiation of Basques today. This aspect is defined by the difference between cultural and political, or by understanding identity as a result of memory, the present and of what one wishes to be, seeking the recovery of patrimonies, their recognition and enjoyment. It can also be defined as the commitment to a rich societal life with cultural expressive manifestations of our different and hybrid *modus vivendi*, generators of new traditions for the future. It can also be represented by making the use of Basque in products, services, and communications correspond to general or territorial sociolinguistic means, thus avoiding, in many cases, that cultural activities take a back seat position, or worse still, become a hindrance to existing uses and programs in the process of language normalization.

d) The commitment to modernization lies in special attention paid to new cultural trends, new style education, communication open to other cultural latitudes and with internal plurality, and the use of new techniques, formats and technologies in experimentation, creation, production, dissemination and cultural development of the community.

e) Cultural projection abroad, beyond Euskal Herria, requires Basque culture to turn towards the communities and markets of the Spanish and French States, both specially close by and with a singular historic connection, towards the convergence with Europe as a basic cultural destination and towards countries where the Basque diaspora is more numerous (Latin America and the USA), with which we have special bonds.

Brief Synthesis of the Philosophy of the Basque Culture Plan

There are several important elements in the Basque Culture Plan such as basic factors that affect Basque culture in the 21st century: the commercial exploitation of culture, the internationalization of creative processes and markets, the small size of the Basque Country, the conjugation of institutional support with the involvement of a very active civil society, and coming to terms with the migratory phenomenon in terms of respect and inclusive citizenship.

The document conceives culture as a way of life for communities and, as a result, their identity. Cultural identity is not the repetition of the same characteristics throughout history, but a result that gives a sense of continuity to the generations surrounding a base population, to a nucleus of more or less preserved cultural features, a historic memory and permanently changing social dynamics.

The plan considers that Basque culture is a different culture located between two strong cultures, Spanish and French, the cultures of two nation states, obviously identifiable. Moreover, in its different territorial versions, it is not unaware of them because it interiorizes them in part; both from the outside influence and from the inner presence in Basque culture itself.

Basque culture is understood here to be the result of inherited nuclear culture, assimilated and own cultures, and the culture of the current Basque citizenship as a whole.

The Basque Culture Plan is committed to building a common cultural identity and political society from the concept of collective citizenship and a basic shared cultural project, regardless of the particular degree of cultural or political feelings.

It also considers that Basque culture or Basqueness (Basque generic identity) must be built from the present, understood as a more or less balanced result between cultural legacy and present, and as a strictly cultural concept, located on a different plane to other concepts that incorporate cultural effects and projects (Basquism) or political identities (national Basque identity, etc.).

The plan also expresses the decisive importance of the institutions (public autonomous power and civil society institutions) in strengthening a culture in modern societies insofar as they mould it and may guarantee its feasibility, development and opportunities, more so in the case of minority cultures.

But culture, besides embodying values and trends, is also economic in nature. This is expressed in the plan, stating that culture is also a productive *input* and generates an important market in an era which should be called the "Society of Information, Knowledge, and Culture." Artistic and industrial creation and culture production is thus added to patrimony accumulated through history and to its practical value.

The Basque Culture Plan considers that a country such as the Basque Country, with its potential and its needs, should not hesitate to commit strongly to specializing in the generation of culture for both cultural and identity reasons and to developing economically and socially. The cultural sector is, moreover, intensive in skilled labor and creative and highly important for current and, above all, future employability.

With regard to territory, the small size of Euskal Herria (Basque Country) and the proximity between the outer points means it can be conceived as Euskal Hiria (Basque Town), using the words of the writer Atxaga. It can be conceived as a global village that makes the exchange of knowledge and close contact possible between people and activities, and weaves a complex and deep relational system with growing returns; or as a Euro region and above existing political-administrative structures; or as a revitalizing center of a Euro region that encompasses the whole of Atlantic Europe. These approximations are not only compatible but necessary.

Therefore the plan understands Euskal Herria to be a historic cultural body that, despite its differences in territorial development, shares patrimony, art, culture, and history. It is supposed that the political-administrative institutions safeguard this as a legacy for each territory, but also as common shared patrimony belonging to a wider cultural community. Based on this premise, one of the clear objectives of the plan is to foster the strengthening of common cultural institutions and promote that which unites us.

In this sense, one of the sections that the plan gives special attention to is the Basque language as one of the central pillars of Basque culture. Besides being the language of the Basque people, together with Spanish or French, it is one of the tools that is used and has been used throughout history to create Basque culture. The narrow interrelation between Basque language and Basque culture makes the future of the latter depend on Basque language and on a global development of culture in the areas of creation, production, and dissemination of Basque culture, in whatever language it may be; and of course, the very future of Basque requires the continuance and strengthening of culture in all its manifestations.

5
Environmental Strategy: Committed to Sustainability

We have to consider the "benefits of early action on energy." The European Commission took this position in 2005 to win the battle against climate change:

> "We are aware that the effects of climate change could be very serious, could affect basic elements of the lives of people all over the world: access to water, food production, health and the environment. Hundreds of millions of people could starve, suffer droughts and coastal flooding as the planet heats up. Faced with this panorama, fortunately, although perhaps too late, the idea has caught on that the benefits of early action on energy will far exceed the costs of passiveness and inaction."[364]

The Basque Autonomous Community had reached this reflection some time before the Commission, defining sustainability and the defence of the environment as a "third prong" in the sustainable human development strategy.

The General Law to Protect the Environment of the Basque Country[365] was approved in 1998 and represented a milestone, as it set sustainable development as an objective for the whole of environmental policy developed in the territory of the Basque Autonomous Community. The Law

---

364 Communication from the European Commission to the European Council, European Parliament, Committee of the Regions and European Economic and Social Committee. "To win the battle against climate change," COM (2005) 0035 final. More recently, November 2006, the STERN REPORT, commissioned by the British Government, assessed the serious consequences for the immediate future of passiveness in the face of this phenomenon.

365 LAW 3/1998 of February 27, General on Environment Protection in the Basque Country, Basque Parliament.

stated that the use of air, water, land, landscape, flora and fauna would be sustainable,[366] and assumed the commitment to guarantee sustainable development that satisfied the needs of the present without jeopardizing the capacity of future generations to satisfy their own needs.[367]

Leadership and institutional commitment at the highest level in the new model for growth, which considers the environmental dimension to be a fundamental reference in public policies, were clearly expressed with the signing of the Commitment to Sustainability of the Basque Country in January 2001,[368] which included the following principles to guide the concept of Basque environmental strategy:

- Ethical code: Our way of thinking, values, lifestyle and consumption habits must be modified.
- Social cohesion and participation: All sectors of society play a role in the process towards sustainability.
- Principle of precaution: We must promote action every time there is a threat of damage against the environment.
- Comprehensive focus: The environment variable should be included in all sectorial policies.
- Eco-efficiency: There may and must be a reduction in the use of natural resources, while increasing productivity.
- Strategic planning: Environmental objectives must be the fruit of the process of reflection by Basque society on the new model of development.

---

366 LAW 3/1998 of February 27, General on Environment Protection in the Basque Country, Basque Parliament, article 1.

367 LAW 3/1998 of February 27, General on Environment Protection in the Basque Country, Basque Parliament, article 2.

368 IBARRETXE J.J., Basque Country Commitment to Sustainability. Bilbao January 22, 2001.

Medium Term Strategic Planning: Basque Environmental Strategy on Sustainable Development 2002–2020

In compliance with the 1998 Law to Protect the Environment of the Basque Country, and following the diagnosis on the situation of the environment in the Autonomous Community of the Basque Country carried out in 2001,[369] a global strategy for the defence of environmental sustainability[370] was approved in 2002. For the first time a regional European community had a long-term strategic tool for the following 20 years.

This long-term strategy was completed with the "Environmental framework programs"[371] which defined the 5 environment goals we set as a Country for 2020.

These five environment goals set as a Country are:

1. Guarantee clean and healthy air, water and land.
2. Responsible management of natural resources and waste.
3. Protection of nature and biodiversity.
4. Balance territory and mobility: a common focus.
5. Limit the influence of climate change.

The environmental framework strategy 2002–2020 was presented publically in June 2002 and stated:

> "With environmental subjects we cannot wait to act and we cannot make mistakes. The legacy for our children is at risk. Sustainable Development means ensuring a better quality of life for everyone, now and for the future. Therefore, we want to build our

---

369 BASQUE GOVERNMENT, Environment in the BAC. 2001, Diagnosis.

370 BASQUE GOVERNMENT, "Basque Environmental Strategy of Sustainable Development 2002–2020." Government Council June 4, 2002.

371 BASQUE GOVERNMENT, "First Framework Environmental Program 2002–2006." Government Council June 4, 2002; "Second Framework Environmental Program 2007–2010." Government Council June 5, 2007.

quality of life on the foundations of sustainability."[372]

The Basque Environmental Strategy for Sustainable Development responded to the commitment taken on at the Summit meeting in Río to develop sustainable development strategies locally. The added value is that of establishing environmental goals that Basque society must reach in order to guarantee the achievement of an optimum level of quality of life for the current generation, without endangering the welfare of future generations, setting the common guidelines of action for citizens, productive agents, and the administration.

In this way, besides the five environmental goals described above, the Strategy is organized around:

> Objectives: To reach environmental goals requires gradual advances adapting to new situations as they are detected. The formulation of objectives associated to each environmental goal was based on the principles of caution and preventive action, correction of damage preferably at the source and environmental recovery as set by Law 3/98.
> Commitments: The assignation of quantitative values and deadlines for the achievement of environmental objectives and goals leads to specific commitments.

The development process was based on commitment and active cooperation between public institutions and social agents in the definition and defence of a model of sustainable development. The document involved the participation of over 150 experts and representatives from all institutional levels and Basque economic and social agents.

Finally, six necessary conditions were set to advance towards sustainability in the Basque Country:

---

372 IBARRETXE J.J., Presentation "Basque Environmental Strategy for Sustainable Development 2002–2020." June 2002.

1. Improve environmental legislation and how it is applied.
2. Encourage the market — companies and consumers — to act in favor of the environment.
3. Integrate the environmental variable in all other policies.
4. Make citizens, companies, and institutions jointly responsible for modifying habits in favor of sustainability.
5. Promote research in environmental areas.
6. Environmental cooperation on an international level.

The result of this strategy, according to the assessment report on the second environmental framework program 2007–2010,[373] is positive, but we still have a low score in some significant indicators regarding the reduction in the consumption of waste, sustainable mobility, and the emission of greenhouse gases.[374]

A Local Experience with Citizen Participation: Udalsarea 21

The Second Environmental Framework Program (2007–2010) establishes and recognizes Agenda Local 21 (AL21) as the key tool to articulate improvements in the environment and deploy the program locally.

The delay in the introduction of AL21 on a world level is evident precisely due to a lack of material and human resources at town councils to carry out the development of environmental policies locally.[375]

---

373 *Report on Environmental Sustainability in the Autonomous Community of the Basque Country*. June 5, 2007, which serves as a final balance of the first framework program 2002–2007 and as an Introduction to the Second framework environmental program 2007–2010.
374 *Report on Environmental Sustainability in the Autonomous Community of the Basque Country*. June 5, 2007.
375 BASQUE GOVERNMENT, *Report on local sustainability in the BAC*, 2008. Executive summary; and BARRUTIA, J.Mª., "Network of policies to disseminate the Agenda 21 local in the Basque Country." Research article supported by the UPV/EHU (32.321-

For this reason, the initiative of the Basque Government, through the public company IHOBE and the joint commitment of the Provincial Councils and the Association of Basque Municipalities (EUDEL), has been key to achieving progress in this process in the Basque Autonomous Country, so much so that it is at the head of Agendas Locales 21 in Europe.

Udalsarea 21 signed the Aalborg Commitments in 2004 together with another 110 local bodies, at the IV Sustainable Cities and Towns Conference, Aalborg Plus 10.[376]

According to the latest available data in early 2009,[377] 218 Basque towns have AL21 Local Action Plans, which represent 98.8% in population terms. Practically all of the inhabitants of the BAC live in a municipality with AL21 integrated in the network "Udalsarea 21."

Fight against Climate Change

The "Basque Plan against Climate Change 2008–2012"[378] was approved by the Basque Government in December 2007. The aim was to coordinate, strengthen and intensify the measures that were being taken, giving them focus and a comprehensive approach; the main goal being to reach the objective of reducing the average level of emissions between 2008 and 2012 by 14% with regard to the reference year 1990.

The Basque Plan against Climate Change arose, therefore, as a Basque Government response to the trend of

---

15908/2004) and UNESCO for Sustainable Development (Unesco 05/2006)

[376] AALBORG +10: *IV Sustainable Cities and Towns Conference,* held in Denmark June 9–11, 2004, ten years after the ratification in the same city of the Charter of Sustainable Cities and Towns, Aalborg Charter.

[377] According to EUDEL data 218 towns, 98.8% of the Basque population have agenda local 21 action plans. And 199 towns are integrated in the Network Udalsarea 21 – Basque Network of Sustainable Municipalities.

[378] BASQUE GOVERNMENT, "Basque Plan against Climate Change 2008–2012." Government Council December 4, 2007.

increasing greenhouse gas emissions and to the evidence acknowledged by the international scientific community of the serious consequences that this trend will have on climate conditions both locally and globally in the immediate future. The plan was designed along two lines:

- The first aimed to counteract the greenhouse effect by reducing the emission of the gases that cause it. To do so the Plan defined the general objectives for the Kyoto period (2008–2012) and subsequent objectives, following European Union Guidelines for 2020.
- The second aimed to mitigate the consequences of climate change that will occur through action plans to tackle future climate conditions.

Therefore, Basque self-government did not ignore one of the greatest problems facing western society at the end of the 20th century and beginning of the 21st: the fight against climate change and sustainability as a basic tool for all productive processes.

The decade of the nineties is characterized by a boost in social awareness and by positive actions to preserve the Basque environment. The following decade was that of the promotion of effective policies to seek efficiency and sustainability in sectors such as energy, transport or industry, and to program strategies to reduce greenhouse gases.

In fact, during the Presidential Investiture Debate held in June 2001 a commitment was made on the "creation of wealth, innovation and sustainable growth," stating the following:

> "Our final aim to create wealth and employment is an objective consciously committed to the concept of sustainable growth. Our horizon is to go much further than the mere application of environmental legislation. It is a case of integrating the environment in economic and social policies to get the concept of sustainability to also be a fundamental criterion that guides urban development and that of the different economic

sectors: industry, agriculture, energy and transport. If making growth sustainable requires a boost in environmental policies, making growth with guarantees possible involves developing new strategies in accordance with the times."[379]

Already by 2002, as we have seen, the "Basque Environmental Strategy on Sustainable Development 2002–2020" had been approved with its five environmental goals. The different operational programs developed led to the five strategic goals turning into specific commitments.

The First Environmental Framework Program (2002–2006) formulated a series of commitments focused mainly on four areas: energy, transport, industry, and the construction sector. Subsequently, the new Environmental Framework Program came into effect in June 2007 for the period 2007–2010. Among its commitments we should mention a specific group, approved previously in Energy Strategy 3E2010,[380] to advance in the fight against climate change in the Basque Autonomous Community:

- achieve a saving in energy in 2010 of 975,000 tons of oil equivalent (TOE)
- achieve 29% of electricity consumption from renewable energy and cogeneration
- achieve annual consumption of 177,000 TOE of biofuel in transport

379 IBARRETXE, J.J., President's Investiture Speech, Basque Parliament. Diary of sessions July 11, 2001, VII Legislature, no 4, p. 21.

380 In the Basque Government publication from March 8, 2006: *Towards sustainable development: With regard to Basque energy policy.* It was already stressed in 2001 that a global review of energy strategy 2005 was necessary, with a new approach arising on November 14, 2001 in the Basque Parliament, through the approval of the motion on the Basque energy strategy with a view to 2010, which would consequently lead to approval of the Basque Energy Strategy on Sustainable Development E3 2001–2010 by the Basque Government in December 2001.

- reach 35% recycling of the total urban waste generated and zero non treated urban waste prior to final deposit
- stop the loss of biodiversity, for which measures were proposed, including restoring 50 Ha of wetlands
- increase the forestry area by 10,000 Hectares with regard to that existing in 2006 and reduce the presence of invasive exotic species
- rechannel the distribution of public transport passengers and goods transport, towards rail transport

Sustainable Energy Strategy

The fields where progress is needed to advance towards a model of production, supply and consumption of energy less dependent on oil and more sustainable were identified in the "Energy Strategy of the Basque Country 2010: 3E-2010"[381] and were as follows:

a) Improvement in energy efficiency with an aim to reducing energy consumption in global terms, and a reduction in energy intensity, in accordance with the objectives established by the EU.
b) Intensify efforts to increase the supply of renewable energy (hydraulic, biomass, solar, wind, biofuels, etc.) to reach the objective set by the EU for these types of energy.
c) Energy infrastructures to improve the security of the supply, competitiveness and quality of the energy system. With regard to thermoelectric generation, guarantee more energy efficient and environmental

381 BASQUE GOVERNMENT, "Basque Energy Strategy on Sustainable Development E3 2001–2010." Approved by the Government Council in December 2001, according to Basque Parliament guidelines November 14, 2001.

production by means of combined cycle power stations.

d) Promote R&D in the Basque energy sector to improve energy efficiency and to progress towards alternative energy sources.

The "Energy Strategy of the Basque Country 2010: 3E 2010" aimed to advance towards a sustainable energy model with the criteria of efficiency, competitiveness, quality and safety and improvement of the environment.

Sustainable Transport and Mobility Strategy

This strategy was conceptually defined in the "Master Plan for Sustainable Transport 2002–2011."[382] The challenge, as stated in the "White Paper on sustainable transport in the EU"[383] is to disconnect demand for transport from economic development.

The most serious problems were derived from the exaggerated weight of the private vehicle in the mobility of individuals[384] and from road transport as the means for goods transport. The solutions considered had to rebalance

---

[382] BASQUE GOVERNMENT, "Transport Master Plan: Common transport policy of the Basque Country 2002–2010." Government, Council November 19, 2002.

[383] EUROPEAN COMMISSION, Common European transport policy. *White Paper on Transport.* September 12, 2001.

[384]The data refers to 2007 ("Sustainable Transport Master Plan 2002–2012," indicators TMA, DTOP-DMAOT), conclude that mobility increases and that the car, means of transport that emits more CO2 into the atmosphere, continues to gain ground as a means to satisfy this need, with generalized presence in all geographic areas and regardless of the reason for travel. The comparison between 2003 and 2007, using the same indicators, reveals an increase in mobility, measured in terms of trips per person and day, from 2.75 to 2.98, and an increase in the presence of the car, which increased from 34.6% to 38.6% of total trips. Public transport, over the same period 2003 to 2007, also progresses, although rising slightly from 13.8% to 14.6% of trips, to the detriment of trips on foot. Other modes of transport fell by 0.4%. The modification of this modal share was one of the main objectives of the "Sustainable Transport Plan 2002–2012."

the different means of transport and intermodal transport. Train and public transport must be favored in general for passengers, and train and sea transport for goods.

To achieve this rebalance at different scales, from local and district levels to the international level, measures must include urban development, taxes, technology, mobility demand management, and also the creation of new infrastructures. Solutions must be found that adapt to the needs of the demand for mobility and demands for environmental sustainability.

This concern about sustainable mobility was present in the review the institutions carried out on the guidelines on land regulation, the decree on the authorization of large stores and the new tax system to give incentives to a low carbon economy.

These measures had to be tackled in a coordinated way by different administrations and on different scales, from local to global. Sustainable transport is a field where the application of the principles of multilevel governance is particularly suitable.

The Basque Government, besides leading the development of the whole of the system of sustainable transport, developed, in accordance with its competences and through a 2006 agreement with the Spanish Government, the execution of a strategic project for the future of the Country: the Basque "Y" high speed rail network. This high speed rail project, to transport passengers and goods, will constitute a real intercity connection between Basque cities in little over twenty minutes and will transform these Basque cities into future "stations" connected with the rest of the "city stations in the European metro" (Paris, Madrid, London, Berlin, etc.) which will be joined through this rail infrastructure.[385]

In short, the "Sustainable Transport Master Plan 2002–2012" assumed the challenge shared with the EU to dissociate demand for transport from economic development, to achieve universal accessibility, promote a rebalance between modes of transport, strengthen the

---

[385] Besides the Basque "Y" the Bilbao Tramway and Metro Plan was undertaken (urban and district areas) and what are known as the "Sea Motorways" were promoted.

strategic position of the Basque Country in Europe, and advance towards a model of sustainable transport that is respectful with the environment. Two basic pillars were proposed for this aim:

- The Transport Authority as a coordinating body of different administrative competencies, of different economic interests and the endemic atomization of the sector.
- The Logistics Platform the Basque Country-Aquitaine, as a tool to assert the strategic position of the Basque Country in north-south European communications.

Comment and Assessment

Many of these actions contributed to lower greenhouse gas emissions in the Basque Autonomous Community than in Spain. The Basque community has a Climate Change Office that has taken measurements continually since 1990, illustrating the level of awareness that has existed in the country for decades. As can be seen in Table 3, the Autonomous Community of the Basque Country reached 2002 with annual increases in greenhouse gas emissions.

Starting in 2002, the Autonomous Community of the Basque Country started a phase of decreasing CO2 emissions, as a result of the institutional policies introduced, as well as public-private collaboration. These results brought the Basque Country, in the first decade of the 21st century, closer the objectives set in the Kyoto Protocol, even to fulfill it from 2009. In any case, the results reached in recent years are moving the Country in the right direction.

Table 3: Greenhouse gas emissions (1990-2013).

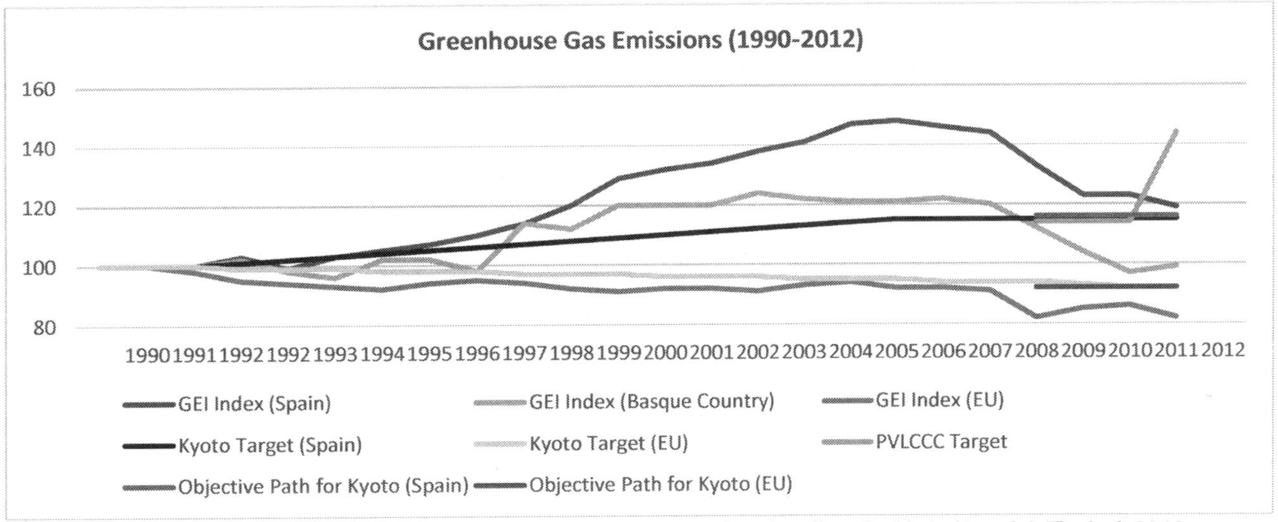

Source: Basque Government, Department of Environment and Regional Policy, *Perfil Ambiental de Euskadi 2013*.

6
Results of the Strategy of Sustainable Human Development Applied to the "Basque Case" Statistical Annex

In this chapter we will assess the results of the "Basque case": an applied experience of sustainable human development. We will analyze, thus, the results of the Economic Strategy, the results of the Environmental Strategy and the results of the Strategy of Social Cohesion.

We will do this by using the indices and indicators usually used in analyses of this nature, based on official statistics and data from the European Union (EUROSTAT), from the Spanish State (INE), from the Basque Autonomous Community (EUSTAT), from the statistical institutions of different Basque Government Departments, and our own. Placing special emphasis on the analysis of the Structural Indicators of the EU Lisbon Strategy, defined in 2000[386] and revised in 2005.[387]

Economic Strategy Indicators. Indicators of Economic Results

The rates of growth of GDP of the Basque economy were, as can be seen in Table 4, from the mid 90s, with the exception of 2009, always outstanding and permanently higher than the growth rates, also positive, obtained by Spanish and European economies.

---

386 EUPROPEAN COUNCIL, Presidency conclusions, Lisbon. March 23–24, 2000.

387 EUPROPEAN COUNCIL, Presidency conclusions, Brussels. March 22–23, 2005.

Table 4: GDP growth % rates, in nominal and in real terms

	Nominal Δ				Deflator				Real Δ			
	BAC	Spain	Euro Zone	EU 27	BAC	Spain	Euro Zone	EU 27	BAC	Spain	Euro Zone	EU 27
1996	6.7	6.0	4.2	5.2	3.6	3.5	2.7	3.4	3.0	2.4	1.6	1.8
1998	9.0	7.1	3.9	4.8	2.9	2.5	1.0	1.7	5.9	4.5	2.8	3.0
2000	7.9	8.7	5.3	7.2	2.6	3.5	1.3	3.2	5.2	5.0	3.9	3.9
2002	5.2	7.1	3.5	3.8	2.7	4.3	2.6	2.6	2.4	2.7	0.9	1.2
2004	8.3	7.4	4.1	4.9	4.4	4.0	1.9	2.3	3.7	3.3	2.2	2.5
2006	7.8	8.3	5.0	5.6	3.3	4.1	1.9	2.3	4.4	4.0	3.0	3.2
2008	3.0	3.4	2.9	1.2	1.2	2.5	2.2	0.4	1.9	0.9	0.7	0.8
2009	-3.2	-3.6	-2.8	-2.7	0.0	0.0	1.3	1.5	-3.3	-3.6	-4.0	-4.1

Source: Eurostat, Eustat, INE and own production.

This performance by the Basque economy over the period 1998–2008 was better than in the region, not only in the EU as a whole, but also in relation to the main countries in the EU, USA, and Japan, as reflected in Table 5. In this table we can see how the Basque economy has lost this trend from 2008 on.

Table 5: Basque Country GDP growth % rate comparison

Evolution of real GPD (1998-2013)						
Country	**1998**	**2001**	**2004**	**2008**	**2011**	**2013**
EU	3.0	2.0	2.5	0.4	1.7	0.1
Germany	2.0	1.2	1.2	1.1	3.3	0.4
Spain	4.5	3.6	3.3	0.9	0.4	-1.2
Italy	1.4	1.8	1.5	1.2	0.4	-1.9
France	3.5	1.9	2.5	0.1	2.0	0.2
UK	3.6	2.5	3.0	0.8	1.1	1.9
USA	4.4	1.1	3.6	0.3	1.8	1.9
Japan	-2.0	0.2	2.7	-1.0	-0.5	1.5
BAC	5.9	3.3	3.7	1.3	0.3	-1.2

Source: Basque Government, Direction of Economy and Planning, *Informe anual 2013* (2014/07/31). Eurostat, Eustat, and own production.

As a consequence, and as reflected in Table 6, the GDP per inhabitant of the Basque Autonomous Community with regard to the EU average[388] has been hugely reappraised over recent years. Thus, it was 108.9% in 1998 (EU-25) and, after a significant increase, 131% in 2008, and 122% according with the last data.

---

388 This is one of the structural indicators of the EU Lisbon Strategy defined in 2000 (EUPROPEAN COUNCIL, Presidency conclusions, Lisbon. March 23–24, 2000) and reviewed in 2005 (EUPROPEAN COUNCIL, Presidency conclusions, Brussels. March 22–23, 2005).

Table 6: GDP per capita comparison by countries

GPD per capita (per year and country)					
Country	1998	2001	2005	2008	2013
EU 28	**100**	**100**	**100**	**100**	**100**
Germany	114.2	116	116	116	122
Austria	122.9	126	125	124	128
Belgium	111.6	124	119	115	119
Croatia			58	64	61
Denmark	123.1	128	123	123	124
Slovakia	47.4	53	60	71	75
Spain	88.6	98	101	102	94
Finland	112.1	115	116	120	113
France	113.1	116	110	106	107
Greece	70.3	87	91	93	73
Ireland	116.3	133	145	132	130
Italy	114.6	119	107	106	99
Luxembourg	193.5	234	242	256	257
Netherlands	121.5	134	133	139	131
Poland	44.9	48	50	55	67
Portugal	77.8	81	80	79	79
UK	111.3	121	125	114	109
Czech Rep.	66.5	73	80	82	82
Sweden	113.6	123	124	127	127
BAC	108,9	120	125	131	122

Source: Eurostat (2015/05/22), Eustat (2015/05/22) and own production.

The following table (Table7) shows that in the European GDP per capita ranking, Basque men and women occupy a leading position among European countries, with an important increase over recent years. We were in ninth position in terms of income in 2001 and moved up to be among the first five countries in 2008 and 2013. This, without a doubt, shows a notable performance by the Basque economy especially during the period 1998-2008.

Table 7: GDP per capita: European top 10 ranking

	2001			**2005**			**2008**			**2013**	
1	Lux.	234	1	Lux.	242	1	Lux.	256	1	Lux.	257
2	Neth.	134	2	Ireland	145	2	Neth.	139	2	Neth.	131
3	Ireland	133	3	Neth.	133	3	Ireland	132	3	Ireland	130
4	Denmark	128	**4**	**BAC**	**125**	**4**	**BAC**	**131**	4	Austria.	128
5	Austria	126	5	Austria	125	5	Sweden	127	5	Sweden	127
6	Belgium	124	6	UK	125	6	Austria	124	6	Denmark	124
7	Sweden	123	7	Sweden	124	7	Denmark	123	**7**	**BAC**	**122**
8	UK	121	8	Denmark	123	8	Finland	120	8	Germany	122
9	**BAC**	**120**	**9**	Belgium	119	**9**	Germany	116	**9**	Belgium	119
10	Italy	119	10	Germany	116	10	Belgium	115	10	Finland	113
…			…			…			…		
14	Spain	98	14	Spain	101	14	Spain	102	14	Spain	94

In the ninth position in terms of income in 2001, Basques moved up to be among the first five countries in 2008 and 2013, showing a notable performance of the Basque economy especially during the period 1998–2008.

Source: Eurostat (2015/05/22), Eustat (2015/05/22) and own production.

Productivity[389] also showed an outstanding performance, with a labor productivity per worker nearly 30 points higher than the community average.

Table 8: Occupied manpower productivity evolution

Occupied manpower productivity evolution					
Country	**2003**	**2005**	**2007**	**2009**	**2012**
Germany	107.8	108.5	108.2	104.1	107.0
Austria	120.5	118.3	116.9	116.1	114.9
Belgium	135.4	130.3	127.5	127.7	128.4
Denmark	106.7	107.1	104.6	106.7	111.9
Slovenia	78.8	83.1	83.0	80.0	80.8
Spain	104.1	101.3	103.0	109.2	109.6
Finland	110.0	111.1	113.5	110.0	109.0
France	116.1	116.3	115.5	117.1	116.1
Greece	101.8	95.8	95.3	98.1	91.7
Netherlands	111.3	114.4	114.3	112.5	108.3
Ireland	137.7	135.8	136.3	132.8	141.7
Italy	116.6	111.9	111.5	112.4	109.3
Luxembourg	168.0	170.1	179.7	159.2	162.4
Poland	60.3	61.7	62.1	65.4	73.6
Portugal	71.1	72.8	73.9	76.0	76.0
UK	114.0	114.9	111.7	106.9	99.2
Czech Rep.	71.1	73.0	76.2	75.8	73.8
Sweden	111.8	111.9	114.7	112.0	114.3
BAC	**126.9**	**125.2**	**129.7**	**129.3**	**128.5**

Source: Eurostat (2014/06/16), Eustat (2014/07/28) and own production.

389 Structural indicator of the European Union Lisbon Strategy.

In Table 9, where Basque society is seen among the leading countries with the highest productivity in the European productivity ranking. The Country is always moving between the leading positions in ranking: third in 2000, fourth in 2005, second in 2008 and third in 2012.

Business investment[390] also deserves special attention due to its importance. Here, gross formation of fixed capital as a percentage of GDP. This is a concept, reflected in Table 10, which was constant over the period 1999–2014 with the Basque Country showing good performance as it was always considerably better than the EU average. Growth was uninterrupted from 1999 — when it was 21.5% — until 2008, when it rose to 30.6% (in 2014 it was 21.9%).

390 Structural indicator of the European Union Lisbon Strategy.

Table 9: Occupied manpower productivity: European top 10 ranking

2000			2008			2012		
1	Luxembourg	176.8	1	Luxembourg	172.8	1	Luxembourg	162.4
2	Belgium	137.3	2	**BAC**	**132.0**	2	Ireland	141.7
3	**BAC**	**133.0**	3	Ireland	131.4	3	**BAC**	**128.5**
4	Ireland	129.3	4	Belgium	124.3	4	Belgium	128.4
5	Italy	127.5	5	France	121.1	5	France	116.1
6	Austria	123.5	6	Finland	119.7	6	Austria	114.9
7	France	119.4	7	Netherlands	115.5	7	Sweden	114.3
8	Finland	115.5	8	Austria	113.5	8	Denmark	111.9
9	Netherlands	115.0	9	Sweden	111.6	9	Spain	109.6
10	Sweden	114.9	10	UK	111.0	10	Italy	109.3
…			…			…		
13	Spain	104.2	12	Spain	104.5			

Source: Eurostat (2014/06/16), Eustat (2014/07/28) and own production.

Table 10: Gross fixed capital formation (investments) in relation to GDP

Country	1999*	2003	2008	2014
EU28	**18.1**	**21**	**22.5**	**19.3**
Germany	19.4	19.6	20.3	20.0
Austria	21.7	24.2	23.4	22.1
Belgium	18.8	20.5	24.3	22.9
Bulgaria	11.3	19.7	33.5	21.0
Croatia	:	25.8	28.1	19.6
Denmark	18.1	20.7	23.0	19.6
Slovenia	22.4	25.2	29.6	20.1
Spain	21.2	27.7	29.2	18.9
Finland	16.2	21.8	24.4	20.0
France	15.8	20.9	23.6	21.6
Greece		24.8	23.7	11.6
Netherlands	19.9	20.7	22.1	18.5
Hungary	20.2	23.7	23.3	21.3
Ireland	20.0	24.4	24.2	16.4
Italy	17.3	20.7	21.2	16.8
Luxembourg	19.2	20.3	19.4	
Poland	20.9	18.2	22.6	19.6
Portugal	22.8	23.7	22.8	15.1
UK	16.1	18.2	17.9	17.2
Czech Rep.	23.8	28.8	29.0	25.3
Romania	16.,0	22.3	38.4	21.8
Sweden	14.4	21.3	24.3	23.1
BAC	**21.5**	**29.0**	**30.6**	**21.9**

*1999 – EU27

Source: Eurostat (2014/04/14) and own production.

This has represented a relative but continuous improvement in the position in the European ranking, as can be seen in Table 11. The Basque Country was always among the European countries with the highest percentages of investment and involvement in constructing economy and society, i.e. the country.

Today the world speaks about observing the real economy to overcome crisis and build the future. This highlights the importance of the economic structure of a country to tackle the changes, challenges and, transformations that must be faced. In the case of Basque society the commitment to the real economy, to industry over recent decades, has consequently led to the industrial sector continuing to represent a great weight in the Basque economy. As can be seen in the following Table 12 the contribution by industry, in terms of GDP, to the Basque economy was, in 2008, 11 points higher than the contribution in the case of Spain and 8 points above the European average. However this tendency has been reduced dangerously, from 2008, in the last six years.

Table 11: Gross fixed capital formation in relation to GDP. European top 10 ranking

2000		
1	Czech R.	24.4
2	Slovakia	23.8
3	Portugal	23.3
4	Latvia	22.9
5	**BAC**	**22.7**
6	Spain	22.7
7	Austria	22.5
8	Slovenia	22.4
9	Estonia	22.0
10	Poland	21.4

2008		
1	Romania	39.4
2	Bulgaria	33.5
3	Latvia	32.0
4	Estonia	31.2
5	**BAC**	**30.6**
6	Slovenia	29.6
7	Spain	29.2
8	Czech R.	29.0
9	Croatia	28.1
10	Cyprus	27.3

2014		
1	Estonia	25.8
2	Czech R.	25.3
3	Latvia	23.0
4	Belgium	22.9
5	Austria	22.1
6	**BAC**	**21.9**
7	Romania	21.8
8	Finland	21.6
9	Hungary	21.3
10	Slovakia	21.1

Source: Eurostat (2015-04-11) and own production.

Table 12: Compartison of sectorial distribution of GDP of Basque Autonomuos Community (1980–2013)

Social Distribution of GDP of Autonomous Community of the Basque Country 1980-2013 Current prices. Base Year 2005, 2010				
BAC	**1980**	**1998**	**2008**	**2013**
Agriculture and Fisheries	3.4	1.8	0.7	0.9
Industry	43.4	31.6	28.0	22.8
EU-27Construction	4.3	6.3	9.6	6.7
Services	48.9	60.3	31.7	69.6
Spain				
Agriculture and Fisheries	3.4	1.8	0.7	0.9
Industry	43.4	31.6	28.0	22.8
EU-27Construction	4.3	6.3	9.6	6.7
Services	48.9	60.3	31.7	69.6
EU27				
Agriculture and Fisheries	3.4	1.8	0.7	0.9
Industry	43.4	31.6	28.0	22.8
EU-27Construction	4.3	6.3	9.6	6.7
Services	48.9	60.3	31.7	69.6

Source: Eurostat, INE, Eustat, (2013 Novenber) and own production.[391]

[391] The Basque economy was promoted by an intelligent use of the instruments of self government. An important strategic component is the opening to foreign markets (see Tables 13, 14, 15 and 16.) Table 13 shows the growth that exports and imports had in this period. The exports to the rest of the State, which stood at 69% over GDP in 1981, decreased to 34% over GDP in 2008, while exports to the rest of the world stood at 22% over the GDP in 1981 and increased to 33% according to GDP, very similar to those to the State, in 2008 (Table 14).

Table 13: Aggregates of Demand of the Basque Autonomuos Community (thousand Euros)

	1981	1989	1998	2001	2005	2008
EXPENDITURE ON FINAL CONSUMPTION	**5.552.87**	**14.667.00**	**28.849.95**	**33.020.95**	**43.691.68**	**52.140.793**
Expenditure on final household expenditure	4.652..101	11.890.60	21.600.307	26.448.751	35.215.76	41.430.793
Expenditure on final consumption of AAPP	900.774	2.776.398	5.249.646	6.572.199	8.475.920	10.710.000
GROSS FORMATION CAPITAL	**1.548.331**	**4.261.788**	**8.753.759**	**11.688.578**	**16.422.80**	**19.818.678**
Gross Formation Fixed Capital	1.329.219	3.984.818	8.199.523	11.171.581	16.079.83	19.657.343
Stock Variations	219.112	276.969	554.236	516.997	342.971	161.335
INTERNAL DEMAND	**7.101.206**	**18.928.79**	**35.603.712**	**44.709.52**	**60.114.495**	**71.959.471**

EXPORTS OF GOODS AND SERVICES	**6.974.781**	**14.060.72**	**23.798.00**	**29.522.48**	**35.764.61**	**45.906.34**
Rest of the State	5.269.881	10.291.61	12.994.781	15.942.337	19.353.91	23.013.305
Abroad	1.704.899	3.769.115	10.803.226	13.580.149	16.410.69	22.893.042
IMPORTS OF GOODS AND SERVICES	**6.477.78**	**13.813.75**	**23.715.634**	**30.301.348**	**35.589.96**	**49.437.133**
Rest of the State	4.552.252	9.685.060	16.316.394	19.571.245	23.939.98	29.094.966
Foreign	1.925.533	4.128.697	7.399.240	10.730.103	14.649.98	20.342.167
FOREING BALANCE OF TRADE	**496.996**	**246.972**	**82.373**	**-778.861**	**-2.825.352**	**-3.530.786**
Rest of the State	717.630	606.554	-3.321.613	-3.628.908	-4.586.061	-6.081.661
Foreign	-220.634	-359.582	3.403.986	2.850.047	1.760.709	2.550.875
GROSS DOMESTIC PRODUCT (at market prices)	**7.598.20**	**19.175.76**	**35.686.08**	**43.930.66**	**57.289.14**	**68.428.68**

Source: INE, Eustat and own production.

Table 14: Exports mix evolution of the Basque Autonomuos Community: Percentages of Exports over GDP.

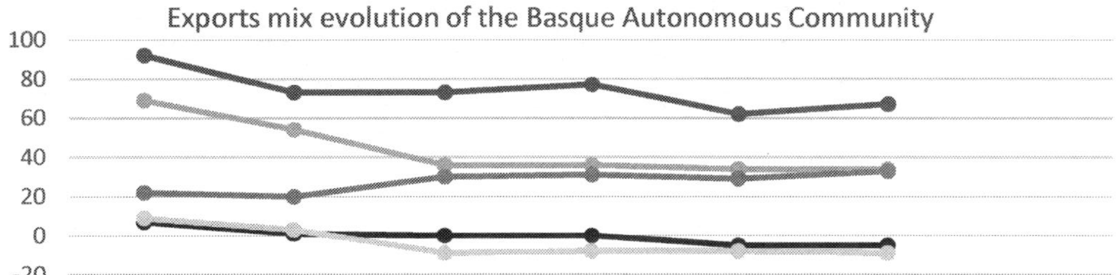

	1981	1989	1998	2001	2005	2008	
Total Export	92	73	73	77	62	67	
Export Rest of State	69	54	36	36	34	34	
Foreign Export	22	20	30	31	29	33	
Total Balance	7	1	0	0	-5	-5	
Rest of State Balance	9	3	-9	-8	-8	-9	

Source: IBARRETXE, Juan J., *Ethical Principle, Democratic Principle and Sustainable Human Development. Foundations for a Democratic Model,* [Doctoral Thesis] University of the Basque Country, Donostia, 2012.

Table 15: Foreign trade of the BAC. Percentages and composition of Imports and Exports in relation to GDP

Foreign trade of the Basque Autonomous Community									
	Total Export	Rest of State Export	Export Abroad	Total Import	Rest of State Import	Import Abroad	Total Balance	Rest of State Balance	Balance Abroad
1981	92	69	22	85	60	25	7	9	-3
1989	73	54	20	72	51	22	1	3	-2
1998	67	36	30	66	46	21	0	-9	10
2001	67	36	31	69	45	24	-2	-8	6
2005	62	34	29	67	42	26	-5	-8	3
2008	67	34	33	72	43	30	-5	-9	4

Source: IBARRETXE, Juan J., *The Basque Case*, Bogotá, La Oveja Negra, 2012[392].

---

[392] The second change which can be seen in Tables 15 and 16 refers to foreign trade balances, because although the balance was positive in relation to the rest of the State (more was exported than imported) and negative with the rest of the world (less was exported than imported) from 1981 to 1989, from 1998 a change in the trend was observed until 2008 when it was negative with the rest of the State (less was exported than imported) and positive with the rest of the world, where more was exported than imported. In fact, whereas Basque exports in terms of GDP were similar to the rest of the State than to the rest of the world (34% and 33%), Basque imports were much greater from the rest of the State than from the rest of the world (43% compared to 30% according to GDP respectively).

Table 16: Foreign trade of the Basque Autonomuos Community: Percentages and composition of Imports and Exports in relation to GDP

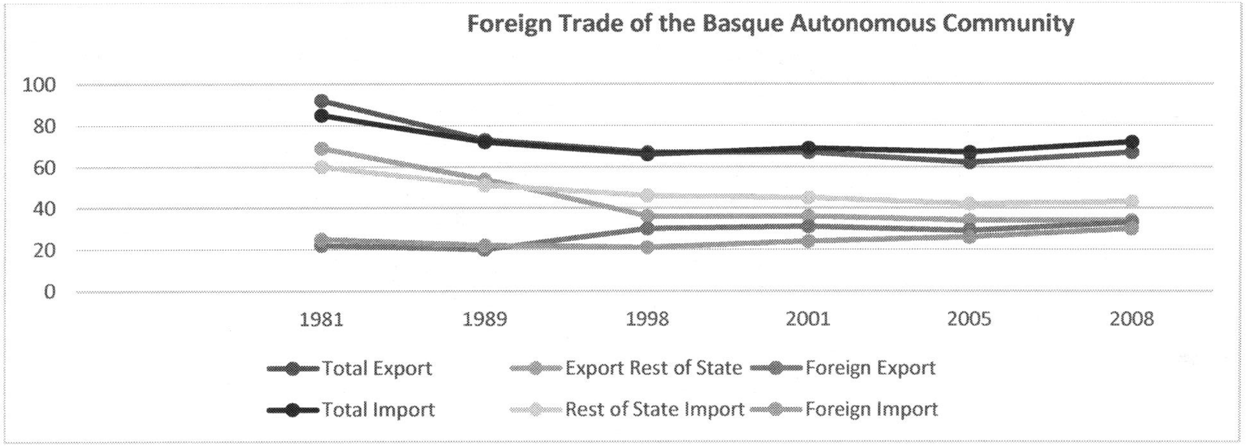

Source: IBARRETXE, Juan J., *Ethical Principle, Democratic Principle and Sustainable Human Development. Foundations for a Democratic Model*, [Doctoral Thesis] University of the Basque Country, Donostia, 2012.

Innovation and Research: Activity R&D

As we have already commented in this results analysis for the sustainable human development strategy of Basque society, another strategic objective of the country, considered over the period 1998–2008, was to achieve technological convergence with Europe.

As the data indicate in Table 17, expenditure on R&D in the EU[393] in 1998 was still far from the objective, but the effort carried out was outstanding[394] and the results in quantitative and qualitative terms were clear, as we have observed in our own analyses.

The first striking point in Table 17 is that while Basque investment rose constantly from 1998, in the case of the EU there was a dangerous stagnation in the area, which may explain, in our opinion, part of the incapacity to react on the part of the EU concerning the current crisis, which in the first part of this paper we defined as polyhedral and axiological.

---

393 Structural indicator of the European Union Lisbon Strategy.

394 We should remember that in 1981, when Prof. Pedro Miguel Etxenike, at that time Minister for Education of the Basque Government born with the Statute of Gernika, took the decision to put into practice in the BAC, with its own means and still without the transfer of science, technology, and innovation, the Basque system of science and technology; investment in R&D was 0.069% of the GDP.

Table 17: R+D expenditure in relation to GDP

R+D expenditure in relation to GDP				
Country	**1998***	**2001***	**2008**	**2013**
EU28	**1.78**	**1.87**	**1.85**	**2.02**
Germany	2.28	2.47	2.60	2.94
Austria	1.77	2.05	2.59	2.81
Belgium	1.86	2.07	1.92	2.28
Croatia	:	:	0.88	0.81
Denmark	2.04	2.39	2.78	3.05
Slovenia	1.33	1.49	1.63	2.59
Spain	0.87	0.92	1.32	1.24
Finland	2.88	3.32	3.5	3.32
France	2.14	2.20	2.06	2.23
Greece	:	0.58	0.66	0.78
Ireland	1.24	1.09	1.39	:
Italy	1.04	1.08	1.16	1.25
Luxembourg	:	:	1.65	1.16
Netherlands	1.90	1.93	1.65	1.98
Poland	0.67	0.62	0.60	0.87
Portugal	0.63	0.77	1.45	1.36
UK	1.73	1.77	1.69	1.63
Romania	0.49	0.39	0.57	0.39
Sweden	:	4.13	3.50	3.21
BAC	**1.11**	**1.42**	**1.81**	**1.99**

*years1998-2001, EU27.
Source: Eurostat (2014/11/13), Eustat (2014/12/26) and own production.

Achieving the objective of technological convergence Basque society with Europe considered in 1998 and 2001 is reflected in Table 18. Here we can observe the important joint effort in a real strategic alliance, carried out by public and private sectors in the Basque Country to achieve their "vision," to become a reference in Europe in the area of innovation.

Table 18: Total R+D expenditure (public and private) in the Basque Autonomous Community in million Euros, and in relation to GDP

R+D Expenditure (public and private)						
% R+D / GPD	**1998**	**2001**	**2005**	**2008**	**2012**	**2013**
BAC	1.11	1.42	1.41	1.81	2.06	1.99
Spain	0.87	0.92	1.10	1.32	1.27	1.24
EU-28	*1.78	*1.87	1.76	1.85	2.01	2.02

*years 1998-2001 – EU27
Source: Eurostat (2014/11/13), Eustat (2014/12/26) and own production.

As a consequence of this investment, defined and developed jointly by the administrations and civil society, as we saw when analyzing the science, technology, and innovation plans, Basque society which was still far from the EU average in 1998 (1.11% according to GDP in the BAC, 1.78% in the EU), reached the European average in 2008, when investment in R&D according to GDP was 1.81% in the BAC, and the EU-27 average which was 1.85% (Data from the INE for the year 2008, published on December 18, 2009, established a percentage of GDP invested in R&D was 1.96%).

Then, in March 2010, official data was published by the European Innovation Scoreboard 2009. It is striking that, the edition of the report for this year shows for the first time the regional dynamics, confirming the dynamics of innovation are produced fundamentally on a regional scale and not on a state level.[395]

Finally, according to the last data published by the European Innovation Index (Table 19), we can confirm an unstoppable rising trend over recent years, and very specifically over the period between 1998 and 2008. This enables us, for the Basque society case, to confirm the diagnosis and at the same time, with intellectual honesty, to show our concern for the change of trend observed since 2008, losing the position with the European average, as seen in the data for the years 2011 and 2014, after the enormous efforts that Basque society did to achieve the technological convergence with the EU in 2008.

---

395 The European Innovation Scoreboard 2009, March 2010, states that the Spanish State is in the group of "Slow growth," and Section 6.4., Regional Innovation Performance, p. 34 states:

- The most innovative regions are typically in the most innovative countries.
- Nearly all the "high innovators" regions are in the group of "Innovation leaders" identified in the European Innovation Scoreboard (EIS).
- Similarly all of the "low innovators" regions are located in countries that have below average performance in the EIS. However, the results also show regions that outperform their country level:
  - Noord-Brabant in the Netherlands is a high innovating region located in an Innovation follower country.
  - Praha in the Czech Republic, Basque Country, Charter Community of Navarre, Community of Madrid and Catalonia in Spain, Lombardy and Emilia-Romagna in Italy, Oslo og Akershus, Sør-Østlandet, Agder og Rogaland, Vestlandet and Trøndelag in Norway are all medium-high innovating regions from Moderate innovators. The capital region in Romania, Bucuresti — Ilfov, is a medium-low innovating region in a Catching-up country.

Table 19: Comparison of European Innovation Index performance by the Basque Country ("C.A. de Euskadi" stands for Basque Autonomous Community)

Innovation Union Scoreboard (IUS)								
Country	2007	Ranking Top EU	2008	Ranking Top EU	2011	Ranking Top EU	2014	Ranking Top EU
BAC	0.37	13	0.49	11	0.46	15	0.50	15
Spain	0.31	18	0.37	17	0.41	19	0.41	19
EU-28	0.45		0.48		0.54		0.56	

Source: Innovation Union Scoreboard (IUS) 2007, 2008, 2011, 2014 (2014/04/14), Eustat and own production.

In conclusion, Basque society's goal to achieve technological convergence with Europe has been a shared objective, and its success was also shared and recognized by third parties in Europe.[396]

Indicators of the Social Cohesion Strategy. Education Indicators

Education, training men and women, is behind all personal and collective success. In the case of Basque society, without any doubt, it has been an explanatory factor for development over the last 25 years and specifically for the development achieved between 1998 and 2008.

---

396 Jean Monnet Group on Competition and Regional Development. Case Study Basque Country. Report made by: J. LÓPEZ-RODRIGUEZ, J.A. FAÍÑA and P. MONTES-SOLLA, 2009. "Main message: The three problems highlighted in the innovation potential hypothesis (lack of R&D drivers on the demand side, barriers to innovation and path-dependence problems in existing old-industrial technologies) were serious handicaps of the Basque economy in the eighties. The main messages to be drawn from our analysis in the particular case of the Basque country are:

1. Measures to support public and technological research centers were very important to tackle the path dependence problems in the traditional industrial sector of the Basque country. Moreover they have also contributed to a diffusion process on the key role played by R&D and innovation as a power tool to build sustainable competitive advantages throughout the entrepreneurial fabric.
2. Measures supporting cooperation and joint R&D projects are effective to smooth innovation barriers especially for SMEs and micro-firms.
3. Measures addressed to SMEs and micro-firms to soften financial barriers to innovation combined with the above measures are very effective to boost R&D drivers on the demand side. This is specially the case with reimbursable aids to fund R&D projects.

As a conclusion we can finally state that hypothesis 4 of the Core Team conceptual model, 'Innovation potential,' is validated in the case of the Basque Country."

Table 20 shows us data on the total level of education[397] by each EU country. We can see that Basque society stays above the European average throughout the period, and above 80%, which is the objective set in the Lisbon strategy for 2010.

[397] The total level of education is one of the structural indicators of the EU Lisbon strategy. It measures the proportion of population aged 20 to 24 that have surpassed secondary level education.

Table 20: Total Level of Education[398]

Population (20-24) that have surpassed secondary level education			
Country	**1999**	**2008**	**2013**
EU27		**78.5**	**80.9**
Germany	74.6	47.1	76.8
Austria	84.7	84.5	87.4
Belgium	76.2	82.2	83.1
Denmark	73.2	68.9	71.8
Slovenia	85.8	90.2	91.5
Spain	65.2	60.0	63.8
Finland	86.8	86.2	85.9
France	80.0	83.8	86.4
Greece	76.6	82.1	86.5
Netherlands	72.3	76.2	78.2
Ireland	82.0	87.7	89.5
Italy	66.3	76.5	77.9
Luxembourg	71.2	72.8	76.4
Poland	81.6	91.3	89.7
Portugal	40.1	54.3	69.9
UK	75.3	78.2	82.9
Czech Rep.	91.8	91.6	90.2
Sweden	86.3	85.6	86.2
BAC	**79.0**	**81.6**	**85.5**

Source: Eurostat (2014/06/13), Eustat (2014/07/28) and own production.

---

398 Population aged 20 to 24 that have surpassed secondary level education). Comparison by countries ("C. A. de Euskadi" stands for Basque Autonomous Community.)

Table 21: Total Level of Higher Education (population aged 30 to 34). Comparison by countries

Total Level of Higher Education (population aged 30 to 34)			
Country	**2000**	**2008**	**2014**
EU27	**22.4**	**31.2**	**37.9**
Germany	25.7	27.7	31.4
Austria		21.9	40.0
Belgium	35.2	42.9	43.8
Croatia		18.5	32.2
Denmark	32.1	39.2	44.1
Slovenia	18.5	30.9	41.0
Spain	29.2	41.3	42.3
Finland	40.3	45.7	45.3
France	27.4	41.2	44.1
Greece	25.4	25.7	37.2
Ireland	27.5	46.3	52.2
Italy	11.6	19.2	23.9
Luxembourg	21.2	39.8	52.7
Netherlands	26.5	40.2	44.6
Poland	12.5	29.7	42.1
Portugal	11.3	21.6	31.3
UK	29.0	39.7	47.7
Czech Rep.	13.7	15.4	28.2
Sweden	31.8	42.0	49.9
BAC	**30.5**	**38.7**	**48.9**

Source: Eurostat (2015/04/22), Eustat (2015-05-18) and own production.

Tables 22 and 23 show data for higher education. It is remarkable that the proportion of women with higher education is higher than men in the BAC. Also, in reference to the EU, the average difference is greater in the case of Basque women.

Table 22: Level of Higher Education for Women

Level of Higher Education of Women (population aged 30 to 34)			
Country	**2000**	**2008**	**2014**
EU28	**22.7**	**34.4**	**42.3**
Germany	22.6	27.0	30.8
Austria		22.4	41.6
Belgium	37.1	48.6	50.2
Denmark	33.6	41.8	50.0
Spain	30.4	46.5	47.8
Finland	47.9	56.6	52.6
France	29.0	45.2	48.4
Greece	26.9	27.8	41.6
Ireland	29.2	52.7	58.6
Italy	12.5	23.5	29.1
Luxembourg	17.7	42.7	55.4
Netherlands	25.6	41.8	47.9
Poland	14.6	35.0	50.2
Portugal	13.5	26.1	38.9
UK	27.4	41.0	51.1
Czech Rep.	13.0	15.9	32.5
Sweden	33.2	47.7	57.9
BAC	**36.5**	**47.5**	**58.0**

Source: Eurostat (2015/04/22), Eustat (2015-05-18) and own production.

Table 23: Level of Higher Education for Men

Level of Higher Education of Men (population aged 30 to 34)			
Country	**2004**	**2008**	**2014**
EU28	**25.3**	**28.0**	**33.6**
Germany	29.1	28.3	32.0
Austria	22.0	21.8	38.3
Belgium	35.8	37.4	37.4
Croatia	14.1	15.3	25.6
Denmark	38.7	36.8	38.4
Slovenia	18.1	24.3	30.0
Spain	33.4	36.5	36.8
Finland	35.0	35.0	38.2
France	32.6	37.1	39.6
Greece	23.6	23.7	32.9
Ireland	35.7	39.9	45.1
Italy	12.8	14.9	18.8
Luxembourg	33.2	36.9	49.8
Netherlands	33.2	38.5	41.3
Poland	17.8	24.4	34.2
Portugal	12.5	16.9	23.2
UK	34.0	38.3	44.2
Czech Rep.	13.2	14.8	24.2
Sweden	28.6	36.6	42.4
BAC	**29.4**	**29.6**	**40.7**

Source: Eurostat (2015/04/22), Eustat (2015-05-18) and own production.

Table 24 shows a summary of the level of qualifications of Basque, Spanish, and European societies. This reflects the huge task that is still to be carried out in this area and at the same time one of the most important reasons to explain the socio economic transformation of the Basque society during this period of time.

Table 24: Percentage of population between 20 to 24 years old which has finished the compulsory secondary education

Country	1999	2003	2008	2013
BAC	79.0	81.0	81.6	85.5
Spain	65.2	62.2	60.0	63.8
EU-27	*76.6	77.1	78.5	80.9

Source: Eurostat (2014/06/13), Eustat (2014/07/28) and own production.

The information shown in Table 25 is equally interesting in relation to people's qualifications, in an ever more scientific-technical society. It shows the percentage of graduates in science and technology by EU country. The BAC ranked second in 2000, and was at the head of Europe in 2005 and 2009.

Table 25: Percentage of graduates in science and technology by countries in Europe

2000			**2005**			**2009**		
1	Ireland	24.2	1	BAC	26.6	1	BAC	26.6
2	BAC	20.2	2	Ireland	24.5	2	France	20.2
3	France	19.6	3	France	22.8	3	Romania	**20.0**
4	UK	18.5	4	UK	19.2	4	Finland	19.0
5	Finland	16.0	5	Lithuania	18.9	5	Lithuania	18.5
6	Lithuania	13.5	6	Finland	18.1	6	UK	17.5
7	Denmark	11.7	7	Denmark	14.7	7	Slovakia	17.5
8	Sweden	11.6	8	Sweden	14.4	8	Ireland	17.2
	EU-27	10.1		EU-27	13.3		EU-27	14.3

Source: Basque Government, Department of Education, Universities and Research, ISEI-IVEI, Rs7, *Graduados en Ciencias, Matemáticas y Tecnología*, December 2011 and own production.

Rates of school failure[399] — reflected in Table 26 for years 2000, 2006 and 2014 in the EU — are fundamental to define the health of an education system. The evolution of the Basque education system is positive; the rate of school failure was 14.3% in 2000, 12%, considerably lower than the European average at 15.4% for 2006 and 7.2% — 12% EU — in 2014. And we should not forget, that among the EU recommendations is that of the rate of school failure, which should be below 10%.

Table 26: School failure rates by countries (population aged 18 to 24). European ranking

2000			2014		
1	Sweden	7.3	1	Croatia	2.7
2	Finland	9.0	2	Slovenia	4.4
3	Austria	10.2	3	Poland	5.4
4	Denmark	11.7	4	Czech R.	5.5
5	France	13.3	5	Lithuania	5.9
6	Belgium	13.8	6	Luxemb.	6.1
7	Hungary	13.9	7	Slovakia	6.7
8	**BAC**	**14.3**	8	Sweden	6.7
9	Germany	14.6	9	Cyprus	6.8
10	Estonia	15.1	10	Ireland	6.9
	EU-27	17.6		**BAC**	7.2
	Spain	29.5		EU-28	11.1
				Spain	21.9

Source: Eurostat (2015/04/22), Eustat (2015-05-18) and own production

399 The rate of school failure measures the abandonment of studies before finishing compulsory secondary education.

A final question in this section refers to schooling quality. In Table 27 we can see the data collected in the Report on Education Policies in Spain, carried out for 2007, 2011, and 2015, under the auspices of the Spanish Ministry of Education. In it the Basque education system is assessed as first in the ranking for education excellence on a State level.

Table 27: School excellence in the Spanish State

2007			2015		
1	**BAC**	**9.37**	**1**	**BAC**	8.80
2	CCN	7.41	**2**	CCN	7.64
3	Asturias	7.28	**3**	Castilla L.	7.39
4	Madrid	6.63	**4**	Madrid	7.08
5	Castilla L.	6.51	**5**	Asturias	6.78
6	Aragón	6.29	**6**	Galicia	6.45
7	Cantabria	6.09	**7**	Cantabria	6.31
8	Galicia	5.68	**8**	La Rioja	5.72
9	Catalonia	5.54	**9**	Aragon	4.87
10	La Rioja	4.89	**10**	Catalonia	4.74
11	Valencia	3.96	**11**	Andalusia	3.53
12	Balearics	3.08	**12**	Extremad.	3.39
13	Extremad.	2.71	**13**	Balearics	3.08
14	Castilla M.	2.53	**14**	Valencia	2.71
15	Murcia	2.51	**15**	Murcia	2.48
16	Canary Isl.	2.44	**16**	Canary Isl.	2.16
17	Andalusia	2.09	**17**	Castilla M.	1.88

Source: Profesionales de la ética-Área de Estudios, *Las políticas educativas en España: Ranking de excelencia educativa 2007, 2011 y 2015.*

The conclusion is that over the period studied, the Basque education system has educated and qualified an important percentage (more than 80% above the European average) of men and women aged between 20 and 24, achieving a gradual reduction in the rates of school failure (below the European average) and developing a school of appreciable quality, in relation to our state and European vicinity.[400]

Indicators of Employment and Labor Market

The objective of convergence in income with the European Union[401] was about to be reached in 1998 and social and technological convergence with the EU from that moment on became the important objectives to be reached over the coming years in the Basque Country.

The first social convergence objective was to reach convergence in employment with the EU. As reflected in Tables 28 and 29, the concern was legitimate because in 1998 the rate of unemployment in Basque society was around 17%. This is an aspect that stands out in Table 28, labor market (PRA) produced by the Basque Statistics Institute (EUSTAT), as in Table 29, labor market (EPA) for the BAC, produced by the Spanish Statistics Institute (INE).

In both tables —28 and 29— the evolution between 1998 and 2008 is outstanding, showing a constant increase in the active population and employed population and a significant and constant decrease, as well as in the unemployed population and rates of unemployment. This is reflected in Table 29, incorporating the comparison with the EU top 10 ranking. It can be seen that — after being above in the year 2000 — a lower rate of unemployment was reached in Basque society in 2005 than in Europe, an objective which would continue to be achieved in 2008. Unfortunately we have lost this position in the recent years.

400 In the European EFQM system until 2009: among the 223 institutions recognized with the Silver Q in the Basque Country: 125 are education centers; among the 53 recognized with the Gold Q in the Basque Country: 20 are education centers; among the 10 institutions that were Finalists in Europe: 4 are education centers; among the 13 institutions were recognized with the Prize in Europe: 3 are education centers; and the only institution recognized in Europe as Award was 1 education center (in the whole Basque Country and in the whole State).

401 In 1998, we were on a par with the EU-15 at that time. According to table 6, for 1998, the Basque Autonomous Community was 108.9% and the EU-15 was 109.5% of the EU-25.

Table 28: Labor market evolution in the Basque Autonomous Community (1977–2013)

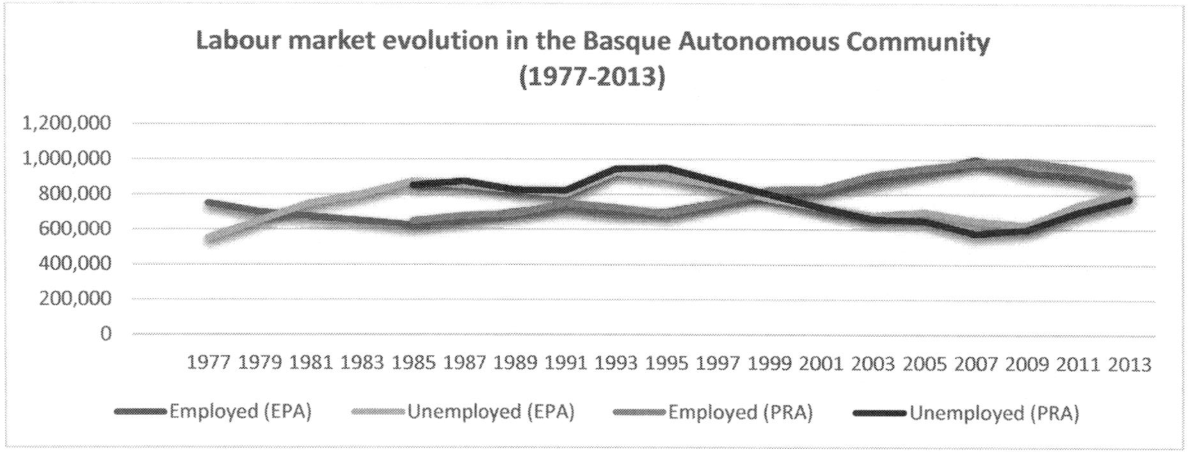

Source: ALBERDI, A., *La economía vasca ante el cambio de era (1955-2015): del crecimiento al desarrollo*, Grupo Vasco del Capítulo Español del Club de Roma, Bilbao, 2014.

Table 29: Unemployment by countries. Europe bottom 10 ranking

2000			2005			2008			2013		
1	Lux.	2.2	1	Ireland	4.4	1	Netherl.	3.1	1	Austria	4.9
2	Netherl.	3.1	2	Lux.	4.6	2	Denmark	3.5	2	Germany	5.3
3	Austria	3.6	3	UK	4.8	3	Cyprus	3.7	3	Lux.	5.9
4	Ireland	4.2	4	Denmark	4.8	4	**BAC**	3.8	4	Malta	6.4
8	Czech R.	5.4	**8**	**BAC**	**5.7**	8	Lux.	4.9	8	Romania	7.3
10	Hungary	6.4	10	Hungary	7.2	10	UK	5.6	10	Finland	8.2
	BAC	**12.2**		**EU**	**9.0**		EU	7.0		**BAC**	**14.6**
	EU	**8.8**		Spain	9.2		Spain	11.3		**EU**	10.8
	Spain	11.7								Spain	26.1

Source: Eurostat (2014/06/10), Eustat (2014/07/28) and own production.

There are still some aspects of employment susceptible to improvement. In Table 30 we can see one of them: temporary employment. A reduction over recent years does not avoid concluding that we continue, however, to present a notable and prejudicial difference in relation to the European average and therefore, it constitutes a subject for serious reflection in the future.

Table 30: Temporary Employment Comparison[402]

Temporary employment comparison			
Country	**2004**	**2007**	**2013**
BAC	31.6	21	21.7
Spain	32.4	31.2	:
EU-27	13.3	14.5	13.8

Source: Eurostat, Basque Government, Direction of economics and planning, *Informe anual 2013* (2014/07/31-Eustat data) and own production.

By contrast, another outstanding element is the employment rate, a structural indicator of the Lisbon strategy,[403] which is reflected in Table 31, and which clearly shows the positive evolution of this rate in Basque society. In fact, starting with a 60% rate of employment in 1999, far from the European average, the Basque Autonomous Community achieved convergence with the EU in 2004, 67.7%, and reached 71%, higher than the EU average (70.3%), in 2008.

However, the Basque Country has lost the position in 2014, and it constitutes another subject to reflect on.

[402] Temporary employed people/total employed people.

[403] Proportion of employed persons aged 15 to 64 in relation to the total population of the same age group.

Table 31: Employment rate by countries

Employment rate by countries (population aged 20 to 64)			
Country	**1999**	**2008**	**2014**
EU28	**66.2**	**70.3**	**69.2**
Germany	68.3	74.0	77.7
Austria	71.4	73.8	74.3
Belgium	64.5	68.0	67.3
Croatia		64.9	59.2
Denmark	77.7	79.7	75.9
Slovenia	68.1	73.0	67.8
Spain	58.3	68.5	59.9
Finland	70.8	75.8	73.1
France	66.6	70.4	69.8
Greece	61.4	66.3	53.3
Hungary	60.6	61.5	66.7
Ireland	68.8	72.2	67.0
Italy	56.4	62.9	59.9
Luxembourg	66.2	68.8	72.1
Netherlands	73.5	78.9	76.1
Poland	63.9	65.0	66.5
Portugal	72.6	73.1	67.6
UK	73.8	75.2	76.2
Czech Rep.	71.5	72.4	73.5
Romania	69.4	64.4	65.7
Sweden	76.5	80.4	80.0
BAC	**67.7**	**71.0**	**67.55**

Source: Eurostat (2015/04/22), Eustat (2015/05/18) and own production.

It is also necessary to make a reflection in relation to the case of the female employment rate.[404] The data from Tables 32 and 33 speaks for themselves. They show firstly, and this is positive, that in 2008 the female employment rate in the BAC was more or less the same as the European average (61.9% in the BAC, 62.8% in the EU), which occurred for the first time in our recent history. Secondly, the positive evolution is striking, because the rate was 44.8% just in 1999, far from the European average which was 56.6%. Thirdly, the differential with the male employment rate, although still very important in 2008 — the female employment rate was 61.9% and the male rate was 18 points higher, at 80% — it was much higher in 1999, when the female rate was 44.8% and the male rate was 74.9%, slightly over 30 points higher. These differences, as we can see in tables 32 and 33, have been narrowed, in 2014, due to the economic crisis.

A final question in relation to the male employment rate in the BAC, Table 33, is that a higher rate than the European average (80% compared with 77.9%) was seen in 2008 and that the evolution was positive both quantitatively, the rate was 74.9% in 1999, and qualitatively, Basque men then had a lower rate than in the EU. This trend broke, as we see in 2013, in which we lost male employment within the country (71.6%) and in relationship with the European average (75%).

The conclusion of this section is that, even though the Basque Country has lost positions in the recent years, over the period 1998–2008 the Basque society reasonably fulfilled the objective set to achieve convergence in employment with Europe.

---

404 The female employment rate is a structural indicator in the EU Lisbon strategy, which measures the proportion of women employed aged 15 to 64 in relation to the female population of the same age group.

Table 32: Employment rate of Women by countries

Country	1999	2008	2014
EU28	**56.6**	**62.8**	**63.5**
Germany	60.2	67.8	73.1
Austria	62.2	68.6	70.1
Belgium	54.7	61.3	62.9
Denmark	72.3	75.5	72.2
Slovenia	63.1	68.5	63.6
Spain	41.6	58.3	54.8
Finland	67.6	73.1	72.1
France	59.2	65.5	66.2
Greece	44.8	52.5	44.3
Hungary	53.2	55.1	60.2
Ireland	56.1	64.2	61.2
Italy	40.9	50.6	50.3
Luxembourg	52.1	60.1	65.5
Netherlands	63.1	72.2	70.7
Poland	56.7	57.3	59.4
Portugal	63.9	67.0	64.2
UK	66.3	68.8	70.6
Czech Rep.	62.3	62.5	64.7
Romania	63.2	57.3	57.3
Sweden	74.1	77.2	77.6
BAC	**44.8**	**61.9**	**63.4**

Source: Eurostat (2015/04/22), Eustat (2015/05/18) and own production.

Table 33: Employment rate of Men by countries

Country	1999	2008	2013
EU28	**75.8**	**77.9**	**75.0**
Germany	76.4	80.1	82.3
Austria	80.7	81.7	78.3
Belgium	74.1	74.7	71.6
Denmark	83.0	83.9	79.5
Slovenia	72.4	77.4	71.6
Spain	75.2	78.1	65.0
Finland	73.9	78.4	74.0
France	74.2	75.5	73.6
Greece	78.5	80.4	62.6
Hungary	68.3	69.0	73.5
Ireland	81.4	80.4	73.0
Italy	72.2	75.4	69.7
Luxembourg	79.9	77.2	78.4
Netherlands	83.6	85.5	81.4
Poland	71.4	73.0	73.6
Portugal	81.8	79.4	71.3
UK	81.2	81.8	81.9
Czech Rep.	80.8	82.0	82.2
Romania	75.9	71.6	74.0
Sweden	78.9	83.5	82.2
BAC	**74.9**	**80.0**	**71.6**

Source: Eurostat (2015/04/22), Eustat (2015/05/18) and own production.

Indicators in Social Protection and Equality

Table 34 measures the risk of poverty[405] for the different countries in the EU over different years for which homogenous data exists. The evolution of data for the BAC is outstanding, because in 2000 it had a rate of risk of poverty of 19.9%, higher than the European average which was 16%. In 2008 the rate of poverty in the Basque society was 17.9%, below the European rate of 23.8%. In 2013 the rate was 22.7% in the BAC and 24.5% in EU.

---

[405] The poverty risk rate is a structural indicator of the EU Lisbon strategy. It measures the proportion of persons with equivalent available income, after receiving social transfers, which are below the threshold of poverty set at 60% of the national average of equivalent available income.

Table 34: People at risk of poverty after social transfers (% of total population)

Country	2005	2008	2013
EU28	***25.7**	***23.8**	**24.5**
Germany	18.4	20.1	20.3
Austria	17.4	20.6	18.8
Belgium	22.6	20.8	20.8
Denmark	17.2	16.3	19.9
Slovenia	18.5	18.5	20.4
Spain	24.3	24.5	27.3
Finland	17.2	17.4	16.0
France	18.9	18.5	18.1
Greece	29.4	28.1	35.7
Hungary	32.1	28.1	33.5
Ireland	25.0	23.7	29.5
Italy	25.0	25.3	28.4
Luxembourg	17.3	15.5	19.0
Netherlands	16.7	14.9	15.9
Poland	45.3	30.5	25.8
Portugal	26.1	26.0	27.5
UK	24.8	23.2	24.8
Czech Rep.	19.6	15.3	14.6
Romania	:	44.2	40.4
Sweden	14.4	14.9	16.4
BAC	**(1) 19.6**	**17.9**	**(2) 22.7**

Source: Basque Government, Department of Employment and Social Policies, *Encuesta de pobreza y desigualdades sociales*, Eurostat (2015/05/05), Eustat (2015/05/05) and own production.

In the same way, we have in table 35 the distribution of income in the year 2011 (Gini index and extreme poverty), in which the Basque Community appears among the most egalitarian in the EU.

Table 35: Distribution of income 2011 among the most egalitarian countries in the EU

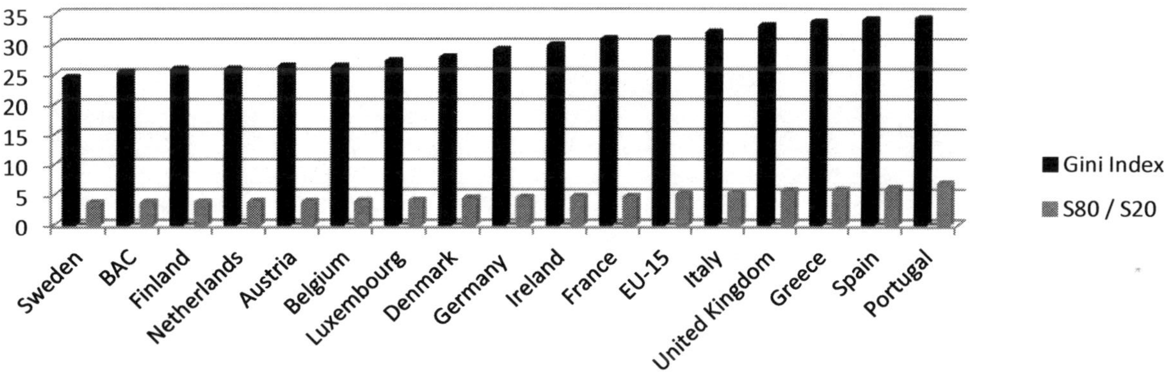

Source: ALBERDI. A., *La economía vasca ante el cambio de era (1955-2025): Del crecimiento al desarrollo*, 2014.

Table 36 shows the dispersion of regional employment rates[406] in the Basque case by districts. The coefficient in this case decreased slightly with the passage of time, until it reached 3.7 in 2008 (4.1 in 2013), and therefore, far below the community average which was 11.2 for the same year (14 in 2013).

Table 36: Dispersion of regional employment rates

Country	1999	2008	2013
EU28	**13.0**	**11.2**	**14**
Germany	5.5	4.6	4.2
Austria	2.0	3.8	3.9
Belgium	7.8	8.6	9.3
Slovakia	8.3	8.3	7.9
Spain	10.8	7.7	11.3
Finland	1.3	6.2	4.7
France	7.1	6.4	6.8
Greece	5.7	3.5	5.2
Ireland	9.2	9.7	7.3
Poland	4.8	4.5	4.8
Portugal	3.4	3.3	4.1
UK	7.2	5.1	5.2
Sweden	4.8	2.4	2.8
BAC	**6.5**	***3.7**	**4.1**

Source: Basque Government, Department of employment and social policies, *Censo del mercado de trabajo*, Eurostat (2015/01/07) and own production.

406 The dispersion of regional employment rates is a structural indicator of the EU Lisbon strategy. It shows the variation coefficient of regional employment rates (level 2 of the NUTS) for each country. In the case of the BAC a comparison is made of the indicator by districts.

The following analysis data refers to long-term unemployment rates,[407] Table 37, by countries in the European Union. According to data offered in the BAC the long-term unemployment rate was 6.5% in 2000, considerably higher than the rate in Europe which was 4.1%. The reduction was drastic over the period analyzed up to 2008, which it fell to 0.9%, below the 2.6% average rate in Europe. But this has changed, according to the last data, and in 2012 it was 6.1 in the Basque Community, 4.6 in the EU. Another subject to reflect on.

Table 37: Long-term unemployment rates by countries

Country	2000	2008	2012
EU27	**4.1**	**2.6**	**4.6**
Germany	4.1	4.0	2.5
Austria	1.0	0.9	1.1
Belgium	3.7	3.3	3.4
Spain	4.9	2.0	11.1
France	3.5	2.9	4.1
Ireland	3.1	3.6	4.9
Italy	1.6	1.7	9.1
Netherlands	4.5	2.5	3.0
Portugal	1.9	4.0	7.7
UK	1.4	1.4	2.7
Sweden	1.4	0.8	1.5
BAC	**6.5**	**0.9**	**6.1**

Source: Eurostat (2014/02/07), Eustat (201/02/14) and own production.

407 The long-term unemployment rate is a structural indicator of the EU Lisbon strategy. It reflects long-term unemployed, over 12 months, as a percentage of the total active population aged 15 to 64.

Tables 38 and 39 refer to expenditure on social protection per inhabitant and to the European ranking in social protection respectively.

Table 38: Expenditures Per Capita in Social Protection

Expenditures per capita in social protection					
Country	**2000**	**2002**	**2004**	**2007**	**2010**
BAC	3,616	4,110	4,719	5,785	7,209
Spain	3,130	3,900	4,126	4,536	5,198
EU-28	:	:	:	*6,224	6,742

Source: Eurostat (2014/06/13), Eustat (2014/07728) and own production.

We should highlight that between 2000 and 2007 (despite not counting all Basque expenditure on social protection due to methodological reasons), an appreciable convergence with Europe took place with regard to expenditure on social protection. Data for 2010 shows that this convergence was already overcome by that time.

Table 39: Expenditure in Social Protection: European Ranking.

2002			2006			2010		
1	Luxemb.	12,516	1	Luxemb.	14,328	1	Luxemb.	16,114
2	Denmark	10,586	2	Denmark	11.556	2	Denmark	13,229
3	Sweden	9.552	3	Sweden	10,474	3	Netherl.	10,690
4	Austria	8,403	4	Netherl.	9,315	4	Sweden	10,640
5	Netherl.	8,378	5	Austria	8,687	5	Ireland	10,129
6	Germany	8,216	6	France	8,674	6	Austria	9,502
7	France	8,080	7	Finland	8,202	7	France	9,366
8	Belgium	7,389	8	UK	8,100	8	Finland	9,196
9	UK	7,210	9	Germany	8,053	9	Belgium	8,860
10	Finland	7,140	10	Belgium	7,934	10	Germany	8,804
11	Italy	6,196	11	Ireland	7,210	11	UK	8,250
12	Ireland	5,940	12	Italy	6,563	12	BAC	7,209
13	BAC	4,110	13	BAC	5,394	13	Italy	7,001
14	Spain	3,900	14	Greece	4,488	14	Spain	5,198
15	Greece	3,601	15	Spain	4,393	15	Greece	4,980
16	Portugal	3,335	16	Portugal	3,637	16	Cyprus	4,127
17	Slovenia	3,136	17	Cyprus	3,515	17	Portugal	4,069

18	Cyprus	2,763	18	Slovenia	3,430	18	Slovenia	3,765
19	Malta	2,034	19	Malta	2,233	19	Malta	2,632
20	Czech R.	1,707	20	Hungary	2,059	20	Czech R.	2,229
21	Hungary	1,582	21	Czech R.	1,948	21	Hungary	1,963
22	Slovakia	1,196	22	Poland	1,323	22	Croatia	1,819
23	Poland	1,173	23	Slovakia	1,246	23	Slovakia	1,566
24	Estonia	785	24	Estonia	1,147	24	Poland	1,561
25	Lithuania	621	25	Lithuania	938	25	Estonia	1,551
26	Latvia	614	26	Latvia	863	26	Lithuania	1,316
27	Romania	366	27	Romania	549	27	Latvia	1,135
28	Bulgaria	:	28	Bulgaria	478	28	Romania	930
29	Croatia	:	29	Croatia	:	29	Bulgaria	709
	EU-28	:		EU-28	*6171		EU-28	6,742

*EU 27

Source: Eurostat (2014-06-13), Eustat (2014-07-28) and own production.

Life Expectancy Index

The life expectancy index is one of the three parameters used by the United Nations to measure the Human Development Index (HDI). Table 40 reflects the HDI produced on a world level by the United Nations for 2007, in which, as we will later analyze, the Basque Country occupied third position, disaggregated in its three components: life expectancy index, education index, and GDP index.

Table 40: Human development index world top ranking as of 2007

Human development index world top ranking as of 2007				
Country	Human develop. index	Life expect. index	Education Index	GPD Index
Iceland	0.968	0.94	0.98	0.99
Norway	0.968	0.91	0.99	1.00
BAC	0.964	0.93	0.99	0.97
Australia	0.962	0.93	0.99	0.96
Ireland	0.959	0.89	0.99	0.99
Sweden	0.956	0.93	0.98	0.97

With regard to Table 41, life expectancy is analyzed and a world ranking by countries is established for 2007 and 2013. It is therefore striking that life expectancy in the Basque Country was 80.9 years in 2007 (with the same position as in the human development index on a general level, third place in the ranking on a world level, in this case just behind Japan and Iceland) and 82.7 in 2013.

Table 41: Life expectancy index world top ranking

2007			2013*		
1	Japan	82.3	1	Monaco	86.5
2	Islandia	81.5	2	Japan	84.6
3	BAC	80.9	3	Andorra	84.2
4	Switzerland	81.3	4	Singapore	84.0
5	Australia	80.9	5	Hong Kong	83.8
6	Sweden	80.5	6	San Marino	83.5
7	Spain	80.8	7	Iceland	83.3
8	Canada	80.3	8	Italy	83.1
9	Italy	80.3	9	Austrlia	83.0
10	Israel	80.3	10	Sweden	83.0
11	France	80.2	11	Switzerland	82.8
12	Norway	79.8	12	BAC	82.7
13	New Zeal.	79.8	13	Canada	82.5
14	Austria	79.4	14	Spain	82.5
15	Netherlands	79.2	15	France	82.3

Source: PNUD and Eustat - 2007 data. *OMS and Eustat – 2013 data and own production.

Commitment to Gender Equality

The commitment to equality between men and women in our society deserves a special reflection due to its importance. For this reason Tables 42, 43, and 44 provide us with information to assess the commitment of Basque society to equality.

Firstly, in Table 42 we can conclude that the law on equality, approved by the Basque Parliament in February 2005, was the key to increasing the presence of women in elected positions of public office. The influence of the Basque regulations, reflected in 2005, 2009, and 2014, in contrast to the presence of women in the Basque Parliament (53%, 46%, 46%), with that of women in the Spanish Congress and Senate (36% and 29% respectively) or in the European Parliament, which was 36%.

Table 42: Women equality (% of elected women at the Basque, Spanish and European parliaments)

	2001	2005	2009	2014
BAC	37.3	53.3	46.7	46.6
Spain: Congress	29.9	36	36.3	14.1
Spain: Senate	24.3	25.1	28.2	29.0
European Parliament	30	31	36*	36*

Source: Emakunde, Inmujeres, European Parliament and own production, April 2015.

With regard to Table 43, this measures the Gender Development Index (GDI)[408] on a State level and refers to the years between 1985 and 2005. Here we can observe how in 2005 the Basque Country was at the head of the state in the GDI.

Table 43: Gender Development Index in the Spanish State

GDI	1985	1995	2000	2005
BAC	0.854 (2nd)	0.902 (3rd)	0.926 (2nd)	0.938 (1st)
CCN	0.852 (3rd)	0.904 (2nd)	0.925 (3rd)	0.936 (2nd)
Madrid Community	0.860 (1st)	0.912 (1st)	0.940 (1st)	0.936 (3rd)
State	0.825	0.873	0.895	0.903

Source: Rev. Esp. Salud Pública 2010. Vol. 84, N° 1, *Geopolitical Development Inequalities in Gender in Spain 1980–2005. A Structural Determinant of Health* and own production.

[408] The Gender Development Index is the non-weighted average of the indices of life expectancy at birth, education, and income equally distributed between women and men.

In the third table, Table 44, a deeper analysis of the GDI and its three factors is shown. It can be clearly seen that more emphasis must be made in the future to redress the balance: income, i.e. the salary gap.

Table 44: BAC "Gender Development Index" composition

GDI of Basque Autonomous Community		
GDI	**1985**	**2005**
Compound index	0.854	0.938
Life Expectancy index	0.876 W (0.826 M)	0.946 W (0.893 M)
Education index	0.809 W (0.923 M)	1.000 W (0.998 M)
Income index	0.711 W (0.908 M)	0.876 W (1.000 M)

Source: Revista Española de Salud Pública, 2010, vol. 84, No. 1, *Geopolitical Development Inequalities in Gender in Spain 1980-2005. A Structural Determinant of Health* and own production.

Indicators of Environmental Strategy. Energy Efficiency and Environmental Sustainability

Table 45 includes the data on total "greenhouse gas emissions"[409] for all the countries of the EU. It reflects an unstoppable increase up to 2002 and a reduction and containment from then on. It also reflects the great effort that the Basque society made, particularly to regards to control emissions produced by transport,[410] a specific issue

---

409 Total "greenhouse gas emissions" is a structural indicator of the EU Lisbon strategy. This indicator measures the evolution from the base year 1990=100, of the percentage variation of the volume of gas emissions equivalent to CO2, and Kyoto objective for 2010.

410 In May 2007 the Basque Government approved the Program of Economic Context and Reforms for Growth and Social Progress 2006–2009, as realization of the coalition agreement for the Government 2005–2009 inspired by the renewed Lisbon strategy, in which it states, "sustainability is at risk mainly in the management of energy policy and the transport sector which

for the Basque Country,[411] over the following years to 2007 in order to reach the Kyoto commitment[412] and to fulfill the objective established in the "Basque Climate Change Plan 2008–2012."[413]

---

should respond to the energy and mobility needs posed by the globalized economy and today's society and do so in such a way that minimizes the effects of climate change and the damage to the quality of life, health and the urban environment."

411 The latest data refer to 2007 (Sustainable Transport Plan 2002–2012, indicators TMA, DTOP-DMAOT), and conclude that mobility is increasing and cars are the means of transport that emit most CO2 into the atmosphere. They continue to gain ground as the main satisfaction for this need, with generalized presence in all geographic areas regardless of the reason for the trip. The comparison between 2003 and 2007, according to the same indicators, reveals an increase in mobility, measured in terms of trips per person and day, from 2.75 to 2.98, and a modal division with an increase in the presence of the car, which increases from 34.6% to 38.6% of total trips. Public transport, over this same period 2003 to 2007, also progresses, although slightly, rising from 13.8% to 14.6% of trips, in detriment to trips on foot. Other modes of transport fell 0.4%. The modification of this modal division was one of the main objectives of the "Sustainable Transport Plan 2002–2012."

412 The Kyoto objective for the Spanish State is 115 for 2010, with regard to 1990=100.

413 "The Basque Plan Against Climate Change 2008–2012," approved by the Basque Government on December 4, 2007 sets the objective of reducing the average level of emissions between 2008 and 2012 to 14% with regard to the reference year, i.e. 114 with regard to 1990=100.

Table 45: Evolution of greenhouse gas emissions by countries. Year 1990 is 100 precent

Country	1998	2002	2008	2011
EU 27	**93.4**	**91.8**	**90.3**	**83.0**
Belgium	106.04	101.1	96.4	85.1
Czech Rep.	74.0	72.3	72.9	68.4
Denmark	110.4	101.2	94.3	83.4
Germany	86.6	83.4	79.3	74.5
Ireland	118.4	125.4	125.1	105.8
Greece	117.1	120.9	124.6	109.6
Spain	119.9	140.5	143.0	126.4
France	104.2	100.2	97.1	88.9
Italy	104.8	108.1	105.4	95.3
Luxembourg	71.8	91.5	101.6	100.2
Netherlands	103.6	103.3	99.1	94.7
Austria	105.3	110.6	112.8	107.6
Poland	89.5	80.8	87.8	87.6
Portugal	126.6	144.4	129.9	116.5
Slovenia	104.7	108.3	116.3	105.9
Finland	101.7	108.9	100.8	96.6
Sweden	101.8	97.2	88.9	86.0
UK	92.8	87.7	85.0	74.8
Australia	109.8	120.3	129.9	131.4
Belarus	62.3	55.5	62.7	64.3
Canada	113.7	120.3	126.7	118.6
Switzerland	99.1	97.6	101.3	94.4
USA	110.4	112.4	117.1	110.1
Russia	60.6	61.8	65.6	66.1
Japan	106.2	104.0	107.8	99.3
Norway	107.0	111.0	112.5	109.1
New Zeal.	114.3	120.8	124.7	120.4
Turkey	145.5	148.2	202.2	213.4
Ukraine	46.0	43.0	46.9	41.2
Iceland	100.6	109.5	130.9	131.6
Liechtenst.	108.9	110.6	106.0	101.7
BAC	109.6	128.8	120.0	99.3

Source: Eurostat (2014/03/19), Eustat (2014/07/28) and own production.

Table 46 presents the indicator of the energy intensity of the economy.[414] We can see that the investment in the Basque economy maintains energy intensity rates well below the community average.

Table 46: Energy Intensity of Economy by Countries

Country	1998	2002	2008	2011
EU 27	**93.4**	**91.8**	**90.3**	**83.0**
Belgium	106.04	101.1	96.4	85.1
Germany	86.6	83.4	79.3	74.5
Ireland	118.4	125.4	125.1	105.8
Greece	117.1	120.9	124.6	109.6
Spain	119.9	140.5	143.0	126.4
France	104.2	100.2	97.1	88.9
Italy	104.8	108.1	105.4	95.3
Netherlands	103.6	103.3	99.1	94.7
Austria	105.3	110.6	112.8	107.6
Poland	89.5	80.8	87.8	87.6
Portugal	126.6	144.4	129.9	116.5
Finland	101.7	108.9	100.8	96.6
Sweden	101.8	97.2	88.9	86.0
UK	92.8	87.7	85.0	74.8
Australia	109.8	120.3	129.9	131.4
Canada	113.7	120.3	126.7	118.6
Switzerland	99.1	97.6	101.3	94.4
USA	110.4	112.4	117.1	110.1
Russia	60.6	61.8	65.6	66.1
Japan	106.2	104.0	107.8	99.3
New Zeal.	114.3	120.8	124.7	120.4
BAC	109.6	128.8	120.0	99.3

Source: Eurostat (2014/03/19), Eustat (2014/07/28) and own production.

---

414 The indicator of "energy intensity of the economy" is a structural indicator of the EU Lisbon strategy. It measures gross domestic energy consumption (measured in kilograms of equivalent oil) divided by GDP (in the table, at constant prices 1995=100) per thousand euros.

As seen in Table 47, the Basque economy occupies a privileged position in the European ranking. Although we should also notice that ahead of the Basque economy in the ranking are economies with deep rooted industries and high consumers of energy, such as Ireland.

Table 47: Energy intensity of economy. Top 10 European rnking

2003		
1	Ireland	101.2
2	Denmark	105.2
3	Italy	130.9
4	UK	132.0
5	BAC	135.1
6	Austria	139.4
7	Luxembourg	153.0
8	Germany	156.4
9	Spain	158.9
10	Netherlands	163.2
	EU 28	169.2

2009		
1	Ireland	89.5
2	Denmark	94.1
3	UK	109.9
4	Italy	121.2
5	BAC	121.6
6	Austria	125.7
7	Spain	137.2
8	Luxembourg	137.4
9	Germany	138.9
10	France	148.8
	EU 28	148.9

2012		
1	Ireland	82.8
2	Denmark	87.2
3	UK	105.1
4	BAC	111.4
5	Italy	117.3
6	Austria	123.9
7	Germany	129.2
8	Luxembourg	133.8
9	Spain	136.4
10	France	142.9
	EU 28	143.2

Source: Eurostat (2014/06/16)), Eustat (2014/07/28) and own production.

The conclusion of this section is clear, we must persist. But the Basque society is making a huge effort, within a transversal and comprehensive strategy to fulfill the objective pathway for emissions agreed in Kyoto and the results reached over recent years are heading in the right direction.

Summary-conclusion of Results. Human Development Index

The Human Development Index (HDI) is a synthetic indicator of the level of development relating to a country and is produced by the United Nations. It is an indicator that, in our judgement, presents limitations to diagnose the degree of development of a country, which is relevant in terms of the modern concept of human development,[415] but which, bearing in mind that it also assesses income, education, and life expectancy, offers us a much more "human" measurement than usual, a question which was incidentally called — "from production to well-being" — in 2010 by the Commission presided over by Joseph E. Stieglitz and which reported to President Sarkozy.[416] This was the fundamental reason for the Basque Government requesting from the United Nations the chance to incorporate the Autonomous Community of the Basque Country as a country in the report on the HDI.

---

[415] The limitations of the HDI are clear, as we have shown in section V.3.2. Growth does not always generate development, either because income is concentrated among few people, or because of unequal living conditions between men and women, or because a system of liberties, participation and democracy either does or does not exist, or because there is no commitment to sustainability, etc.

[416] "The Commission on the Measurement of Economic Performance and Social Progress," created in February 2008, proposed by the President of the French Republic, Mr. Sarkozy, under the Presidency of Mr. Joseph Stiglitz and the Coordinator being Jean Paul Fitoussi, concludes his report, made public in June 2010, among many other things with the following recommendation: "From production to well-being... to shift emphasis from measuring economic production to measuring people´s well-being."

Table 48: World Ranking Evolution of the "Human Development Index" of United Nations

2001			2005			2007		
1	Norway	0.939	1	Norway	0.963	1	Iceland	0.968
2	Australia	0.936	2	Iceland	0.956	2	Norway	0.968
3	Canada	0.936	3	BAC	0.955	3	BAC	0.964
4	Sweden	0.936	4	Australia	0.955	4	Australia	0.962
5	Belgium	0.935	5	Luxembourg	0.949	5	Canada	0.961
6	USA	0.934	6	Canada	0.949	6	Ireland	0.959
7	Iceland	0.932	7	Sweden	0.949	7	Sweden	0.956
8	Netherlands	0.931	8	Switzerland	0.947	8	Switzerland	0.955
9	BAC	0.930	9	Ireland	0.946	9	Japan	0.953
10	Japan	0.928	10	Belgium	0.945	10	Netherlands	0.953
11	Finland	0.925	11	USA	0.944	11	France	0.952
12	Switzerland	0.924	12	Japan	0.943	12	Finland	0.952
13	Luxembourg	0.924	13	Netherlands	0.943	13	USA	0.951
21	Spain	0.908	22	Spain	0.928	15	Spain	0.949

Source: PNUD, Eustat and own production

The request was accepted by the United Nations, in the following table (Table 48) we can observe the performance of the country over time (unfortunately the last report in which the Basque Community was measured was in 2007, so it is necessary to recover the measurement of this index by UN) and in the world ranking.

The evolution is clear in the HDI: the index rose from 0.930 in 2001 to 0.955 in 2005 and to 0.964 in 2007. With regard to the world ranking, we occupied 9th place in 2001 and moved up to 3rd place, behind Iceland and Norway, in 2007. It is, therefore, an outstanding evolution in the global context.

Confidence in the Basque Public Administration Index

The Basque public administrations have generally carried out a rational use of the instruments and resources that derive from the Basque self-government, particularly from the Economic Agreement. It could be no other way, because the mechanism of fiscal co-responsibility which, expressed in the Economic Agreement, presides over the relation between the Basque and Spanish administrations, "rewards" whoever manages the agreement well and "penalizes" whoever does so badly. The Basque administrations live off their own resources, they therefore have to take care of revenue as well as be rigorous in relation to public expenditure.

In Table 49 we observe the evolution of the Basque Government outstanding debt from 1998 to 2014. Here a rigorous performance can be observed in relation to public deficit and a cautious one with regard to debt. Indebtedness was recurred to more during the mid 90s — industrial policies, social policies and investment in infrastructures — due to the crisis suffered at that time and to play an anticyclic role as required of administrations when things go wrong. This caution is noticeable once again in the accounts of the Basque Government when in the second half of the 90s and first years of the 21st century, with an improvement in the economy, the percentage of outstanding debt was reduced. This attitude has enabled — the anti cyclic role of the administration — as we can see in the figures for 2014, again resort to public debt to combat the crisis in recent years.

Table 49: Evolution of "Outstanding Public Debt" of the Basque Government (% GDP)

	1995	2000	2005	2008	2012
Public Debt	12.9	8.2	7.2	5	15.2

Years 2004-2009: SEC 95. Years 2010-2012: SEC 2010.
Source: Eustat (2014/10/23) and own production.

We should stress that cautious and rigorous management of public finances by all the Basque administrations in general enabled the BAC to reach some of the lowest levels in Europe of gross consolidated debt in the Basque public sector, as reflected in Table 50. What is more important is to transmit the image of a responsible country that generates confidence and possesses the resources to develop ideas.

Table 50: Gross consolidated debt of Basque public sector in relation to GDP. European Ranking

2000			2005			2012		
1	Estonia	5.1	1	Estonia	4.6	1	Estonia	9.7
2	Luxembourg	6.2	2	Luxembourg	6.1	2	**BAC**	15.2
3	**BAC**	8.2	3	**BAC**	7.2	3	Bulgaria	18.0
4	Latvia	12.4	4	Latvia	12.5	4	Luxembourg	21.4
5	Czech Rep.	17.8	5	Romania	15.8	5	Sweden	36.4
6	Romania	22.5	6	Lithuania	18.3	6	Romania	37.3
7	Lithuania	23.6	7	Slovenia	26.7	7	Lithuania	39.9
8	Slovenia	26.3	8	Ireland	27.3	8	Latvia	40.9
9	Ireland	35.1	9	Bulgaria	27.5	9	Czech REp.	45.5
10	Poland	36.8	10	Czech Rep.	28.4	10	Denmak	45.6
	Spain	59.4		Spain	43.2		Spain	84.4
	EU27	61.9		EU27	62.8		EU27	83.5

Source: GPD base 2010, Eurostat (2014-10-21), Eustat (2014/10/22), *Cuentas económicas de las administraciones vascas* and own production.

The two effects of this rigorous management of resources are: firstly — up to the downgrading (from AAA to AA+ with a negative outlook) of the Rating by Standard & Poor's[417] — in April 2010, the Basque Government and its financial performance were assessed to have the maximum qualification by international rating agencies.[418] Secondly, there is the paradox that the Basque Country was the only stateless nation in the world that had a higher rating than the Spanish state.

In conclusion to this third chapter in which we have analyzed the results of the Basque strategy of sustainable human development, Table 51 shows some of the features of the socio-economic evolution of the Autonomous Community of the Basque Country, from the beginning of self government in 1980, with a reference to the year — 1986 — when we formally joined Europe, another reference to the period from 1998 up to 2008.

We should highlight the huge growth in per capita income of Basque citizens since the introduction of self-government until 2008. In absolute terms per capita income increased tenfold, rising from 3,132 euros in 1980 to 30,917 euros in 2008. With regard to convergence in income with Europe, the increase has been striking. When we joined Europe in 1986, per capita income for Basque citizens was 90% of average European income, and in 2008, only twenty-two years later it was 134%, placing the Basque Country among the top three countries in Europe with regard to per capita income.

In order to understand this huge transformation, to give it concrete meaning, we should take a look at the enlightening data shown in Table 52 ("Training Level of Workers in Employment in the Basque Country, 1977–

---

417 Standard & Poor's, Global Credit Portal, Ratings Direct, Research Update: Spain's Basque Country Downgraded To 'AA+' On Sizable Debt Burden Growth; Outlook Negative. Rating Action, on April 29, 2010, Standard & Poor's Ratings Services lowered its long-term issuer credit rating on Spain's Autonomous Community of the Basque Country to 'AA+' from 'AAA'. The Outlook is negative.

418 Up to April 2010 the Ratings were: Standard & Poor's, AAA Outlook stable; Moody's, AAA Outlook stable; Fitch, AAA stable.

2013"): from my point of view they show the tremendous creation of human capital and give meaning to this whole experience.

The conclusion is therefore clear: the results confirm the hypothesis that self-government in the "Basque case" has meant more welfare, and that things can be done differently. The "Basque experience" shows that a strategy of sustainable human development can be developed, that the social state is not an illusion, but something desirable and practicable.

Table 51: Main indicators evolution of the BAC from the beginning of its political autonomy

Indicator	New auton. in 1980	Entry in Europe 1986	1998	2003	2008
GDP Per Capita, Current prices, €	3,132	6,132	16,4	23,306	29,959
Convergence in income with Europe (EU=100)	89	90	108.9	125	129
Investment to the R&D (%)	0.07	0.5	1.11	1.39	1.99
Unemployment	12.54	24.57	17.8	8.6	14.6

Source: Eurostat, Eustat and own production.

Table 52: Training Level of Workers in Employment in the Basque Country (1977–2013)

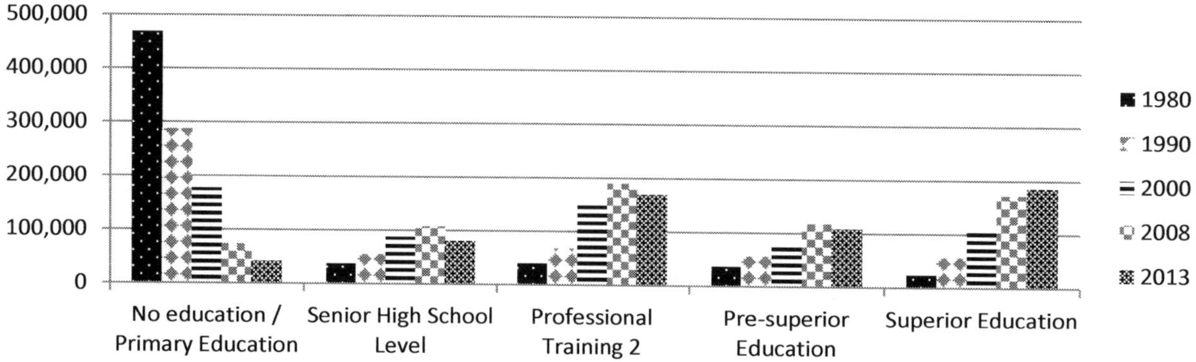

Source: ALBERDI, A., *La economía vasca ante el cambio de era (1955-2015): del crecimiento al desarrollo*, Basque Group of the Spanish Chapter of the Club of Rome, Bilbao, 2014, Fundación Bancaja e IVI (Instituto Valenciano de Investigaciones Científicas), *Capital humano en España y su distribución provincial*, Januari, 2014.

7

Keys to the Success of the Basque Experience of Sustainable Human Development

We have emphasized that the Basque people are an ancient people who have adapted to the changing times to be among the world leaders in sustainable human development. The priority objective for the near future is to consolidate as a people among the leading group in the world with regard to sustainable human development. This will only be possible if the project is based on two pillars: identity and innovation. Roots and wings in a world ever more characterized by relations between cultures, rather than between States, and in which "culture is both a divisive and unifying force."[419] Identity to guarantee our survival as a people, open to the world and innovation, to project our people creatively and collectively towards the future. Prof. Boudreaux states, "the Basque Case presents an ancient people who have embraced modernity, who have neither forgotten their roots nor allowed them to prevent innovation."[420]

---

[419] HUNTINGTON, S.P., *The clash of civilizations and reconfiguration of the world order.* Barcelona, ed. Paidós, 1997, p. 23: "In the cold post war world, culture is both a divisive and unifying force. People separated by ideology but united by culture unite, as the two German states did (…) Societies united by ideology or historic circumstances, but divided by civilization, either break up (like the Soviet Union, Yugoslavia and Bosnia) or are subject to great tension, such as the case of Ukraine, Nigeria, Sudan, India, Sri Lanka and many others. The countries with cultural affinities collaborate economically and politically."

[420] BOUDREAUX, K., contribution made in relation to "The Basque Case: A Comprehensive Model for Sustainable Human Development." Research program at the bilateral meeting held at Mercartus Centre, George Mason University, Washington, January 28, 2011.

In a world characterized by a design of globalization that is full of imbalances and turbulences[421] we have analyzed "the Basque case" and how it reflects a model of a country brought about through sustainable human development. A strategy that is in tune with the EU Lisbon Strategy[422] and which emphasizes productivity and quality employment. The success of this policy has favored higher social expenditure and made the sustainability of public finances possible. Sustained success in the commitment to a powerful system of innovation has turned out to be fundamental in raising the speed of growth in productivity and contributing decisively to sustainability and to solving environmental problems. Thus, Prof. Colomer highlights the importance of self-government and fiscal autonomy: "The Basque Model represents a potential governance structure in the emerging European Union system."[423]

In the last chapter we reviewed the results that endorse the strategy of sustainable human development developed in Basque society. Results which objectively show that beyond "economic rationality,"[424] in the "Basque case,"

---

[421] SOROS, G., *The crisis of global capitalism: Open society in danger.* Madrid, ed. Debate, 1999, ps. 21 and 22: "The development of a global economy has not coincided with the development of a global society. The basic unit of political and social life is still the nation-state. International law and international institutions where they exist, lack the necessary power to stop war or large scale abuses against human rights in some countries. Ecological threats are not tackled appropriately. Global finance markets are largely out of the control of national and international authorities. I maintain that the current situation is not very solid and is unsustainable."

[422] Lisbon strategy adopted by the European Union in 2000 for the whole decade, reviewed in 2005.

[423] COLOMER, J., contribution made in relation to "The Basque Case: A Comprehensive Model for Sustainable Human Development." Research program at the bilateral meeting held at Georgetown University, Washington, January 25, 2011.

[424] BUARQUE, C., *Un nuevo mundo feliz.* Madrid, Santillana Ediciones Generales, 2010, p.221, states that: "Economic rationality is logical, which, without taking into consideration the social objectives or ethical values, explains how to achieve a greater

it has been possible "to look the market in the eye" while "looking people in the eye" at the same time.

The current chapter aims to go further and condense and define the reasons for the satisfactory results of the "Basque experience," the key differentials that have made the strategy of sustainable human development in Basque society possible over the last 35 years, and specifically over the first years of the 21st century. These were, in our opinion: conception and vision of a country; shared leadership; and commitment to the real economy; social state; and identity and innovation.

One: Conception and Vision of a Country

From a convinced and militant Europeanism and in a Europe unfinished and imperfect but apart in that it's "very windy and very cold for all," the Basque people and the Basque Autonomous Community have claimed active protagonism, their own place and their own voice. We have tried to contribute, humbly but with conviction, with our culture, language, way of understanding work, education, companies, savings, solidarity, society, our "model" of sustainable human development. The Basque experience has been possible because a vision of a country existed.[425]

---

economic performance during the process to transform nature into goods and services for man."

[425] TAYLOR, Ch., "Why democracy needs patriotism." In NUSSBAUM, M.C., *The limits of patriotism: Identity, belonging and `world citizenship.'* Barcelona, ed. Paidós, 1999, ps. 145 and 146: "in the modern world we cannot do anything without patriotism. (…) A citizen democracy can only work if most of its members are convinced that their political society is a common Enterprise of considerable transcendence, and that the importance of this enterprise is so vital that they are willing to participate as far as possible to ensure it continues to work like a democracy. Such participation not only requires that citizens commit to the common project, but that they also feel a special bond with those other people who participate in the project. maybe this is the point that most threatens the solidity of the most contemporary democracies. (…). and these policies demand a high degree of mutual commitment. (…). In short, patriotism is as necessary as

A country open to the world but with roots. The aim is integration, to participate in our own space in the globalized world and portray our identity as a people; to defend the Basque identity, not in confrontation, but in collaboration with other identities. In this respect Prof. Aligica underlines "how the document had managed to distance from chauvinistic interpretations of identity. In its own right the example of the Basque identity in economics could be used as a separate example of good practice."[426] Indeed, "we can love what we are, without hating what we are not" as Kofi Annan[427] wisely put it. To be enriched through universal culture and contribute with our own unique culture. As Prof. Cowen points out: "cultures that place a high value on human capital create more resistant economies."[428] All of this helps form the reasoning for the road we have taken.

Two: Shared Leadership: Strategic Public-private Alliance

A vision of country is indispensable, "when there is no vision, the people perish" Franklin D. Roosevelt said with undoubted effect.[429] Without vision there is no leadership,

---

cosmopolitism because the modern democratic States are particularly demanding enterprises with self government. They demand their members contribute greatly, as they require a much greater solidarity towards compatriots than towards humanity in general. And the success of these enterprises depends on its members experiencing a strong feeling of mutual identification."

[426] ALIGICA, P., contribution made in relation to "The Basque Case: A Comprehensive Model for Sustainable Human Development." Research program at the bilateral meeting held at George Mason University, Washington, January 26, 2011.

[427] ANNAN, K., Ex Secretary General of the United Nations. Speech made in the Nobel Prize Award Ceremony, Oslo, Norway, December 10, 2001.

[428] COWEN, T., contribution made in relation to "The Basque Case: A Comprehensive model for Sustainable Human Development." Research program at the bilateral meeting held at the Mercartus Center, George Mason University, Washington, January 24, 2011.

[429] ROOSEVELT, F.D., Inaugural speech to the 32nd presidency of the United States, Washington, March 4, 1933.

but with a vision of a country the most successful of leaderships is possible: leadership shared between the public administration and social initiative.

The Autonomous Community of the Basque Country, starting with its federal structure, needs complicity between different public institutions and between the latter and society. Thus the country and its agents have configured a closely woven network of relations over the last 35 years of the development of Basque self-government, which has enabled the design and planning of a whole range of innovative legal initiatives or socio-economic plans and programs (Plan against poverty, Science, technology and innovation plan, Plan against climate change, etc.). They have all had a common attribute that conferred upon them substantial strength: they were produced, developed, and led by a shared effort.

Indypaul Johar, underlines "the serious need for radical institutional reform in Western societies; particularly in the way we view or relationship with natural and social capital" and expresses "a need for a radical democracy model that will see a greater diffusion of power and decision making." In this sense Mr. Johar states, "this radical democracy has been manifested in the mechanisms that create the Basque sense of solidarity and enabled policies focused on the concept of improving the Basque Country as a whole." And adds that "the Basque Case is an exceptional example; it has an interdependent economy, a diffused distribution of power, has enacted considerable institutional change that has kept both the government and the private sector close to the people, and there is genuine social responsibility in the private sector."[430]

As has been highlighted in our previous discussion we concede, in our approach, a central role to the institutions in the explanation of how economies work. We are not only saying that no economy can work in the absence of a suitable institutional framework, but that economic results will

---

[430] JOHAR, I., CEO of Project 00, London, a contribution made in relation to "The Basque Case: A Comprehensive Model for Sustainable Human Development." Research program at the bilateral meeting held in London, March 29, 2011.

depend, fundamentally, on their capacity to create an institutional framework that acts as a driving force for vitality and creativity in the society which it must serve. In short, and following the criteria of D. North, we can say that political, economic, and social institutions constitute the regulations to define the restrictions and incentives that guide the action of agents, and we insist, paraphrasing the author, that the differential performance of economies through time is fundamentally influenced by the way that institutions evolve.[431]

In this sense we are recognizing the value of the institutionalist approach, more in terms of fundamental principles and specific practical recommendations than as a body of thought with enough capacity to become a theoretical framework of reference. It should be said, in fact, that we are not identified by an established theory capable of providing a determined, more or less complete vision of the working of the economy, but that we are facing a set of "under construction" approaches with a growing level of interdisciplinary contributions that prevent us, citing Oriol,[432] from formalizing a compact and consistent classification.[433]

In any case, we should identify some of these original principles that constitute the common patrimony of all visions and the principles we adhere to as vectors of our economic activity.

Firstly, we propose the evolutionary character of economic dynamics ("history matters"), compared to "ahistorical" methodological individualism that presents conventional visions, particularly the traditional neoclassicism of perfect markets and the benevolent

---

431 NORTH, D., *Institutions, institutional change and economic performance.* Mexico, *Fondo de Cultura Economic*, 1993, p. 13.

432 ORIOL, J., "Revision crítica de los aportes del institucionalismo a la teoría and la práctica del desarrollo." *Revista de Economía Institucional*, v. 9, no. 16, First semester, 2007, ps. 121–148.

433 Some qualifying approaches may be seen in: NIELSEN, K., "Review of Institutionalism: Approaches in the Social Sciences; Typology, Dialogue, and Future Prospects." *Research papers 7/01*, Department of Social Sciences, Roskilde University, 2003; PETERS, G: "Institutional Theory in Political Science: The 'new institutionalism.'" London, Rouledge, 1999.

planner.[434] In line with this conception we must recognize, as a consequence of the political, social and economic transformations that are taking place, the growing role to be played by the state in modern times to govern an ever more complex reality. It is true that interventionist approaches can take on many forms, as we can witness with existing differences between, (for example) the Swedish or European variants of this policy, but, in keeping with Heilbroner and Milber, the most probable horizon of a new "classic situation" in economic thought in advanced countries will be marked by a greater application of government power and greater recourse to social coordination sponsored by the Government than was acceptable in the past.[435]

Our work in the field of innovation — an area of economic operations to which we have given key importance and which, in addition, presents a high level of operational complexity — has enabled us to detect the huge insufficiencies that traditional analytical visions present and to adopt a vision that takes into account institutionalist aspects to articulate, explain, and manage our economic reality. It is precisely in the field of innovation where an evolutionary vision of economic activity originates. J. A. Schumpeter brilliantly pointed this out in his *Theory of Economic Development*, consolidated with the work of other authors who have worked in this field.[436] An approach that obliges us to speak of Innovation Systems and the need for institutions and the central role of the public administration

---

[434] See DIXIT, A., *The Making of Economic Policy: A Transaction-Cost Politics Perspective*. Cambridge, MIT Press, 1996.

[435] HEILBRONER, R., and MILBERG, W., *Crisis of vision in modern economic thought*. Barcelona, ed. Paidós, 1998, p. 158.

[436] SCHUMPETER, J.A., *Theory of economic development: Research on profits, capital, credit, interest and economic cycle*. México, Fondo de Cultura Económica, 1967. Work published for the first time in 1912 and which was not understood or acclaimed until the second half of the 20th century. Clearly economic literature offers us a pile of references to justify the line of thought that is consolidated in the field of innovation and technical change; an example is this title, perhaps the most common of all economic texts: NELSON, R., and WINTER, S., *An evolutionary theory of economic change*. Cambridge, Harvard University Press, 1982.

in the construction of these institutions, as seen in the Basque Innovation System.

Logically, institutional change is presented as a fundamental driving force for development and is the fruit of interaction between institutions and organizations (groups of individuals united with a common purpose) in areas of uncertainty and competence. But institutional change will be efficient, if the political and institutional reforms we introduce describe a coherent sequence between institutional change, organizational change, and public policies. We must not forget that the institutional context is the expression of the social structure such that for institutions, especially legal institutions, to be efficient they must be accepted and socially recognized. In the same way and as Oriol says, institutional development policies that merely "transplant" institutions from one context to another, cannot guarantee they will function correctly without the context in which they are confined mattering.[437]

In this sense, each economy, including the Basque economy, must seek its own institutional framework, which must be specific to its own political, social, and economic reality, in order to be efficient. In this regard Prof. Hughes-Hallet praises the efforts of the Basque Country in creating an authority specifically to motivate innovation and expressed a belief that "it was this combination of an investment in human capital and commitment to innovation that enabled a country to change its industrial focus.[438]

Therefore, shared public leadership committed to people and their welfare, together with an unequivocal commitment to building a strategic public-private alliance to generate wealth and progress in Basque society, has enabled this country to boast a very powerful transformation lever that has given us a competitive advantage in our region.

---

[437] ORIOL, J., "Revision crítica de los aportes del institucionalismo a la teoría and la práctica del desarrollo." *Revista de Economía Institucional*, Vol. 9, nº 16, Primer semestre, 2007, p. 143.

[438] HUGES-HALLE, A., contribution made in relation to "The Basque Case: A Comprehensive Model for Sustainable Human Development." Research program at the bilateral meeting held at the School of Public Policy, George Mason University, Washington, January 26, 2011.

Three: Commitment to the Real Economy

Rowing on many occasions upstream against neoliberal intellectual and political thought prevailing in Spain and Europe since the 80s — and against savage criticism from certain media at the service of those political and economic ideologies — the Basque Autonomous Community decidedly and bravely committed to industry and the productive economy through the instruments of self-government acquired at the beginning of the 80s.

This renewed industrialization, commitment to technology and associated knowledge, the recovery of social knowledge leading to the role of the "entrepreneur," the centrality of industry, the company in economic policy, social awareness, and the development of advanced and specialized services for production[439] have all formed part of the foundation on which the strategic development of the Basque Country has been built. The contribution of Lucy Goodhart is noteworthy when she highlights three key factors: "active industrial policy focussed on an innovative economy; clusterisation of industry in productive chains; and the role of government to facilitate the relationship between the economy and society."[440] Also worth mentioning are the comments of Prof. Dube who remarks that "the Basque model is not only defined by a commitment to the real economy but also to its openness to trade and its strong human capital."[441]

---

[439] AZUA, J., *Clusterizar y globalizar la economía: "La magia del proceso."* Bogota, ed. Oveja Negra, 2008, p. 230„ "evolving the concept of innovative manufacturing…beyond simplified labels around the industry dichotomy (manufacturing) against services."

[440] GOODHART, L., Columbia University, New York contribution made in relation to "The Basque Case: A Comprehensive Model for Sustainable Human Development." Research program at the bilateral meeting held in New York, May 12, 2011.

[441] DUBE, O., New York University, contribution made in relation to "The Basque Case: A Comprehensive Model for Sustainable Human Development." Research program at the bilateral meeting held in New York, May 13, 2011.

The decided commitment to industry, to the "real economy", understood as the driving force behind the Basque economic and social project, underwent a moment of great cost in terms of "political erosion", more serious for being unjust, for Basque institutions, but, and this is what is really important, of great social and economic benefit to Basque society as a whole. Furthermore, seeing how each economy is weathering the storm of the crisis we are suffering today, maintaining an economic structure with a large industry component, close on 30% according to GDP, unlike the Spanish and European economies, it has turned out to be a decision with enormous strategic significance today.

Four: Social State; a Strategy with "Eyes and Faces"

The strategy developed would not have been possible without putting people, men and women, at the center of the project. Why build with only 50% of society, if we can do it with 100% of men and women working together? Are soulless projects possible? Is a project possible in which many contribute a lot and a few get almost everything? Is it possible to carry out a project if there is no citizen participation, if people feel left out, if as Koldo Saratxaga and Jabi Salcedo say, people do not feel like they are "co-owners"?[442] People, everybody, are the heart of any political, economic, and social project. [443]

---

[442] SARATXAGA, K. and SALCEDO, J., *El éxito fue la confianza: Una historia real ocurrida en el Pais Vasco en plena crisis del 2008*. Bilbao, ed. K2K, 2010, p. 72: "Just as friendship is not forged through the orders of a long serving sergeant, people do not commit to a project because the Director of the moment or the Strategic Plan or the corresponding Mission, Vision and Values tell them that their commitment to people is total and absolute. This commitment is only possible in a non hierarchical, non militarized structure, based on freedom, trust in people, responsibility; in short, a structure that enables people to participate and be the owners of the project in which they are working."

[443] STIGLITZ, J.E., *Unease in globalization.* Madrid, Santillana Ediciones Generales, 2002, p. 313: "Policies are needed for sustainable, fair and democratic growth. This is the reason for

This is one of the clearest failures of the neoliberal economic-political thought we have suffered in recent years, especially since the oil crisis in the 70s which resulted in the loss of State power to the market, and which was well reflected in that thought attributed to the International Monetary Fund (IMF) that "what does it matter if people are having a hard time, if the economy is doing well."

For this reason, faced with the sacralisation of indispensable macroeconomic policies, although they do not explain the strategic differences in the world, the Basque Autonomous Community committed clearly and energetically, optimizing the instruments of self-government, to sound macroeconomic policies, but always looking into the face and eyes of people. In short, committed to our own and different project, to alternatives in a world in which physical dimensions — who is big? And who is small? — or units of economic efficiency form part of the debate of the past. It is not a question of promoting charity policies, which, as Robert B. Reich says, rarely help the poorest,[444] but of

---

development. Development does not consist of helping a few individuals to get rich or create a handful of absurd protected industries that only benefit the elite of a country; it does not consist of bringing Prada and Benetton, Ralph Lauren or Louis Vuitton to cities for the benefit of the rich, abandoning the countryside poor to their misery (…) Development consists of transforming societies, improving the lives of the poor, allowing everyone the opportunity to progress and have access to health and education."

444 REICH, R. B., *The work of nations: Towards the capitalism of the 21st century*. Madrid, Javier Vergara ed., 1993, p. 276: "No nation is more vividly proud of their charitable acts than the United States; none are committed to such a great number of charity dances, sales and auctions or adhere to good causes. Most of these gestures are sincere; many are admirable. But a more detailed analysis reveals that they and other types of charity rarely truly help the poorest. Between a third and half the donations that come from the Americans that are in the high band of income tax are particularly suspicious. Investigations have revealed that these donations are not directed mainly at social services for citizens with few resources, to improve schools, health care or recreation areas. Instead of this, the contributions end up in places where the rich are inspired, cured or educated: to art museums, concert halls,

guaranteeing people's rights. Speaking of rights, Baroness Noala O' Loan underlines "the strong relationship between self-governance and improved well-being in Basque society."[445]

The building of the Basque Country project can be based on proximity, on what is found nearby, and on understanding the problems to be solved.[446] Based on the conviction that it is well educated people — by paying attention to the education system — and well cared for — by paying attention to the health system and construction of the socio-health space — who guarantee a successful ending to family, company, or country projects. Projects with a critical capacity to discern that banish social, political, economic, and democratic corruption, carrying out a true task of "informal social control."

Consequently, we must consider that there is no economic project without a life project: "a market without values is not a real market, but a flea market." We must not resignedly accept that everything is in the hands of macroeconomic policies, but that there is room for microeconomic policies, to develop our own Basque project. This evidence, which has been emphasized by the current crisis, helped Basque society enormously to find its own way over the last years of the 20th century and at the start of the 21st century.

---

theatres, symphonic orchestras, dance troupes, private hospitals (whose patients have health insurance) and elitist universities."

[445] BARONESS O'LOAN, N., Member of the House of Lords, in a contribution made in relation to "The Basque Case: A Comprehensive Model for Sustainable Human Development." Research program, at the bilateral meeting held at the House of Lords, Westminster, London, March 28, 2011.

[446] GUIBERNAU, M., *Nationalisms.* Barcelona, ed. Ariel, 1996, ps. 150 and 151: "Renewed emphasis acquired by the national identity arises from the need for an identity, both collective and individual. (…) It is crucial to show the fact that nationalism that at present shows renewed strength and energy are mainly emanates from nations without states. The identity policy includes a progressive element, and nationalist movements that represent it are located alongside pacifist, ecologist or feminist movements insofar as they defend those who are different, the weak."

The "Basque case" transmits the idea that the sustainable human development strategy is feasible. The idea that "Yes we can!" That we can look the market in the eye, without having to avoid looking people in the eye. Compared to the resigned attitude in the face of the statement that neoliberalism is the "nature of things," and even represents a "scientific reading of reality,"[447] the Basque experience shows that these suppositions are not correct. Clearly the "Basque case," far from inviting resignation,[448] represents an eloquent manifestation that "Yes, we can!" We want to and we will![449] With regard to the Basque experience Mr. Campbell underlines "the importance of integration of the three agenda; economic, social, and environmental," suggesting that "the Basque Case focus on relationship between social capital and natural capital could play a revolutionary role in the 21st Century."[450]

---

447 JAUREGUI, G., *Democracy in the 21st century: A new world, new values*. Oñate, IVAP, 2004, ps. 144 and 145: "neoliberalism grants itself a natural and inevitable character, considering it to be an almost inevitable factor to which society is predestined. Neoliberalism bases its strategy on the profound conviction that there is only one road to which there is no possible alternative. The degree of determinism is such that it impregnates its ideology which even reaches the point of rejecting not just any kind of opposition to its strategy, but even rejects a simple discussion about it."

448 SOTELO, I., *The social State: Background, origin, development and decline*. Madrid, ed. Trotta, 2010, p. 392: "if a social rebellion does not occur in the medium term, there will be a slow dismantling of the social State, (…). This forecast, (…) does not imply the thesis that nothing can be modified, because with a capitalist market economy and representative democracy we will have reached the end of history in the sense that whatever happens has to happen within these parameters. In no way do I believe that capitalism will last forever, nor that the basic forms of our democracies may not be modified."

449 In Basque there is a beautiful expression to reflect this: "Ezina ekinez egina."

450 CAMPBELL, C., Founder & Executive Director, Assist Social Capital, United Kingdom, a contribution made in relation to "The Basque Case: A Comprehensive Model for Sustainable Human

Five: Identity and Innovation; Self-government

Self-government is the key to "Basque country strategy," it soars high above, shelters the rest of the reasons that explain the success reached in the sustainable human development strategy applied in the Basque Autonomous Community over the last 35 years and more specifically over the period analyzed 1998–2008.

A statement that is ever more valid for a global society — "competing with roots," "cooperating with roots," "innovating with roots," and "social construction with roots" — therefore makes full sense for Basque society. In fact, one of the most significant changes in the globalization paradigm occurs between "global annuls local," from a few years ago, and the current "local moves the World" or growing protagonism of what is small and well structured politically, culturally, and economically in the world, reflected in the works of Alberto Alesina[451] and his colleagues or Guillermo de la Dehesa.[452] In other words from "small is beautiful" as

Development." Research program at the bilateral meeting held in London, March 31, 2011.

[451] See ALESINA, A. and SPOLAORE, E., *The Size of Nations.* Massachusetts, MIT Press, 2005; ALESINA, A. and SPOLAORE, E., "On the Number and Size of Nations," *The Quarterly Journal of Economics,* v. 112, n. 4, November, 1997, ps. 1027–1056; ALESINA, A., SPOLAORE, E. and WACZIARG, R., "Economic Integration and Political Disintegration." *American Economic Review,* v. 90(5), December, 2000, ps. 1276–1296; ALESINA, A. and WACZIARG, R., "Openness, country size and the Government." *National Bureau of Economic Research* (6024), May, 1997.

[452] DE LA DEHESA, G., *Understanding globalization.* Madrid, ed. Alianza, 2002, ps. 109 and 110: "there is another repercussion that has huge political importance for many countries, including Spain. In an increasingly more globalized and more open world it is easier for situations of political disintegration to arise (Alesina, Spolaore and Wacziarg, 1997). Globalization will tend to favour separatism processes. Many small homogeneous regions from a cultural, linguistic or ethnic point of view may try to democratically negotiate to live independently from the country in which they are integrated, In a more democratic and more open world, minorities will be able to choose their future more freely, becoming more autonomous or, even, independent."

E. F. Schumacher[453] said in 1973, we move to "small is possible," in the words of George McRobie[454] in 1976, because "interest in Intermediate Technology has grown quickly" as Schumacher himself recognized,[455] to the current "nano explosion," based on "small is different," which led Prof. Pedro Miguel Etxenike to state that we are "facing the great challenge of everything small." [456]

However, basically this is nothing new, because J.J. Rousseau himself remarked, in the 18th century in his first version of the *Social Contract* on the generalized cliché that nations believed they increased their power and prosperity by increasing their territory, stating that the opposite occurs, as besides relaxing the social tie in this process —he wrote — "in general a small State is always proportionally more powerful that a large State."[457]

The will to make one's own and different decisions together with the real capacity to face up to responsibility have been the key differentiating elements in the Basque strategy.[458] In this way, initiatives, laws, fiscal regulations,

---

453 SCHUMACHER, E.F., *Small is beautiful* (1ª Edition 1973). Madrid, Tursen S.A.-Hermann Blume ed., 1990.

454 McROBIE, R., *Appendix: Small is possible*, in Schumacher, E.F., *Small is beautiful.* Madrid, Tursen S.A. – Hermann Blume ed., 1990, ps. 264 to 306.

455 SCHUMACHER, E.F., *Small is beautiful.* Madrid, Tursen S.A. – Hermann Blume ed., 1990, pg. 265, Schumacher E.F., in the introduction to the Appendix to McRobie, *Small is possible*, states, "since the publication in English of *Small is Beautiful* in 1973, interest in Intermediate Technology has grown quickly (...) based on these experiences, certain conclusions have been drawn that make it possible to establish that *Small is Possible.*"

456 ETXENIKE P.M., Conference "Crisis: Education and Science." AICE-IZEA XXV Anniversary, Guggenheim, Bilbao, May 8, 2009.

457 ROUSSEAU, J. J., *Social Contract* (Primera version). O.C., v. 3, ed. De La Pléiade, 1964, p. 320.

458 STIGLITZ, J.E., *Unease in globalization.* Madrid, Santillana Ediciones Generales, 2002, p. 309: "Globalization of the economy has benefitted countries that took advantage of this opportunity opening new markets for their exports (...) But the countries that benefitted most were those that took charge of their own destiny and recognized the role that the State can play in development,

strategic plans, instruments, and our own resources and finance have been articulated from a conception of self government in all the policies designed and implemented. Mr. Addari states, "the Basque Case presents more than just 'self-governance,' it presents a radical form of grass roots democracy through its bottom up vision."[459]

Therefore, the advance of Basque self-government, defence of the Basque political, cultural, and economic identity, was not only behind the claim for a legitimate political project, but also behind, as an inseparable element, the development of a different model in relation to its situation, of a strategy of sustainable human development for the Basque Autonomous Community.

---

without trusting the notion that a self-regulated market resolves its own problems."

[459] ADDARII, F., Executive Director, Euclid Network, London, a contribution made in relation to "The Basque Case: A Comprehensive Model for Sustainable Human Development." Research program at the bilateral meeting held in London, March 31, 2011.

8
A "Road Map" to Increase Prosperity and Happiness among Individuals and Peoples

Diametrically opposed to the thesis held by Hayek in his well known work *The Road to Serfdom*,[460] our "road map" is also a road, but one to prosperity. This is the fundamental justification for a new framework of self-government.

The development of self government and the use made of it, as shown, has enabled development and progress in Basque society to be different, from the approval of the Statute of Gernika. It made an unmistakable commitment to the State social possible, to our own model of "competitiveness in solidarity." The question is now "Why more self-government?" and the answer is clear "because we need it to continue advancing."[461]

The institutional framework has deep repercussions, without a doubt, on the socio-economic performance of countries, compared with neoliberal theories that advocate a reduction in the State,[462] as we have witnessed in the Basque experience since the approval of the Statute of Gernika.

---

460 See HAYEK, F. A., *The road to serfdom.* Madrid, ed. Alianza, 2002.

461 OSBORNE, D. and GAEBLER, T., *The reinvention of Government: The influence of the business spirit in the public sector.* Barcelona, ed. Paidós, 1995, p. 65: "To be successful in the global super-competitive market of today, corporations need the different factors of production to be the best quality possible: the best trained workers, the most advanced research, the cheapest capital and the best infrastructure. This means that the different roles of Government as educator, trainer, financier of scientific research, establisher of regulations and infrastructure operator are today much more important than thirty years ago."

462 See NOZIK, R., *Anarchy, State, and Utopia.* New York, Basic Books, 1974; and for another vision BUARQUE, C., *A new happy world.* Madrid, Santillana Ediciones Generales, 2010, p.185: "neoliberals defend the total opening of national economies, absolute supremacy of the market and the systematic disappearance of the State as a promoter of social policies. The result of this

The political and social debate today in the Basque Country, whether or not it is desired politically because citizens demand it over the head of political parties, laws and Governments, is whether we need a new legal framework of self government to live up to, from our own unique model, the future.[463]

New Governance

The term "governance" arose in the 80s and 90s. Numerous studies and recommendations by the United Nations (PNUD), the World Bank, and the OECD back up 20th century studies on state realities and ever more studies on international and European political and administrative science.

---

policy is social international segregation: the creation of an international world of the rich and an international gulag archipelago formed by those excluded. Neoliberalism constitutes the new religion of this new reality, a product of a divided society. Proof thereof is that neoliberals are liberals in the trade of goods but defend a tight control on migratory flows. Their proposal consists of applying economic liberalism to the wealthy part of the world, regardless of national borders, and establishing a tight control of social frontiers, even inside each country."

[463] RIFKIN, J., *The European Dream: How the European vision of the future is eclipsing the American dream.* Barcelona, ed. Paidós, 2004, p. 301–304: "What is important is that culture is not, and never has been, a prolongation of the market or Government. Quite the opposite, markets and Governments are prolongations of culture. They are secondary, not primary, institutions. They exist by virtue of the cultures that created them. (…). Following a long period colonized by the market and the Nation State, civil society — together with the even deeper underlying cultural forces — is being noticed for its effort to recover its central role in the scheme of public life. (…). In a globalized economy made up of impersonal market forces, civil society has become an outstanding social refuge. It is the space where people generate a perception of familiarity and confidence, and have the sensation of possessing a shared goal and a collective identity."

The reflection tackled by the European Commission in the "White Paper on European Governance,"[464] in relation to the principles and instruments to make decisions in the context of the Union, has led to a multiplying effect in that it has been understood that the promotion of new types of governance and the principles involved are not the exclusive responsibility of European institutions, but of all levels of public administration. Private companies and organizations are also associated with social corporative responsibility, and the same applies to civil society organized under the concept of active citizenship.

In reality it is a new way of understanding not only the performance and organization of all public administrations, but also their interaction with civil society, considering the person as the last reference of Government and as a co-participant in it.[465]

We have to rethink democracy itself as a political and social model and that means the reconstruction of a new world order.[466] For this reason, the concept of governance is

---

464 Communication of the Commission to the European Parliament, to the Council, to the Economic and Social Committee and the Committee of Regions published in the DOCE COM (2001) 428 end.

465 Interactions between public-private-civil are shown to be fundamental in the concept of governance and in the very definition that the Diccionario de la Lengua de la Real Academia Española establishes defining it as "the art or way of governing that proposes as its goal the achievement of lasting economic, social and institutional development, promoting a healthy balance between the State, civil society and the market of the economy."

466 JAUREGUI, G., *Democracy in the 21st century: A new world, new values*. Oñati, IVAP, 2004, ps. 124 and 125, shows relation with the question "An order based on a complex legal code in which it is possible for the coexistence of diverse legal orders not sustained, necessarily, in hierarchical relations of supra or subordination, but in criteria for sharing, coordination and subsidiarity. World democracy demands a constraint or limitation of sovereignty of states, but, to the contrary of what happens frequently at present; this limitation cannot and must not be exercised by other states. (...) it is necessary for transnational organizations to exercise their authority and be capable of limiting the power of states. Quite the opposite to what is occurring right now, when certain international

presented by the European Commission as a new approach to the question of how the EU uses the powers it is given by the citizenship. Which converts citizenship — compared to Member States — into the source of sovereignty in the EU and at the same time the controller of how the powers conferred are exercised.

The model of governance[467] proposed in the "White Paper on European Governance"[468] is a European Commission strategy to respond to a gradual and inexorable distancing of European citizenship with regard to the European institutions and a crisis in citizens' confidence in the process of European Integration. This model of governance leads, in the words of Juan-Cruz Alli, to "in advanced societies the State and society are two systems interwoven by complex networks and links, (...) that need cooperation, collaboration and coordination."[469] It is necessary to differentiate this from the neoliberal model of governance — corporate governance — developed by the

---

institutions, such as the UN, have become, due to inertia, a docile instrument in the hands of the most powerful nations."

[467] "White Paper on European Governance." Communication of the Commission to the European Parliament to the Council, to the Economic and Social Committee and the Committee of Regions published in the DOCE COM (2001) pg. 428: "The concept of European governance designs the rules, processes and behaviors that influence the exercise of powers on a European level, especially from the point of view of opening, participation, responsibility, efficiency and coherence."

[468] The origin of the "White Paper on European Governance" is one of the strategic Objectives set by the Commission for the period 2000–2005 (COM (2000) 154 end), which consists of "promoting new European forms of Government". This would involve "giving more participation to citizens in European affairs, improving the operation and transparency of the institutions, in particular reforming the Commission and serving as an example for other institutions; adapting institutions to the needs of enlargement; create new forms of cooperation between the different levels of power in Europe and finally, provide an active and specific European contribution to the development of a world Government."

[469] ALLI, J. C., *Administrative Law and Globalization.* Madrid, Civitas ed., 2004, p. 343.

School of Chicago with the main aim to reduce transaction costs of public activity, substituting public interest by economic efficiency, establishing (in terminology used by Wolfgang Reinicke) a kind of "Governing without Government."[470]

The interest of the Basque institutions in the new model of governance was reflected in the "Proposal to reform the Political Statute of the Community of the Basque Country," approved by absolute majority in the Basque Parliament at the plenary session held on December 30, 2004, in which the "Right to good Government and good administration" and to the "participation of civil society" in public affairs were, together with the guiding values of the social and economic framework, the guidelines for the exercise of Basque self-government.[471]

---

[470] See REINICKE, W. H., *Global Public Policy: Governing without Government?* Washington, ed. Brookings Institution Press, 1998.

[471] Proposal to reform the Political Statute of the Community of the Basque Country, approved by absolute majority in the Plenary Session of the Basque Parliament on December 30, 2004, Basque Parliament Gazette, VII legislature, n. 180, 3 January 2005, articles 39 and 40, ps. 22801, 22802 and 22803, state: "Article 39 – Right to good Government and good administration.

Public powers, in the exercise of their functions, will ensure that arbitrariness is not present in the administration, the right to good service and the social function of the political-administrative ends of public management. In accordance, all Basque citizens are guaranteed the right to good Government and good administration, which is materialized through the development of the following contents:

- Transparent working of the Administration, information on rights and procedures, Access to public registers and sufficient motivation in administrative actions.
- Guarantee efficient linguistic co-official nature.
- Functionality, efficiency, and simplicity of administrative procedures and processing without undue delay.
- Application of the presumption that administrated persons will always act in good faith, unless proof to the contrary is provided by the Administration.

Taking as a basis the worrying and growing gap existing between the institutions and the people they serve, Basque self-government aims to configure the concept of Basque governance as a political form to exercise the powers given to it by the citizenship for the citizenship itself to enjoy.

Principles for New Governance: New Self-government

Bearing in mind the conceptual paradigm change that the new European culture of governance[472] represents, we can define what the "new Basque governance" means, also in terms of "new self-government":

- Correspondence in terms of efficiency between the cost of public services, their social justification and the results obtained.
- The duty of the Administration is to ensure in each action the application of quality models, establishing external assessments of the services provided, beyond administrative controls.
- Full and efficient responsibility for administrative operations that are deficient, in accordance with law. (...).
- Article 40 – Participation of civil society

Public powers establish the mechanisms suitable to facilitate and stimulate citizen participation in public affairs, including both in socioeconomic and social, cultural and educational areas, through the instruments determined by a Basque Parliament Law or by sectorial laws. (...)"

[472] JAUREGUI, G., *Democracy in the 21st century: A new world, new values*. Oñate, IVAP, Oñate, 2004, ps. 92 and 93: "Governance constitutes, (...) the quality of a political community according to which Government institutions act efficiently in a way which is considered legitimate by citizens, thus enabling the free exercise of political will through civic obedience by the people. (...) the Government is limited by the territorial area of a state. Governance, however, encompasses a much wider territorial area. For this reason, the distinction between Government and governance is particularly pertinent in the current era of globalization."

First: Bearing in mind the "federal" nature of the BAC, Basque governance unquestionably implies consolidating the inter-institutionalism or co-participation of the three levels of Basque institutions in the planning, execution and assessment of public policies.

Second: It involves advances in general coordination techniques, internal or inter-departmental, for Government action to achieve comprehensive transversal action, through the effective coordination of sectorial policies.

Third: It means integrating in political innovative planning practice the political processes of citizen initiatives, civil society consultations, a search for consensus or solution of conflicts, strengthening the participation of economic and social agents and civil society in the design and elaboration process of public policies.

Fourth: This principle involves at the same time surrendering accounts, institutional loyalty, and co-responsibility of agents and civil society organized in this participative dimension. It also involves the existence of initiative, consultation and debate forums for socio-economic agents which work well, in turn inspired by the principles of governance.

Fifth: This requires perfecting basic methodology to normalize Government action incorporating the constituent aspects of planning: its cause or origin; preparation of potential impacts and alternative action based on an analysis and diagnosis of the initial situation and present and future interests; decision making as a process to select alternatives and prepare and implement strategies to reach goals and, finally, normalize, in terms of quality, the periodical assessment and final balance in terms of efficacy and efficiency in the execution of public policies.

Sixth: It also means adopting measures that make it possible, beyond methods to review governmental decisions foreseen in the legal code and functions to control legislative power, to ensure the double objective of consulting civil society and social interlocutors, and to carry out surveillance and for citizens or non institutional bodies to interrogate the Government at any moment, about the actions planned to be executed according to public policies.

Seventh: This will represent normalizing the possibility of visualizing each and every variable that contributes to guaranteeing efficacy, acceptability, and efficiency of Government action, incorporating private quality and continuous improvement processes to public policies: conception of public policies, choice of instruments and application thereof to reach the goals, communication of policies to society, open debate with society, etc.

Eighth: Another necessary dimension of Basque governance consists of advancing in the integration of the legal code of the BAC for public policies that require regulations, introducing in the planning of Government legislative initiatives and in the legislative process in general, improvements directed at guaranteeing the correct conception of policies, the selection of ideal instruments and a more efficient and rigorous application and compliance with rules.

Ninth: In the supranational framework where the legislative function of the Government is inserted and with regard to the anticipation and proactivity advocated for the position of the Basque Country in Europe, it will be necessary to extend the planning of the internal legislative process. All this will give a solvent and suitable response in the BAC to the processes to co-regulate and assess the possibilities of self-regulation, incorporating applicable guidance to the Legislative Program of the Government that the "White Paper on European Governance" and the Lisbon strategy incorporate to the open method of coordination.

All in all, it is a question of applying to all the agents involved — institutions, organizations, civil society — the principles of good governance summarized in the "White Paper on European Governance" throughout the process to design, formulate, execute, and assess sectorial and transversal public policies.

In parallel to European governance, Basque governance involves a strategic reflection on how to exercise the powers that Basque citizens confer to institutions.[473] If European governance is an attempt to rescue the European project, making it more democratic and more compliant with the five guiding principles,[474] in the same way Basque

---

473 RIFKIN, J., *The European dream: How the European vision of the future is eclipsing the American dream.* Barcelona, ed. Paidós, 2004, p. 285: "A new generation of scientists and analysts promoted a conception process for governance and substituted the hierarchical and closed model with a model of open systems. They argued that the efficiency of governance does not depend so much on imposing up down predefined decisions on passive receivers, but should involve all the actors — Government, companies, civil society agents — in a continuous process of deliberation, negotiation, commitment and consensus, based on the radical proposal that the best decisions are those taken democratically with the participation of everyone affected."

474 The five principles of European governance may be summarized as:

-*Principle of opening*: consists of a more "open" working of the institutions, with more active and efficient communication of this working and the corresponding decisions and in the use of a more accessible language for the public in general.

-*Principle of participation*: appeals to strengthening and the efficiency of the intervention by citizens in all phases of the cycle of European policies (from the design and formulation to the assessment) to bolster their confidence in the European institutions, which will gain in legitimacy to improve the results obtained.

-*Principle of responsibility*: means clarifying the role of each of the European legislative and executive processes and involves the demand for European institutions to explain accounts — and the Member states of their action and consequent assumption of the corresponding responsibility.

-*Principle of efficiency*: seeks the opportunity and efficiency of European policies and measures, understood as obtaining results

governance implies the rebirth of the framework of Basque self-government. A new framework of self-government with more strength, closeness and participation. A Basque self-government that, to respond to new challenges, must contain more political, social and economic power.

Without doubt, Europe from the strictly political and institutional point of view is currently presided over by an economic crisis on the one hand and by an institutional and State territorial model crisis on the other. The debate on the State model, in short, is not taboo at the moment, whether wanted or not, in Spain, in Europe or elsewhere in the world. It is on the global political and institutional agenda today — the cases of Scotland, Flanders, Wallonia, Catalonia, Basque Country, Wales, Greenland or Quebec, are just a sample — and if agreements are not reached it will continue to be there in coming years, with even more political and social violence. Faced with conflict which triggers tension we have to avoid what Peter Coleman identifies as "the natural human tendency to reduce that tension by seeking coherence through simplification."[475]

---

with a double basis: a) clear objectives and b) assessment of the impact of the execution, and the experience accumulated in it. This principle also includes the demand for ideal decision making and proportionality in the measure adopted.

-*Principle of coherence*: Provides simultaneously coherence between policies and actions, as well as a coherent focus on European action (by means of double integration of the sectorial nature and pluralism territorial) in the context of a complex system, whose realization requires political leadership and commitment from the European institutions.

[475] COLEMAN, P.T., *The five percent: Finding solutions to seemingly impossible conflicts*. New York, Public Affairs, 2011, p.63: "It is critical to recognise that we live in an increasingly complex world — biologically, socially, politically, technologically, you name it — that holds many inherent contradictions. In the middle of this complex world are we humans, who have a natural tendency to seek coherence in what we see, feel, think, and do. When we experience conflict, this tendency intensifies. Conflict is essentially a contradiciton, an incompatibility, oppositely directed forces and a difference that triggers tensión. When we ecounter conflict, within the field of forces that constitute it, the natural human tendency that tension by seeking coherence through simplification. (….) this

In the particular case of the Spanish State, rejection by the Government and the Spanish Parliament, without even negotiating on the proposals for a New Basque Political Statute —to negotiate a new framework of self-government for the 21st century between the Basque Country and Spain — and a non-binding democratic consultation — to demand, on the one hand, that ETA put an end to violence and, on the other, that Basque political parties enter into dialogue about solving the Basque political problem — approved by absolute majority in the Basque democratic institutions, and the negative sentences of the Constitutional Court, first on the Basque democratic initiatives,[476] then on the new Catalan Statute[477] — ratified by referendum by Catalan citizens — have placed on the table the need to renew the State and the indispensible constitutional change to bring this about.

In short, the experience and this work show us — with empirical evidence since the approval of the Statute of Gernika — that in the "Basque expience" self-government has been synonymous with welfare for Basque society. They also shows us that, basically, it has been self-government that enabled the Basque Autonomous Community to develop its own different model of sustainable human development, with which it has been possible to build a healthy and socially committed and balanced model of economic development. They also show us that "yes we can!" and that another model is possible.[478] That we are not condemned to the "sole

---

tendency toward simplification becomes even intensified when we are under stress, threat, time constraints, fatigue, and various other conditions all absolutely typical of conflict."

476 CONSTITUTIONAL COURT, Sentence 103/2008 of September 11, on Law 9/2008 of 27 June by the Basque Parliament on Calling and Regulating a Consultation.

477 CONSTITUTIONAL COURT, Sentence 31/2010, of June 28 on the Statute of Catalonia.

478 See GEORGE, S., *Another world is possible…* Barcelona, ed. Icaria, 2004. The author considers in general terms that another world is possible if we know what we are talking about, if we save the planet, if we identify the actors, if we focus on the right adversaries, if Europe wins the war in the West — to which we could add according to WOLTON, D., *The other globalization.* Barcelona, ed. Gedisa, 2004, p. 96 states that another world is

neoliberal economic political way of thinking." That we can definitely "look the market in the eye," while at the same time "looking people in the eye."

And finally, this work: *The Basque Experience constructing Sustainable Human Development*, shows us that to defend and advance in Basque cultural, political, and economic identity is not only the basis of the defence of the democratic principle and a legitimate political project of a nation in Europe, but also inseparably behind the construction of a strategy of sustainable human development in the Basque Community.

possible, if we put into practice "cultural coexistence" based on "relational identity."

9
Conclusions

The passionate road covered in this work, a reflection of our country's path since the start of self-government at the beginning of the 1980s and specifically between 1998 and 2008, has enabled us to verify, with established facts and arguments, *The Basque Experience Constructing Sustainable Human Development.* An open road that required a new paradigm based on foundations such as the ethical principle, the democratic principle, and sustainable human development. The foundations of this "new model" took shape by means of the socio-political-legal-economic initiatives which, led by democratic Basque institutions, were formally presented, debated, and democratically approved during the target period of our study. All of which lead to the final reflections formulated below.

First of all I would like to highlight what in my opinion is the main conclusion of this work: that the hopeful vision for the Basque People is enshrined in the formula: R&D+i+C (Research & Development + Innovation + Culture). This, in the knowledge that magical recipes do not exist in our world. The bad economists are those of us who, regardless of the place and time, apply recipes. When we run out of ideas, we apply recipes. This does not usually work unless we adapt them to our culture, which is our own and different, and also makes our solutions our own and different.

We can learn from the successful experiences applied in other countries around the world in relation to the first part (R&D+i), although the entire polynomial will not work if we do not include the 'C' the cultural element. Another reason, because there is no other way, is that either you incorporate your 'C' — your identity, your way of being and doing things, your knowledge, your ability to innovate — or nobody else will do it. Reaching out to the world without forgetting your roots is the way forward.

Nowadays, in this 'global society' it is the local element that enshrines the real hope that another world is possible. For some time now, people have begun to doubt the processes of transformation and passive change; rather, they get involved in them. The way for the future therefore lies in innovation based on values, and we can only innovate in this way by maintaining the ethics of our roots. In other words, knowing how to see things through to the end and fulfilling our commitments, based on the values that our culture gives us.

In fact we have the knowledge that we are living in 'a new world order' that is ever more interconnected (and leads to a new form of marginalization: 'unconnected' people, for whom we do not have a solution) in which the main change of paradigm is that we have gone from 'choosing' to 'being chosen.' Nowadays, all of us (countries, universities, individuals) are chosen on account of what we offer.

Therefore, in this connected society the objective is not knowing, but understanding. Creativity does not consist of seeing the same thing, but thinking up something different. To be able to think up something different, it is essential to have R&D+i, but also — and above all — the 'C' factor, which becomes the core element of reflection, and with it, self-government and its instruments at the service of the people and the individuals that make up society.

First: The "Basque Case". An Integral Experience Based on Principles

The "Basque case" is the result of development, based on the solid foundations of Basque self-government from its beginnings of a socio-political-legal-economic model built on three principles: the ethical principle, the democratic principle, and sustainable human development.

These are three inseparable principles for Basque society that we cannot forsake. A specific way to understand progress was developed on this basis. Contrasting with the concept of economic growth, which overlooks men and women, a type of progress was favored in which the subject and fundamental end was the person and, from a collective point of view, the Basque people. This is a modern people, who despite their problems — political, secular conflicts and terrorist violence since the mid 20th century — have made significant advances, who have never lost hope, and who have made continuous efforts to build peace based upon social justice and individual and collective liberty.

The development of the three inseparable principles, which together have inspired all the initiatives carried out since the recovery of self-government through the Statute of Gernika, has made the "Basque case" an integral experience of social, political, and economic action. And in this integral character, which has combined rationality, conviction, and capacity for self-government, lies it main strength; to offer the world something personal and different, contrasting with that advocated by the socio-politico-economic neoliberal thought prevailing in our days, based on the social, political and the economic, restoring the person, the people, and competitiveness in solidarity.

Second: Ethical Principle; All Human Rights for Everyone, Reconciliation, and a Dialogued End to Violence

The establishment of the ethical principle as one of the foundations of the model led to the defence of human rights becoming the compass for the actions of Basque society and its public institutions.

Over the period analyzed, advances were made in social pedagogy and the need to accept the indivisible nature of human rights was consolidated in the Basque Country. All human rights for everyone. This is the central belief held by the immense majority of Basque society.

Today the situation has changed in the Basque Country. As of January 11, 2011 ETA declared a permanent ceasefire and fortunately we will have another opportunity to build a peaceful way forward.

The Basque conflict is in a period of transition from destructive cycles of violence to political dialogue, encompassing creative thinking and highly promising initiatives for peace. As in any period of transition, the patterns of behavior of the past and the nascent processes of the future interact in complex and contradictory ways. The old ways have not died out completely, and the new ways have yet to take hold. All the questions that deal with the roots of the Basque conflict are at a crossroads, a moment of uncertainty, and in need of redefinition for the future.

We need to ensure peace in a country that has suffered for many years from the violent activities of ETA. Since the recent ETA ceasefire we now have a fresh opportunity that we have to make the most of.

ETA, therefore, must understand the terrible brutality, futility, and immorality of their violence and must show unequivocal signs of their willingness to abandon this road forever and must also forsake the role of guarantor in any political process.

And the European, Spanish, and Basque institutions as well as the political parties have to reflect upon this too. As the international human rights organizations and the United Nations Rapporteur himself states, the road to peace never passes through torture and mistreatment, nor through legislative initiatives which restrict the civil and political rights of citizens. Neither violence nor terrorism can be overcome with less democracy, but in fact can only be defeated with more democracy. That is to say, with the universalization of the respect for human rights.

Throughout history many directions have been adopted to resolve conflicts. Experience shows us that there is only one road, one method to advance: dialogue. All great or small advances were made, all the hope in Basque society blossomed whenever dialogue and negotiation processes started up. Dialogue is the only valid formula for not failing and the only formulat to achieve basic agreements yet unreached. Dialogue in public and in private, bilateral and multilateral dialogue, dialogue without personal or political vetoes, dialogue without prior conditions, dialogue as a formula to find solutions.

Respect for life and human rights is the starting point. Attacking human life, murder, extortion, or torturing those who think differently is a crime against humanity and there is no room for this in any society. Respect for life and the human fights of everyone has to be the starting point for any peace process and the ethical, moral, and material recognition of the victims of violence and terrorism is an obligation for Basque institutions and society as a whole.

It is therefore, condition *sine qua non* that the rejection of the use of violence as an instrument of political action is made, prior to any process of a dialogued end to violence or as a condition to be fulfilled by part of the participants in any negotiating table for the political conflict. Given these conditions, we continue to defend a dialogued end to violence.

This, therefore, does not imply the spreading of a veil of diffuse obscurity over the past, or inviting the country to a collective amnesty for the inhuman events that took place, but on the contrary, to carry out an analytical and critical reading of them.

Third: Democratic Principle; the Basque People, the Right to Decide and to Negotiate

We are faced with an irrefutable reality: the existence of the Basque people. Furthermore, a very significant and plural part of current Basque society defends that the Basque people exist and that, therefore, it is their role to decide their own future freely and democratically and to have their own place on the European and world stage.

The fundamental priority consists of achieving peace and so Basque society clamours for ETA to give up arms definitively. However, leaving violence to one side, we must recognize the existence of a political problem. This problem must be tackled by Basque society and its political representatives. Because whether political agreements are reached or not, the violence of ETA must disappear, and whether or not ETA exists, agreements must be reached for the coexistence between the Basque Country and the Spanish State.

The conclusion is that a profound political dialogue must take place, with an aim to achieving an agreement on political normalization with regard to fundamental elements for our coexistence, such as identity, sovereignty, territoriality, the right to exercise self-determination, the presence of the Basque Country in Europe and in the world, and the level of desired self-government or the framework of relationship between the Basque Country and the Spanish State. Political problems must have political solutions.

The problem, in political and democratic terms, is the lack of recognition of the Basque people as a political subject with their own identity to which certain historic rights correspond, pre-dating the Spanish Constitution and, in short, with the capacity to decide their own future freely and democratically.

It is therefore necessary to reach a political agreement about the right of Basque society to decide and exercise this right so that — prior ratification by the Basque people — it can be incorporated into the legal code. To achieve, therefore, from mutual respect and within the framework of the European Union, an agreement for a friendly political-social coexistence between the Basque Country and the Spanish State for the 21st century.

From the strictest respect for the democratic essence, the recognition of the right of the Basque people to decide their own future and the commitment to exercise this right through pact and negotiation is the key to the solution.

Fourth: Identity and Innovation; Looking to the Future without Forgetting Our Roots

The defence of Basque identity, culture, and language is not solely related to a legitimate political fact such as the claim for an identity in the current globalized world; it is also related directly to the achievement of sustainable human development.

The Basque people — the Basque Country or Euskal Herria — Basque culture, the Basque language — Euskera — must have their place in Europe and in the world. The defence of Basque identity, not with backs turned or in opposition to other identities but in coexistence with them, is behind, not only a legitimate political claim, but also a sound model of economic, social and political development.

We must look to the future without forgetting our roots. We must compete with roots. We must innovate with roots. The last 35 years have shown us that self-government —"burujabetza" in Basque language — is the same as welfare. To advance in our identity as a people is linked today, yesterday, and more so tomorrow and thereafter, to achieving sustainable human development, through the exercise of self-government.

The *Basque Experience* also transmits the idea that the strategy of sustainable human development is feasible. The belief that it is possible! That we can look the market in the eye while also looking people in the eye. Faced with a resigned attitude to statements that neoliberalism is the "nature of things" or it represents the "scientific reading of reality," the "Basque case" represents a humble but efficient example that shows the bias of these arguments. It is clear that the Basque experience, rather than inviting resignation, represents an eloquent statement that alternatives exist to the neoliberal model. It is possible! If we want to, we can.

The Basque Country is a country, in short, in which humanism and social, scientific, and technical innovation are incorporated into its own identity, open to the world, possessing a powerful lever to bring about a social, political, and economic transformation.

Fifth: Self-government and Sustainable Human Development

Self-government is the key to our country's strategy. Built on ethical and democratic principles, it is an umbrella over the rest of the elements that explain the success reached with the strategy of sustainable human development applied in the Autonomous Community of the Basque Country over the last 35 years.

The empirical evidence in this work — since the approval of the Statute of Gernika and specifically over the period 1998–2008 — shows us that self-government has been a synonym of welfare for Basque society. It also shows us that, basically, self-government has enabled us to develop a strategy of sustainable human development in the Autonomous Community of the Basque Country which made economic and socially committed and balanced progress possible for its people.

The result of the analysis of the Basque experience shows us that defending and furthering Basque self-government, in the defence of political, cultural, and economic Basque identity, has not only been behind the restoration of the legitimate national political project of a people, but also behind — as an inseparable attribute — the development of a strategy of competitiveness in solidarity, which is independent and uniquely different from those of its environment.

It should be stressed that the axis on which the Basque experience pivots is the person. The person understood in the Kantian sense as developing in a specific socio-cultural space and understood as an end in themselves. This means that self-government is orientated firstly and mainly to the achievement of integral progress for its men and women, i.e. the Basque people.

Thus, in parallel to the concept of new European governance, the new Basque governance entails a strategic reflection on how the powers, which the Basque citizens confer on the institutions, are exercised. If European governance is an attempt to rescue the European project, making it more democratic, then in the same way, Basque governance entails the renaissance of the framework of Basque self-government. A new framework which, in order to respond to the new challenges, must contain more political, social, and economic power.

Without any doubt, the new model of self-government needs to come from a new model of governance, based on the establishment of one's own and differentiated project. This is what makes a difference in the modern world: the ability to establish one's own project and to develop one's identity, not through confrontation but through cooperation with other identities nearby and in the wider world.

This is the case, in my opinion, because the great paradigm change of the 21st century is that we have moved from 'choosing' to 'being chosen.' Nowadays we are elected on the basis of what we offer. As a result, we will be chosen depending on the project we are able to define and carry out here — by the Basque people — within Basque society. This leads us to a debate that is currently intensifying in the political world, in terms of 'yes' or 'no' to independence. As Shakespeare said: "We know what we are, but not what we could be."

As a society, we need to hold a debate on this model of dependence, one that is becoming increasingly solid. In other words, from the point of view of the educational model of the laws produced in the Spanish Parliament, is being independent a good or a bad thing? What about the Civil Service Law, or the laws on Social Security and the management of its economic system? Or those referring to taxation, budgeting and public deficit, or healthcare, industrial policy and R&D+i?

If the present model of dependence Spain is perceived by the majority of Basque society as a bad model, one that is devastating for our self-government and stops us from walking our own path in the globalized world. Well, we need to choose another model. We do not know what our ultimate fate will be, but we do know that it will have to be democratically decided here in the Basque Country. We know what we have to change and what is needed to make progress, because the basis on which the world is now being constructed lies in the following concepts: identity and innovation, in other words, roots and wings. You cannot be in the new world without roots, you need an identity to be able to present something different that is yours, and wings to innovate, to teach people skills and reach out to the rest of the world.

In the global society we need, more than ever, a local response, one that is our own and differentiated. Our roots, culture, way of learning, teaching methods, ways of dealing with problems, serious ways of solving problems, not mortgaging the future of the generations to come, together with a long list of other points, are the differential factors we have in the world, where capital, raw materials, technology and new devices continue to appear at an amazing pace. We need to compete using our roots. We need to innovate with our roots and to do this, we need to have the necessary and sufficient capacity for self-government to take the decisions that suit us best.

This quite simply means that the Basque Country, with the same level of independence-dependence that other European Union countries have, would not only be very viable but, in my opinion, highly advisable. The Basque Country´s main problem in its relationship with Spain is not the media-driven debate on an *independence* that we do not know about but the deeper debate on the *obligatory dependence* that we know and suffer in areas such as monetary, fiscal, legal, education, healthcare, employment, Social Security policy, etc. More than ever, we need our own differentiated project, one that shows solidarity with Spain, France, and Europe but is as committed and differentiated as that of any other country in the European Union.

Finally, I would like to finish this reflexion saying that the Basque Experience has been possible because there was the conception of nation which made sense of economic, political, and social self-government. Without this conception of nation, the public-private-society shared leadership is impossible. It is not possible to develop a different and independent model, a strategy for a country shared with social initiative and clear public involvement, capable of generating ethical progress for its people. Without a vision — a conception of Country or Nation — a people will perish.

Conception of Country, self-government and shared leadership go together to make up the "Project for a Country" from proximity, from an understanding of the problems to be resolved.

Bibliography

AGUADO, I., BARRUTIA, J. Mª, and ETXEBARRIA, C., "El desarrollo sostenible a lo largo de la historia del pensamiento económico," presented in *X Jornadas de Economía Crítica: ¿Alternativas al capitalismo?* Barcelona, March 23–25, 2006.

ALÁEZ, R., BILBAO, J., CAMINO, V. and LONGÁS, J. C., *El sector de automoción: Nuevas tendencias en la organización productiva.* Madrid: Civitas, 1996.

ALBERDI, A., *La economía vasca ante el cambio de era (1955–2015): Del crecimiento al desarrollo.* Grupo Vasco del Capítulo Español del Club de Roma: Bilbao, 2014.

ALESINA, A., and WACZIARG, R., "Openess, country size and the Government." *National Bureau of Economic Research* (6024), May, 1997.

ALESINA, A., and SPOLAORE, E., "On the Number and Size of Nations." *The Quarterly Journal of Economics,* v. 112, n. 4, November, 1997, pp. 1027-1056.

ALESINA, A., SPOLAORE, E. and WACZIARG, R., "Economic Integration and Political Disintegration." *American Economic Review,* v. 90(5), December, 2000, ps. 1276–1296.

ALESINA, A. and SPOLAORE, E., *The Size of Nations.* Massachusetts: MIT Press, 2005.

ALLI, J. C., *Derecho administrativo y globalización.* Madrid: Civitas, 2004.

ANNAN, K., Ex Secretario general de Naciones Unidas, Discurso pronunciado en la Ceremonia del Premio Nobel de la Paz, Oslo, Noruega, December 10, 2001.

ARGYLE, M., *Las fuentes de Satisfacción en la Buena Vida.* Londres, CHRISTIE, I., and NASH, L., ed., 1998.

ARRIGHI, G., *El largo siglo XX: Dinero y poder en los orígenes de nuestra época.* Madrid: Akal, 1999.

AZUA, J., *Clusterizar y globalizar la economía: "La magia del proceso."* Bogotá: Ed. Oveja Negra, 2008.

BAIROCH, P., *Cities and Economic Development: From the Dawn of History to the Present.* Chicago: University of Chicago, 1991.

BALZAT, M., *An economic analysis of innovation: Extending the concept of national innovation systems.* Cheltenham: ed. E.E. (Edward Elgar Pub.), 2006.

BARBERO, I., *Hacia modelos alternativos de ciudadanía: Un análisis socio-jurídico del movimiento sin papeles.* Doctoral thesis defence UPV-EHU, 2010.

BARRERE, M. A., *Discriminación, derecho antidiscriminatorio y acción positiva en favor de las mujeres.* Madrid: Civitas, 1997.

BARRUTIA, J. M., "Red de políticas para la difusión de la Agenda 21 local en Euskadi." Articulo de investigación UPV/EHU (32.321-15908/2004) y cátedra UNESCO para el Desarrollo Sostenible (Unesco 05/2006).

BARRUTIA, J. M., ECHEBARRIA, C., AND AGUADO, I., "Una red de políticas para la difusión de la Agenda 21 Local en Euskadi." *Ekonomiaz*, nº 64, 2007, pp. 214-235.

BAUDRILLARD, J., *Pantalla total.* Barcelona: Anagrama, 2000.

BAUDRILLARD, J., "Del antiterrorismo a la guerra: La violencia de la globalización." *Le Monde diplomatique*, Madrid: Spanish Edition, November 2002, p. 17.

BAZTARRIKA, P., *Babel o barbarie: Una política lingüística legítima y eficaz.* Irun: Alberdania, 2009.

BECK, U., GIDDENS, A. and LASH, S., *Modernización reflexive: Política, tradición y estética en el orden social moderno.* Madrid: Alianza, 1997.

BECK, U., *¿Qué es la globalización? Falacias del globalismo, respuestas a la globalización.* Barcelona: ed. Paidós, 1998.

BERGER, P. L., and HUNTINGTON, S. P., *Globalizaciones múltiples: La diversidad cultural en el mundo contemporáneo.* Barcelona: Ediciones Paidós, 2002.

BLANCHFLOWER, D.G., OSWALD, A. J., "Happiness and the Human Development Index: The Paradox of Australia." *Australian Economic Review*, June 2005, pp. 307-318.

BOBBIO, N., *Derecha e izquierda.* Madrid: Taurus, 1998.

BRAINBRIDGE, W.S., *Nanoconvergence: The Unity of Nanoscience, Biotechnology, information technology and Cognitive Science*. New Jersey: Prentice Hall, 2007.

BRONOWSKI, J., *The Ascent of Man*. Boston: Little, Brown and Co., 1973.

BRUNO, F., AND STUTZER, A., *Happiness and economics*. Princeton: Princeton University Press, 2002.

BUARQUE, C., *Un nuevo mundo feliz*. Madrid: Santillana Ediciones Generales, 2010.

CABALLERO HARRIET, F. J., *Algunas claves para otra Mundialización*. Santo Domingo: Fundación Global, Democracia y Desarrollo (FUNGLODE), 2009.

CARLSSON, B., JACOBSSON, S., HOLMEN, M., AND RICKNE, A., "Innovation Systems: Analytical and methodological issues." *Research Policy*, n° 31, 2002, pp. 233-245.

CARROL, L., *Alicia a través del espejo*. Madrid: Gaviota/Everest, 2010.

CASTELLS, M., *La era de la Información, v. II El Poder de la Identidad*. Madrid: Alianza Editorial, 2003.

CASTELLS, M., AND HIMANEN, P., *El Estado de bienestar y la sociedad de la información: El modelo finlandés*. Madrid: Alianza Editorial, 2002.

CASTORIADIS, C., "De la autonomía en política: El individuo privatizado." *Le Monde Diplomatique*. Madrid, Spanish edition, February 1998, pp. 12-27.

CERVANTES SAAVEDRA, M., *El ingenioso hidalgo Don Quijote de la Mancha*. Ed. del IV Centenario, Real Academia Española, Asociación de Academias de la Lengua Española, Alfaguara, Gobierno Vasco, 2005.

CHAKRAVARTY, S. R., "A Generalized Human Development Index." *Review of Development Economics*. Manuscript n° 9165, August 23, 2000.

CHANG, M., "Cornucopianos los ultraneoliberales" in FOLADORI, G. and PIERRI, N., (eds.), *¿Sustentabilidad? Desacuerdos sobre el desarrollo sustentable*. Universidad Autónoma de Zacatecas: Miguel Ángel Porrúa, 2005.

CHOMSKY, N., *El beneficio es lo que cuenta: Neoliberalismo y orden global*. Barcelona: Crítica, 2000.

CHUA, A., *Dayof Empire: How Hyperpowers rise dominance-and why they fall.* New York: Anchor Books, 2009.

COLEMAN, P.T., *The five percent: Finding solutions to seemingly impossible conflicts.* New York: Public Affairs, 2011.

COOKE, P., HEIDENREICH, M., AND BRACZYK, H., *Regional Innovation Systems.* London: Routledge, 2004.

COSTANTINI, V., MONNI, S., "Environment, human development and economic growth." *Ecological Economics* 64, 2008, pp. 867-880.

CURRICULUM VASCO: ITINERARIO CULTURAL, Propuesta de los expertos, San Sebastián, Mitxelena Artes Graficas, 2004.

DE LA DEHESA, G., *Comprender la globalización.* Madrid: Alianza, 2002.

DE LUCAS, J., "Nuevas estrategias de estigmatización: El Derecho frente a los inmigrantes." In PORTILLA CONTRERAS, G., *Mutaciones del Leviatán: Legitimación de los nuevos modelos penales.* Madrid: Akal, 2005.

DIESENDORF, M., and HAMILTON, C., *Human ecology, human economy.* Sydney: Allen and Unwin, 1997.

DIEZ INOA, S. A., *La globalización neoliberal y el fenómeno migratorio: análisis del modelo hispano-dominicano.* Doctoral thesis defense at the UPV-EHU, 2008.

DIXIT, A., *The Making of Economics Policy: A Transaction-Cost Politics Perspective.* Cambridge: MIT Press, 1996.

DODDS, S., "Economic growth and human well-being." *Ecological Economics*, v. 23, noviembre 1997, pp. 95-111.

DOMÈNECH, A., *El eclipse de la fraternidad.* Barcelona: Crítica, 2004.

DORRONSORO, G., "El sistema vasco de innovación ante los nuevos retos." *Revista Madrid + d.*, Monografía nº 22, 2008.

DRUCKER, P. F., *Innovation and Entrepreneurship: Practice and Principles.* New York: Harper & Row, 1985.

DUFOUR, D. R., "En tiempos del capitalismo total. La nueva servidumbre del hombre liberado." *Le Monde Diplomatique*, Spanish edition, Madrid, October 2003, p. 4.

EDQUIST, C., *Systems of innovation: Technologies, Institutions and organizations.* London: Pinter, 1997.

EDQUIST, C., *Systems of Innovation: Perspectives and challenges.* In FAGERBERG, J. et AL. (eds.), Oxford: Oxford University Press, 2005.

EMMONS, R., HORWITZ, J., DIENER, E., "Happiness of the very wealthy." *Social indicators research.* Vol. 16, 1985, pp. 263–274.

ESTEFANÍA, J., *Contra el pensamiento único.* Madrid: Santillana, 1997.

ETXENIKE, P. M., "Comparecencia en el Senado Español para realizar una evaluación de la política científica del Estado y de la Unión Europea." Madrid, *Diario de Sesiones del Senado.* June 18, 2007.

ETXENIKE, P. M., Conferencia "Crisis: Educación y Ciencia." *AICE-IZEA XXV Aniversario.* Guggenheim-Bilbao, May 9, 2009.

ETXENIKE, P. M., "Cerca de treinta años de Ley del euskera." prologue to *Babel o barbarie, una política lingüística legítima y eficaz.* Irun: Alberdania, 2009.

ETXEPARE, B., *Linguae vasconum primitiae, (1545).* Bilbao: Euskaltzaindia, 1995.

EWING, J. A., "Discurso presidencial en la Asamblea de la British Association, 1932." *Versión del Daily Telegraph.* London, September 19, 1932.

EZEIZABARRENA, X., "Scottish Devolution & Basque Historial titles: 2 legal scopes for cosovereignty?" PSA conference on British and comparative politics, Oxford, January 2010.

FAGERBERG, J. et AL. (eds.), *Systems of Innovation: Perspectives and challenges.* Oxford: Oxford University Press, 2005.

FAGERBERG, J., MOWERY, D. C., and NELSON, R. R., *The Oxford Handbook of Innovation.* Oxford: Oxford University Press, 2005.

FERNANDEZ DE LUCIO, I., "El sistema de innovación en Euskadi." *Ekonomiaz* nº 56, 2004. Ps. 296–305.

FIORITO, A. and MURGA, G., *Keynes y sus interpretaciones II.* Madrid: Ediciones cooperativas, 2006.

FORAY, D., and FREEMAN, Ch., *Technology and the wealth of nations.* London: Pinter Pub, 1993.

FORAY, D., *L'économie de la connaissance.* Paris: La Découverte, 2009.

FOX, R. W., and LEARS, J., *El poder de la cultura: Ensayos críticos de historia de América*. Chicago: University of Chicago Press, 1993.

FRIEDMAN, M. and FRIEDMAN, R. D., *Libertad de elegir: Hacia un nuevo liberalismo económico*. Barcelona: Grijalbo, 1980.

FRIEDMAN, M., *Capitalism and Freedom*. Chicago: University of Chicago Press, 1982.

FUKUYAMA, F., *El fin de la historia y el último hombre*. Barcelona: Planeta, 1992.

GALEANO, E., *Las venas abiertas de América Latina*. Madrid: Siglo XXI, 2005.

GANDHI, M., *Democracy Real and Deceptive*. India: Navajivan Publishing House, 1961.

GELLNER, E., *Cultura, Identidad y Política: El nacionalismo y los nuevos cambios sociales*. Barcelona: Gedisa, 1989.

GEORGE, S., *Otro mundo es posible si...* Barcelona: ed. Icaria, 2004.

GEORGESCU-ROEGEN, N., *The entropy law and the economic process*. Cambridge: Massachusetts, Harvard University Press, 1971.

GIDDENS, A., *La tercera vía y sus críticos*. Madrid: Santillana, 2001.

GOETHE, J.W., *Fausto*. Madrid: Cátedra, 2005.

GOODLAND, R., "The Concept of Environmental Sustainability." *Annual Review of Ecology and Systematics*, v. 26, 1995, ps. 1–24.

GRIMM, M., HARTTGEN, K., KLASEN, S., and MISSELHORN, M., "A Human Development Index by Income Groups," documento de trabajo nº 15, Instituto Ibero-Americano de Investigaciones Económicas, University of Göttingen, November 15, 2006.

GUIBERNAU, M., *Los nacionalismos*. Barcelona: Ariel, 1996.

HABERMAS, J., *El discurso filosófico de la modernidad*. Madrid: Taurus, 1989.

HABERMAS, J., *Facticidad y validez: Sobre el derecho y el Estado democrático de derecho en términos de teoría del discurso*. Madrid: Trotta, 1998.

HAMILTON, C., *El fetiche del crecimiento*. Iruña: Laetori, 2006.

HAYEK, F. A., *Derecho, legislación y libertad*, v. II. Madrid: Unión editorial, 1988.

HAYEK, F. A., *Camino de servidumbre*. Madrid: Alianza, 2002.

HEILBRONER, R., and MILBERG, W., *La crisis de visión en el pensamiento económico moderno*. Barcelona: Paidós, 1998.

HELD, D., and McGREW, A., *Globalización / Antiglobalización: Sobre la reconstrucción del orden mundial.* Barcelona: Paidós, 2003.

HERRERO DE MIÑÓN, M., LLUCH, E., (eds.), *Derechos históricos y constitucionalismo útil.* Madrid: Crítica, 2001.

HERRERO DE MIÑÓN, M., "Pactismo y nacionalismo inclusivos." *Conciliar la diversidad: Pasado y presente de la vertebración de España.* VII y VIII Seminarios Ernest Lluch, Euskal Herriko Unibertsitatea-Universidad del País Vasco, 2009.

HICKS, D.A., "The Inequality-Adjusted Human Development Index: A Constructive Proposal." *World Development*, nº 8, 1997, ps. 1283–1298.

HOBBES, T., "*Leviatán o la Materia, Forma y poder de una República Eclesiástica y Civil.*" (Primera Edición 1651), Buenos Aires: Fondo de Cultura económica, 1994.

HOLY FATHER FRANCIS, *Evangelii Ggaudium, Exhortación Apostólica.* Point 53, Vatican City, 2013.

HOLY FATHER FRANCIS. Speech to the European Parliament. Strasbourg, November 2014.

HOBSBAWM, E. J. E., *Entrevista sobre el siglo XXI*. Barcelona: Crítica, 2004.

HOLLANDERS, H., TARANTOLA, S., and LOSCHKY, "Regional innovation scoreboard (RIS) 2009." Programa pro inno Europe, December 2009.

HOLTON, G., *Einstein, historias y otras pasiones.* Madrid: Taurus, 1998.

HUMBOLDT VON, W., *Los límites de la acción del Estado.* Preliminary study, translation and notes de Joaquín Abellán. Madrid: Tecnos, 1988.

HUNTINGTON, S.P., *El choque de civilizaciones y la reconfiguración del orden mundial.* Barcelona: Paidós, 1997.

HUNTINGTON, S. P., *Who are We? The Challenges to America's National Identity.* New York: Simon and Schuster, 2004.

HUTCHINSON, T., *Economía Positiva y objetivos de política económica.* Barcelona: Vicens Vives, 1971.

IBARRETXE, J. J., Discurso de Investidura como Lehendakari, Parlamento Vasco, *Diario de Sesiones,* VI Legislatura, nº 4, December 29, 1998.

IBARRETXE, J. J., Discurso de Investidura como Lehendakari, Parlamento Vasco, *Diario de Sesiones,* VII Legislatura, nº 4, July 11, 2001.

IBARRETXE, J. J., Discurso del Pleno monográfico sobre Pacificación, sobre Normalización Política y sobre el Diálogo, Parlamento Vasco, *Diario de Sesiones,* VII Legislatura, nº 6, September 28, 2001.

IBARRETXE, J. J., Discurso del Pleno monográfico sobre Autogobierno, Parlamento Vasco, *Diario de Sesiones,* VII Legislatura, nº 10, October 25, 2001.

IBARRETXE, J. J., Discurso de Investidura como Lehendakari, Parlamento Vasco, *Diario de Sesiones,* VIII Legislatura, nº 4, June 22, 2005.

IBARRETXE, J. J., Intervención en las Cortes españolas en defensa del Nuevo Estatuto Politico para Euskadi, Congreso de los Diputados, *Diario de Sesiones,* VIII Legislatura, Pleno y Diputación Permanente, nº 65, February 1, 2005.

IBARRETXE, J. J., Discurso de Investidura como Lehendakari, Parlamento Vasco, *Diario de Sesiones,* IX Legislatura, nº 4, May 5, 2009.

IBARRETXE, J. J., Doctoral thesis. *Principio ético: Principio democrático y desarrollo humano sostenible; fundamentos para un modelo democrático.* San Sebastián: Universidad del País Vasco, 2010.

IBARRETXE, J. J., *The Basque Case: A Comprehensive Model for Sustainable Human Development.* Virginia: Georges Mason University, 2012.

IBARRETXE, J. J., *El Caso Vasco: Desarrollo humano sostenible.* Bogotá: La Oveja Negra, 2012.

ILO, *World Report on Social Protection 2014–2015.* Geneva, June 2014.

INTERNATIONAL MONETARY FUND, *Redistribution, Inequality, and Growth* (Jonathan D. Ostry, Andrew Berg, Charalambos G. Tsangarides). Washington DC, February 4, 2014.

JÁUREGUI, G., *La democracia en el siglo XXI: Un nuevo mundo, unos nuevos valores*. Oñate: IVAP (Herri Arduralaritzaren Euskal Erakundea – Instituto Vasco de Administración Pública), 2004.
JIMENEZ HERRERO, L. M., *Desarrollo sostenible: Transición a hacia la coevolución global.* Madrid: Pirámide, 2000.
JUDT, T., *Ill Fares the Land.* London: Allen Lane, 2010.
JULIÉN, C., *Le suicide des democraties.* Paris: Editions Grasset, 1972.
KANT, I., *Sobre la paz perpetua.* (Presentation by TRUYOL Y SERRA, A.,), Madrid: ed, Tecnos, 1998.
KANT, I., *Fundamentos de la metafísica de las costumbres.* Barcelona: Ariel, 1999.
KEATING, M., "Self-determination, multinational states and the transnational order." *The Implementation of the right to self-determination as a contribution to conflict prevention.* Barcelona: Centre UNESCO de Catalunya, 1999.
KEATING, M., "European Integration and the Nationalities Question" in EZEIZABARRENA, X., MACCLANCY, J., (eds.), *Sub-State entities and co-sovereignty within the UE.* Donostia: Eusko Ikaskuntza, 2008.
KEATING, M., *The Independence of Scotland. Self-government and the Shifting Politics of Union,* Oxford, Oxford University Press, 2009.
KELLEY, A. C., "The Human Development Index: Handle with Care."' *Population and Development Review* 17, nº 2, June 1991, ps. 315–324.
KENNEDY, R. F., Address, University of Kansas. Lawrence, Kansas, 1968.
KENNEDY, P., *Auge y Caída de las Grandes Potencias.* Barcelona: Plaza & Janés, 1994
KEYNES, J. M., *Economic Possibilities for Our Grandchildren.* London: Macmillan, 1933.
KEYNES, J. M., *Teoría general de la ocupación, el interés y el dinero.* México: S.L. Fondo de Cultura Económica de España, 2006.
KIERKEGARD, S., *Diario íntimo.* Barcelona: Planeta, 1993.
KLEIN, N., *No logo: El poder de las marcas.* Barcelona: Paidós, 2002

KRIELE, M., *Legitimitätsprobleme der Bundesrepublik.* Munich: Beck, 1979.

KRUGMAN, P., *Vendiendo Prosperidad.* Barcelona: Ariel, 1994.

KRUGMAN, P., *El gran engaño: Ineficacia y deshonestidad: Estados Unidos ante el siglo XXI.* Barcelona: Crítica, 2004.

KYMLICKA, W., *Estados, Naciones y Culturas.* Córdoba: Almuzara, 2004.

LATOUCHE, S., "Absurdo del productivismo y el derroche: Por una sociedad de decrecimiento." *Le Monde Diplomatique.* Spanish edition. Madrid, November 2003.

LATOUCHE, S., *La apuesta por el decrecimiento: ¿Cómo salir del imaginario dominante*? Barcelona: Icaria, 2008.

LOCKE, J., *Segundo ensayo sobre el gobierno civil.* Madrid: Aguilar, 1969.

LOPERENA, D., *Globalización y desarrollo sostenible.* Pamplona: Aranzadi, 2003.

LOPEZ-RODRIGUEZ, J., FAIÑA, J.A., and MONTES SOLLA, P., "*Case Study Basque Country*" *The Basque Country: Strategy for Economic Development.* Edited for Jean Monnet Group on Competition and Regional Development, Harvard, 2009.

LOZANO, S., GUTIÉRREZ, E., "Human Development Index: A Non-Compensatory Assesment." *Cuadernos de Economía,* 28(50), 2009, ps. 223–235.

LUNDWALL, B. A., *Innovation, Growth and Social Cohesión: The Danish Model.* Edward Elgar, 2002

LUNDVALL, B. A, "National Innovation Systems-Analytical Concept and Development tool." *Industry and Innovation,* n. 14, 2007, ps. 95–119.

MAALOUF, A., *Identidades asesinas.* Madrid: ed. Alianza, 1999.

MARITAIN, J., *El hombre y el estado.* Madrid: Encuentro, 2002.

MARTÍ, F., "Introduction" in *The Implementation of the right to self-determination as a contribution to conflict prevention.* Barcelona: Centre UNESCO de Catalunya, 1999.

MAYOR ZARAGOZA, F., "La problemática de la sostenibilidad en un mundo globalizado." *Revista de educación*, número extraordinario April 14, 2009, ps. 25–62.

MAYOR ZARAGOZA, F., "¿Más de lo mismo? NO." Article published on their *blogspot,* January 8, 2010.

MAYOR ZARAGOZA, F., "Los límites del crecimiento." *Temas para el debate*, nº 181, December 2009, ps.10–16.

McROBIE, R., Apéndice "Lo pequeño es posible," in SCHUMACHER, E.F., *Lo pequeño es hermoso*. Madrid: Tursen S.A. – Hermann Blume, 1990.

MEADOWS, D., "Los límites del crecimiento." For the Club de Roma, Instituto tecnológico de Massachussets-MIT, 1972.

MEADOWS, D., MEADOWS, D.L., RANDERS, J., "Los límites del crecimiento: 30 años después." Chelses Green Publishing Company, June 1, 2004.

MILL, J.S., *Principles of Political Economy: With some of their applications to social philosophy*. London: Longmans, Green and Co., 1923.

MIRALLES, M., y ARQUÉS, R., *Amedo: El Estado contra ETA*. Barcelona: Plaza y Janés, 1995.

MISHAN, E.J., *The cost of Economic Growth*. London: Staples Press, 1967.

MISSELHORN, M., "Human Development Index by Income Groups." Instituto Iberoamericano de Investigaciones Económicas, University of Göttingen, November 15, 2006.

MITXELENA, K., *"El largo y difícil camino del euskera": El libro blanco del euskera.* Bilbao: Euskaltzaindia, 1977.

MONDOLFO, R., *Rousseau y la conciencia moderna.* Buenos Aires: Eudeba, 1962.

MONDOLFO, R., *Problemas y métodos de investigación en la Historia de la Filosofía.* Buenos Aires: Eudeba, 1969.

MORIN, E., *El método: La naturaleza de la naturaleza.* Madrid: Cátedra, 1981.

MOSO, M., and OLAZARÁN, M., "Actores, ideas e instituciones: Políticas tecnológicas regionales y creación de un sistema de I+D en la Comunidad Autónoma del País Vasco." In OLAZARÁN, M., and GOMEZ URANGA, M., *Sistemas regionales de innovación.* Leioa: Servicio editorial de la UPV/EHU, 2001.

MUÑAGORRI, I., "Derecho penal intercultural y crisis del principio de soberanía." In PORTILLA, G., (ed.), *Mutaciones de leviathan: Legitimación de los nuevos modelos penales*. Madrid: Akal, 2005.

MYERS, D., "Does economic growth improve human morale." *Center for a New American Dream*. www.newdream.org, 1997.

NAVARRO, M., y ZUBIAURRE, A., "Los centros tecnológicos y el sistema regional de innovación: El caso del País Vasco." Documento de trabajo nº 38. Instituto de Análisis industrial y financiero, Madrid: Universidad Complutense de Madrid, 2003.

NAVARRO ARANCEGUI, M., "Los sistemas regionales de innovación: Una revisión crítica." *Revista Ekonomiaz* nº 70, Primer cuatrimestre de 2009, ps. 24–59.

NELSON, R., y WINTER, S., *An evolutionary theory of economic change*. Cambridge: Harvard University Press, 1982.

NELSON, R. R., *National Innovation Systems: A Comparative Analysis*. Oxford: Oxford University Press, 1993.

NIELSEN, K., "Review of Institutionalism: Approaches in the Social Sciences; Typology, Dialogue, and Future Prospects." *Research papers 7/01*, Department of Social Sciences, Roskilde University, 2003.

NISBET, R., *History of the Idee of Progress*. London: Einemann, 1980.

NORDSTRÖM, K., and RIDDERSTRÁLE, J., *Funky Business*. Madrid: Prentice Hall, 2000.

NOORBAKHSH, F., "A Modified Human Development Index." *World Development*, vol. 26, nº 3, 1998, ps. 517–528.

NORTH, D., *Instituciones, cambio institucional y desempeño económico*. México: Fondo de Cultura Económica, 1993.

NOZIK, R., *Anarchy, State, and Utopia*. New York: Basic Books, 1974.

OLAZARÁN RODRÍGUEZ, M. and GÓMEZ URANGA, M., *Sistemas regionales de innovación*. Leioa: Servicio editorial de la UPV/EHU, 2001.

ORIOL, J., "Revisión crítica de los aportes del institucionalismo a la teoría y la práctica del desarrollo." *Revista de Economía Institucional*, v. 9, nº 16, Primer semestre, 2007, ps. 121–148.

OSBORNE, D., and GAEBLER, T., *La reinvención del gobierno: La influencia del espíritu empresarial en el sector público.* Barcelona: Paidós, 1995.

OXFAM INTERMÓN, *Gobernar para las élites: Secuestro democrático y desigualdad económica.* Barcelona, 2014.

PETERS, G., *Institutional Theory in Political Science: The "new institutionalism."* London: Rouledge, 1999.

PETRELLA, R., *El bien común: Elogio de la solidaridad.* Madrid: Debate, 1997.

PI i MARGALL, F., *Las Nacionalidades (1876).* Madrid: Edicusa, 1973.

PIORE, M. J., y SABEL C. F., *La Segunda Ruptura Industrial.* Madrid: Alianza ed., 1990.

POLANYI, K., *La gran transformación: Crítica del liberalismo económico.* Madrid: La Piqueta, 1989.

POPPER, K. R., *La sociedad abierta y sus enemigos.* Barcelona: Paidós, 1994.

PORTER, M., *The Competitive Advantages of Nations.* New York: Free Press, 1990.

PORTILLA CONTRERAS, G., *Mutaciones del Leviatan: Legitimación de los nuevos modelos penales.* Madrid: Akal, 2005.

RAMÓN Y CAJAL, S., Discurso de entrada en la Real Academia de Ciencias Exactas, Físicas y Naturales, 1897.

RAMONET, I., et al., *Pensamiento Crítico vs. Pensamiento Único.* Madrid: Le Monde Diplomatique, 2001.

REICH, R. B., *El trabajo de las naciones: Hacia el capitalismo del siglo XXI.* Madrid: Javier Vergara ed., 1993.

REINICKE, W. H., *Global Public Policy: Governing without Government?* Washington: Brookings Institution Press, 1998.

REQUEJO, F., "Una democracia plurinacional a medio hacer: el Plan Ibarretxe y el Estado de las Autonomías." In *Estudios sobre la propuesta política para la convivencia del Lehendakari Ibarretxe.* Oñate: Instituto Vasco de Administración Pública, 2003.

RHULEN, M., *A guide to worlds languages: Classification.* Stanford: Stanford University Press, 1987.

RHULEN, M., *On the origin of languages.* Stanford: Stanford University Press, 1994.

RUHLEN, M., Department of Anthropological Sciences, "The origin of languages; an interview with Merritt Ruhlen." Stanford University, May 2009.

RIFKIN, J., *El fin del trabajo: Nuevas tecnologías contra puestos de trabajo; el nacimiento de una nueva er.* Barcelona: Paidós, 1996.

RIFKIN, J., *La economía del hidrógeno: La creación de la red energética mundial y la redistribución del poder en la tierra.* Barcelona: Paidós, 2004.

RIFKIN, J., *El sueño europeo: Cómo la visión europea del futuro está eclipsando el sueño Americano.* Barcelona: Paidós, 2004.

ROCO, M. C., "National Nanotecnological Iniciative-Past, present, future." In *Handbook on Nanoscience, Engineering and Technology,* 2nd ed., Taylor and Francis, 2007.

ROOSEVELT, F. D., Discurso inaugural de la 32 presidencia de los Estados Unidos, Washington, March 4, 1933.

ROUSSEAU, J. J., *Du Contract Social* (Primera versión), O.C., v. 3, Paris, ed. De La Pléiade, 1964.

ROUSSEAU, J. J., *Émile, L, IV, O. C.* Paris: Editions de la Pléiade / Gallimard, 1969.

ROUSSEAU, J. J., *Extrait du Projet de Paix Perpetuélle de Monsieur l'Abbé de Saint Pierre, L.III, O.C.* Paris: Editions de la Pléiade /Gallimard, 1969.

RYFF, C., "Happiness Is everything, or is it?" *Journal of Personality and Social Psychology,* v. 57, 1989, ps. 1069–1081.

SAID, E. W., *Cultura e imperialismo.* Barcelona: Anagrama, 1996.

SAMPER, E., *El salto global: Retos de América Latina ante la globalización.* Bogotá:. Taurus, 2004.

SAMUELSON, P. and NORDHAUS, W., *Economía.* Madrid: McGraw-Hill, 1999.

SÁNCHEZ INAREJOS, J. J., *La globalización al desnudo.* Madrid: Chaos-Entropy, 2001.

SARAMAGO, J., *La caverna.* Madrid: Santillana, Suma de letras, 2002.

SARATXAGA, K. and SALCEDO, J., "El éxito fue la confianza: Una historia real ocurrida en el País Vasco en plena crisis del 2008."Bilbao, ed. K2K emocionado, 2010.

SCHUMACHER, E. F., "*Small is beautiful: Economics as if people mattered.*" New York: Perennial Library, 1973.

SCHUMACHER, E. F., *Lo pequeño es hermoso*. Madrid: Tursen S.A.-Hermann Blume, 1990.

SCHUMPETER, J. A., *Teoría del desenvolvimiento económico: Una investigación sobre ganancias, capital, crédito, interés y ciclo económico*. México: Fondo de Cultura Económica, 1967.

SCHUMPETER, J. A., *Historia del análisis económico*. Barcelona: Ariel, 1995.

SCOTT, A. J., *Regions and the world economy: The coming shape of global production, competition, and political order*. Oxford: Oxford University Press, 1998.

SCOTT, A. J., STORPER, M., "Regions, Globalitation, Development" documento para el grupo de trabajo Globalitation, Regions, and Economic Development sponsored by the Center for Comparative and Global Research, International Institute, UCLA, published, *Regional Studies, v. 37,* 2003.

SEMPERE CARRERAS, J., and TELLO ARAGAY, E., *El final de la era del petróleo barato*. Barcelona: Icaria, 2007.

SIERRA LUDWIG, V., "Desarrollo sostenible: acotaciones conceptuales y revisiones estratégicas." *Boletín Económico de ICE*, nª 2749, November 25 – December 1, 2002, ps. 13–23.

SOROS, G., *La crisis del capitalismo global: La sociedad abierta en peligro*. Madrid: Debate, 1999.

SOTELO, I., *El Estado Social: Antecedentes, origen, desarrollo y declive*. Madrid: Trotta, 2010.

STIGLITZ, J. E., *El malestar en la globalización*. Madrid: Santillana Ediciones Generales, 2002.

STORA, B., y TEMIME, E., *Immigrances: L`immgration en France au XXe siècle*. Paris: ed. Hachette, 2007.

STORPER, M., *The regional world: Territorial development in a global economy*. New York: The Guildfor Press, 1997.

SUNDERLIN, W. D., *Ideology, social theory and the environmental.* Lanham: Rowman and little field Publishers, 2003.

TAMAYO, V., *Autogobierno de Vasconia: Desarrollo y crisis (1978–2006); Documentos*. Donostia-San Sebastián: Fundación para el Estudio del Derecho Histórico y Autonómico de Vasconia, Diputación Foral de Bizkaia, 2006.

TAYLOR, Ch., *Sources of the Self: The Making of Modern Identity.* Cambridge: Cambridge University Press, 1989.

TAYLOR, Ch., "Por qué la democracia necesita el patriotismo." In NUSSBAUM, M.C., *Los límites del patriotismo: Identidad, pertenencia y `ciudadanía mundial.'* Barcelona: Paidós, 1999.

UGALDE, M., *Nueva Síntesis de la Historia del País Vasco.* Donostia: Ttarttalo, 2004.

URIARTE, P. L., "Euskadi es la autonomía española más rica tras superar una grave crisis," rev. *Fomento de la Producción*, n. 1298, Barcelona, January 2010.

VENCE, X., *Economía de la innovación y del cambio tecnológico.* Madrid: Siglo XXI, 1995.

WALLERSTEIN, I., *El futuro de la civilización capitalista.* Barcelona: ed. Icaria, 1997.

WALLERSTEIN, I., *Utopística o las opciones históricas del siglo XXI.* México: Siglo XXI, 1998.

WEARING, A., y HEADEY, B., "Who enjoys life and why?" In ECKERSLEY, R., (ed.) *Measuring Progress: Is life getting better?* Coollingwood, Victoria: CSIRO Publishing, 1998.

WEBER, M., *El trabajo intelectual como profesión.* Barcelona: Bruñera, 1983.

WEBER, M., *La ética protestante y el espíritu del capitalismo.* Barcelona: Península, 1989.

WILKINSON, R. and PICKETT, K., *The Spirit Level: Why Greater Equality Makes Societies Stronger.* New York: Bloomsbury Press, 2010.

WORLD ECONOMIC FORUM, *Perspectivas de la Agenda Mundial 2014.* Geneva, November 2013.

ZAKARIA, F., *El mundo después de USA.* Madrid: Espasa Calpe, 2009.

ZALLO, R., *El Pueblo Vasco, hoy: Cultura, historia y sociedad en la era de la diversidad y del conocimiento.* Irán: Alberdania, 2006.

Made in the USA
Columbia, SC
05 December 2022

72756056R00198